Numbers–The Powerful Bridge Beyond

Chaldean Numerology for the New Millennium

ISBN-10 1-60145-079-6
ISBN-13 978-1-60145-079-1

Printed in the United States of America.

Published by:
SACRED STAR ENTERPRISES in collaboration with *Numbers R U*

Contact Information:
Joanne Justis
Numbers R U
inquiries@NumbersRU.com
www.NumbersRU.com

William Mykian
inquiries@TheOriginalFirstPlace.com
www.TheOriginalFirstPlace.com

Numbers–The Powerful Bridge Beyond

Chaldean Numerology for the New Millennium

By Joanne Justis and William Mykian

Dedication

This book is dedicated to Betty Gibson for making this publication possible through her contribution and work that has led to the advancement of Chaldean Numerology; to Cynthia R. Cole, an incredible editor, who we owe our gratitude to for making our book "letter" perfect, and to our clients who have trusted us with their personal stories that allowed us through their experiences to bring Numerology to new levels way beyond, beyond.

Numbers–The Powerful Bridge Beyond

Chaldean Numerology for the New Millennium

TABLE OF CONTENTS

Illustration No.	Characteristics and Development Areas
6.A	Destiny
6.B	Soul/Heart's Desire
6.C	Personality
6.D	Purpose
6.E	Life Goal
6.F	Birthdate Cycles
6.G	Challenges
6.H	Pinnacles
6.I	Soul Qualities

Chapter 7 provides sections for each characteristic and development area as listed, including a written description of a step-by-step process for calculating each of the characteristic and development numbers, as well as illustrations and/or examples of the real-time calculations.

Illustration No.	Characteristics and Development Areas	Finding the Assigned Number
7.A	Destiny	Numbers of the Birthdate
7.B	Soul/Heart's Desire	Numbers of the Vowels
7.C	Personality	Numbers of the Consonants
7.D	Purpose	Numbers of the Full Name
7.E	Life Goal	Numbers of the Birthdate Plus Full Name
7.F	Birthdate Cycles	Numbers of the Month, Day, Year of Birth
7.G	Challenges	Numbers of the Challenges

7.H	Pinnacles	Numbers of the Pinnacles
7.I	Soul Qualities	Numbers of the Letters of the Full Name

In the sections of Chapter 8, we provide you with what is called the "interpretive language" of numbers, the in-depth meaning and description of both the "root" (single-digit) numbers and special (high importance) double-digit compound numbers for each characteristic. The language of numbers is the basis for and is essential to interpreting and understanding the vibrational patterns of your numbers.

Illustration No.	Characteristics and Development Areas	Finding the Assigned Number
8.A	Destiny	Numbers of the Birthdate
8.B	Soul/Heart's Desire	Numbers of the Vowels
8.C	Personality	Numbers of the Consonants
8.D	Purpose	Numbers of the Full Name
8.E	Life Goal	Numbers of the Birthdate Plus Full Name
8.F	Birthdate Cycles	Numbers of the Month, Day, Year of Birth
8.G	Challenges	Numbers of the Challenges
8.H	Pinnacles	Numbers of the Pinnacles
8.I	Soul Qualities	Numbers of the Letters of the Full Name

In addition to listing the meanings of the Compound Numbers 10 through 54, Chapter 9 addresses the interacting influences of the single-digit numbers within the compound number. It also contains a discussion of the nature and sense of the positive and negative vibrations of selected numbers as a means for understanding such patterns. And an introductory analysis is

Year numbers. You can be informed about the years to come or, if you are interested, you can understand the patterns of past years. You can learn about things that are happening "now" or soon to be happening. You can find what specific experiences are unfolding, what may be in store for you, based on the vibrational patterns of your Personal Years.

Chapter 14 addresses the influence of the Personal Months, which are calculated using the number of your Personal Years. You get specific information about the months coming up, potential experiences, influences, conditions, and situations which may present themselves depending upon the vibrational patterns that form the personal and unique numbers of your Personal Months. You can learn how to take advantage of the best that the month has to offer, prepare for the events of the month, and maximize the use of your resources.

Chapter 15 gives you access to information never before addressed at this level of detail—learn how to calculate the numbers and patterns of the Personal Days and Hours and reveal their influence and impact on the events and situations that you experience on a day-to-day basis. You will find that the vibrations and patterns of each day and hour are not the same. You will find that each day presents you with new and different actions, influences, and conditions that were not present around you yesterday. You will learn how to get invaluable detailed information that tells you about the energies and patterns that surround a particular day's or hour's influences.

Chapter 16 discusses the meaning of the "Universal" numbers and how they impact your life. It will also discuss Universal Years (calendar years), Universal Months (calendar months), Universal Days (calendar days), and Universal Hours (clock hours), and the use of a 24–hour day in finding the numbers of your Personal Hours. Included are tables for the year, month, day, and "clock" hour numbers.

Chapter 17 is dedicated to showing you "mini-charts" for each of the Celebrities listed. Five of the major Numerology characteristics are calculated using either the "birth" or "stage" name for each celebrity, with brief descriptions of the vibrational patterns revealed by their numbers showing through a blueprint (chart) how each celebrity is designed.

Celebrity	Name Used to Calculate Mini-Charts
Walt Disney	Stage Name
Bill Gates	Birthname
Steve Jobs	Birthname
David Letterman	Birthname
Shirley MacLaine	Stage Name
Marilyn Monroe	Stage Name
Colin Powell	Birthname
Ronald Reagan	Birthname
Robert Redford	Birthname
Steven Spielberg	Birthname
Oprah Winfrey	Birthname

Numbers–The Powerful Bridge Beyond

Chaldean Numerology for the New Millennium

Author's Story

Joanne Justis
Chaldean Master Numerologist
Principal, NumbersRU.com

This book is truly a miracle and a labor of love for me. It's the personal story behind its origin, and the collaborated efforts of two Master Numerologists who dared to write the untold story of Chaldean Numerology so that we could share our findings and work with the world. Our book is based on discoveries, studies, and stories of real people. It is written to take Numerology to higher levels of understanding and accuracy, and to dispel misinterpretations falsely perpetrated throughout history about the science of numbers.

My story begins in the 1980s when my mother, Betty Gibson, discovered Numerology in her search for knowledge and truth. She wanted to know whether life's experiences were attracted to us, or happened at random. This journey took her first to studying "Modern" Numerology and then to developing her Numerology charts based on that system.

She soon discovered that the Modern system was inaccurate (based on consultation feedback through her readings), but was not willing to walk away from years of work because of this discovery and her disappointment. She was, in fact, determined to solve the mystery in finding the number system that was most accurate regardless of what the popular consensus was for using the Western system.

Through more research and in time, my mother was introduced to Chaldean Numerology through a book titled *Numerology Made Easy* and written by W. Mykian, a Master Numerologist using the Chaldean number system. After learning that the formula for the Chaldean number system was based on sound and phonics versus the Western system that is based on the Western alphabet, my mother knew she had solved the mystery as to which system was more accurate. Upon mastering the science of Chaldean Numerology, she developed a computer software program to ensure the accuracy of her charts. From 1984 into the new millennium, my mother gifted charts to people seeking guidance and clarity in their lives.

During the years that my mother devoted herself to her work, W. Mykian was always a part of our life, but of course he never knew this. His book was the only reference material we referred to since he was the known authority on Chaldean Numerology. His book detailed the instructions on how to calculate all aspects of Numerology. We always talked about meeting him one day but little did we know that would not come about until years later and under unexpected new circumstances.

My mother hoped that her work would be preserved by a family member since she had made many independent discoveries over the years based on feedback from research, case studies, and actual readings. My mother's coaching and teaching of the art of Numerology interpretation allowed me to naturally and smoothly take the baton that she passed to me.

Due to circumstances and events that happened beyond my mother's control, she had to set aside her dream of perfecting her computer software program for many years. But once the baton was passed to me, we began reconstruction of the formulas and enhancements she used in her original program, as well as totally having to rewrite the entire material content for this new computer software program.

This was a more difficult task than at first appearance. Reviewing and interpreting my mother's original documentation was a test of character and I was unsure we could succeed identifying and verifying all of the formulas and enhancements that my mother had incorporated in her original program. The process was arduous. But finally, our goal was accomplished. The formulas and specifications were ready for developing the computer software program. My programmer, using the latest technologies available, designed a one-of-a-kind, state-of-the-art, sophisticated computer software program that has the ability to calculate dates between 1900 and 3004, a span of over a hundred years.

While my computer software program was being completed, I was also finalizing the content and design of my Web site. As soon as that was finished, I sent a letter to W. Mykian letting him know I was carrying on my mother's work and wanted his approval to use his name and work on my Web site. His approval led us to eventually communicating full-time, and finally, meeting for the first time. The rest of the story is the book. We have now combined forces to write our book, *Numbers–The Powerful Bridge Beyond: Chaldean Numerology for the New Millennium* (The Definitive Word on Numerology) to set the history records straight and to share the correct system of numbers with the world.

Numbers–The Powerful Bridge Beyond

Chaldean Numerology for the New Millennium

I would like to acknowledge William Mykian for his major contribution as a Master Numerologist as well as being a "brilliant" historian who researched the records of history in order to bring you the most factual details available today on Numerology and for his devotion in working with me to produce this book so others could benefit from our work. I will always be deeply grateful to William for the opportunity of co-authoring our book and probably many more to come—but especially for his friendship, knowledge, and guidance along our journey together to bring you the most complete book on the accuracy of Chaldean Numerology.

A special thanks goes to my family for their encouragement and loving support. First, there is my mother, Betty Gibson, who was way beyond her time in paving the road for advancing Chaldean Numerology and laying the foundation for making my work and my writing of this book possible. Next, I am thankful to my sisters, Gwen, Karen, and Patti Justis for our close and unique relationships with each other and to my twin sons, Charles and Stephen Endweiss, whose birth groomed me in such a special way that would eventually lead me to pursuing my work as a Master Numerologist and fulfilling my dreams in the second half of my life. Most especially, I give my thanks in honor of the glory of our Spanish ancestors. And, special thanks also go out to my many friends who have always been supportive of my work.

I am grateful to all of those wonderful people along the way, who know who they are, who allowed me to demonstrate my charts and readings, and to my clients who have trusted me with their personal stories which allowed me, through their experiences, to bring Numerology to new levels way beyond, beyond.

Wishing all of you the very best that life has to offer.

Joanne Justis
Chaldean Master Numerologist
Principal, NumbersRU.com

Numbers–The Powerful Bridge Beyond

Chaldean Numerology for the New Millennium

Author's Story

William Mykian
Chaldean Master Numerologist
Author, *Numerology Made Easy*

The Universe has blessed me with an opportunity to participate in the writing of a very unique and important book, *Numbers–The Powerful Bridge Beyond: Chaldean Numerology for the New Millennium*. When I wrote *Numerology Made Easy*, I wasn't aware, at that time, that it was the first book that had ever been written to include formulas, calculations, and explanations of a very unique and very accurate system of Numbers, called Chaldean Numerology. It was accurate at its beginnings circa 4,000 BCE, or earlier. It is still accurate and has always been the only accurate system of numbers.

Prior to my discovering Chaldean Numerology, and to the publication of *Numerology Made Easy,* I had reached a frustrating impasse trying to get accurate results from what was called Modern or Western Numerology, particularly when it came to interpreting the patterns of Names. I was at a loss as to how to resolve the inaccuracies in Modern Numerology's treatment of Names. In my search, I was led to two books which introduced me to what was called Chaldean Numerology. One book was titled *Numbers Will Tell* written by Gerun Moore, a student of Count Louis Hamon. Count Louis Hamon, who was known as Cheiro, wrote a book titled *Cheiro's Book of Numbers*. Once I read and studied these books describing Chaldean Numerology, an ancient system of numbers, I tested the claims and results with clients whom I had already worked with using the Modern system of numbers.

Numbers–The Powerful Bridge Beyond

Chaldean Numerology for the New Millennium

What I learned gave me the keys to determining the true design and blueprint of one's life experiences. I discovered that the story of Chaldean Numerology was also *the* true story of Numerology.

In 1984, I received a letter from Betty Gibson, a Numerologist from California informing me that after many years of being mislead by the so-called Modern system of numbers, she had come to realize that the science of Chaldean Numerology as discussed and revealed in *Numerology Made Easy* was the true science of numbers. She was developing a Chaldean Numerology computer software program, and asked to use *Numerology Made Easy* as a basis for her program which also included her enhancements and new discoveries. We then communicated for a few years, but by 1990 we lost touch. Now, here's the rest of the story.

In 2003, I received an interesting e-mail from someone named Joanne Justis. At that time, I had no idea whatsoever who she was, and was surprised to find out that she was the daughter of Betty Gibson, as Betty and I had never discussed our families at all. Joanne was in the process of rewriting and upgrading the computer software program that her mother had developed almost 20 years before, and had written to ask me for confirmation of permission to use my book as a reference along with her work.

At the same time, Joanne was developing the content and design of her Web site (NumbersRU.com), which has turned out to be one of the most unique, profound, and important developments in Numerology, today. The software, which generates her Web site's Numerology charts, contains everything one needs to "see" their life's design and blueprint. While Joanne was finishing her Web site, I was considering a follow-on book to *Numerology Made Easy*, but was unsure as to the feasibility of undertaking such a project.

As the months rolled by, Joanne and I communicated more and more to discuss how to improve the accuracy of the charts, and investigate ways to enhance the methodologies and techniques to utilize Numerology to its fullest potential. I finally realized that the best possible follow-on book could only come about if we both wrote it. In late 2004, we decided to co-author a new and exciting book about Chaldean Numerology. The rest is now history. I am privileged and honored to have worked with Joanne's mother Betty, and to be co-authoring this book with Joanne, a Master Numerologist extraordinaire. Joanne is a brilliant and cognitive Master Numerologist who has an intuitive understanding and insight into the Language of Numbers and its connection to us and the world around us.

For most of my life, I have been naturally attracted to numbers, philosophy, and spiritual studies. As my experience with numbers grew, I sensed a "link" between mathematics and philosophy, and numbers and language, that would, I felt, open doors to new avenues of knowledge and understanding about our lives and our world. On my path, I have made a commitment to the continued study and practice of Metaphysical and Spiritual disciplines. I graduated from Penn State University with majors in Mathematics and Philosophy. In addition to Numerology, my career has ranged from business, financial, and performance management to nutritional therapy and political consulting.

I am deeply thankful to my loving family—my daughters Cathlene, a "Master" healer in her own right, and Indeia Anne, whose own success will be greater than she realizes, and to my son Joshua, for his loving soul and intuitive heart. Also, I thank my longtime friend Cynthia, whose compassionate heart tolerated me while I was discovering what life was all about, including unconditional love. And, I thank all who have crossed my path, who were excited and encouraging about the work I was undertaking, and honored the path that I chose to walk upon.

Joanne and I believe that this book will greatly benefit people who want to live their lives smarter and better. They will be amazed by the incredible accuracy of Chaldean Numerology and the potential for understanding themselves, their path in life, and the things that matter most to them, as well as building a lifetime of informed choices, intelligent decisions, and right action.

William Mykian
Chaldean Master Numerologist
Author, *Numerology Made Easy*

Numbers–The Powerful Bridge Beyond

Chaldean Numerology for the New Millennium

Special Tribute and Acknowledgement to Betty Gibson

Betty Gibson
Chaldean Master Numerologist
Original Founder of Numbers R U

This is a special tribute to my mother, Betty Gibson, for her contribution and work that led to the advancement of the science of Chaldean Numerology. The results of her work have been incorporated into this book.

In the early 1980s, Betty developed and wrote the first-of-its-kind Chaldean Numerology computer software program. Her dream was to develop a software program to generate accurate Numerology charts that would provide insight and clarity on one's life journey and give guidance to those seeking to find and confirm the path toward their greatest good.

Betty's work is made more valuable by the fact that she had originally studied and generated Numerology charts using the so-called Modern Numerology, only to find out later through feedback that her Modern charts were inaccurate. Because she had invested so many years in using the Modern number system, she was not willing to give up on her dream. She felt there was a logical explanation for the inaccuracies. And indeed there was!

But, it wasn't until a friend gave her a copy of W. Mykian's book, *Numerology Made Easy*, which explained the Chaldean system of numbers, that she discovered why. She became an expert in this system, recognizing the vast differences between the Chaldean and Modern systems, and realizing that Chaldean Numerology was the only accurate system of numbers.

Since then, the feedback from her charts and readings has continuously confirmed the accuracy of her discovery.

Betty is very intuitive and way ahead of her time. Her research and case studies have taken Numerology to new levels of advancement. Betty is credited with enhancements in the interpretation of Numerology, for developing her unique computer software program in 1984, and creating the "Essence" charts, which are available only through NumbersRU.com.

Blending my mother's work, Mykian's, and mine, we applied our collective years of experience with Numerology, results from case studies, and discoveries we have made to reveal advancements far beyond the work of any other numerologist. The Chaldean number system is based on sound, resonance, and vibrational patterns that describe our life's path, whereas Modern Numerology does not take into consideration the vibrational essence of the "sound" of our names, therefore producing inaccurate readings. We know that the science of Chaldean Numerology is the only correct system of numbers, based on the historical facts presented in this book and well over 75 years of collaborative work by three Chaldean Master Numerologists.

Joanne Justis
Chaldean Master Numerologist
Principal, NumbersRU.com

Timeline of Historical Events

TIMELINE	DESCRIPTION
Pre-Modern Civilization	Old Pharaonic Dynasties, Pre-Historic/Neanderthal, Paleolithic/Mesolithic/Neolithic/Chalcolithic, Homo Sapiens, etc.
Modern Civilization	The Recorded History of Homo Sapiens (Modern Humans)
4,004 BCE (Based on the calculations of Archbishop James Usher of Ireland, circa 1650 AD, from the book of Genesis.)	Aramaean, Sumerian, Chaldean Culture (Fertile Crescent/Tigris & Euphrates River Valleys/Mesopotamia) ➢ Mathematics, astronomy/astrology, physics, chemistry, medicine, numerology; ➢ Chaldean Book of Numbers; ➢ Engineering, the wheel, bridges, boats, ships; ➢ The kiln, brick, high-rise buildings, architecture; ➢ Writing, schools, scribes, laws, judges, juries, citizen councils.
3,760 BCE	The first calendar. The beginning of Hebrew history.
3,450 BCE	The date of the "Tower of Babel" story. Human civilization expands and moves out into the world in all directions. The beginning of the "NILE Valley" civilization.
2,400 BCE	The beginning of the "INDUS Valley" civilization.
2,193 BCE	Birth of Terah, father of Abraham. Moved from Aramaea to Ur, ancient capital city of Chaldea/Sumeria.
2,123 BCE	Birth of Abraham. Became a Chaldean Kabbalist/Hebrew Mystic.
1,000 BCE	The Story of Creation (circa 4004 BCE) was written down on 7 stone tablets in ancient Babylonia/Sumeria.
570 BCE	Birth of Pythagoras (Greek Mathematician/Philosopher, Chaldean Numerologist).
475 BCE	Death of Pythagoras.

450 BCE	The supposed founding date of the false system of numbers, so-called "Modern/Western" Numerology, by a self-proclaimed "student" of Pythagoras. A student who was not born until after the death of Pythagoras.
Seventeenth Century (~1650 AD)	Archbishop James Usher of Ireland determined that human civilization started in 4,004 BCE, based on calculations from the book of Genesis.
1851 AD	Rev. Charles Forster, author of *The One Primeval Language,* published in London in 1851, demonstrates that there was only one original language, Aramaic/Sumerian.
1876 AD	G. Smith, British Museum, published a book *The Chaldean Account of Genesis,* revealing that the biblical story was a summarization of this original account.
1902 AD	L. W. King, Archeologist, presented *The Seven Tablets of Creation*, which were found in the area of ancient Babylon/Sumeria. They were written 3,000 years ago.
1979 AD	*Numerology Made Easy* by W. Mykian, a first-of-its-kind Chaldean Numerology primer, explains formulas and application of the Chaldean System of Numbers.
2003 AD	Comprehensive Web site NumbersRU.com created by Joanne Justis, including a first-of-its-kind, state-of-the art Chaldean Numerology computer software program that spans 100 years.
2006 AD	*Numbers–The Powerful Bridge Beyond*, authors Joanne Justis and William Mykian, will present to the world sacred knowledge in a form never seen before. It will be known as the most definitive work ever compiled and written about Numerology.

###

Numbers–The Powerful Bridge Beyond

Chaldean Numerology for the New Millennium

Chapter 1:
Introductory Summary

Overview

Numbers–The Powerful Bridge Beyond: Chaldean Numerology for the New Millennium is a particularly unique book, in that, for the first time ever in the history of Numerology, it will explain the heretofore untold story of the history and development of Numerology, and the legacy of Chaldean Numerology science that the ancient Chaldean priest-scientists left us, for our use and benefit. You are being introduced to the story of an ancient but new science that will tell you of the power and gift of numbers. Chaldean Numerology is a science that will reveal secrets and answers that lie within the numbers of your Name and Birthdate. And, it will allow you to claim your birthright, the right to know the true story of the design and blueprint of your life.

To our knowledge, out of the hundreds of books on Numerology previously published, there has been only one Chaldean Numerology book, *Numerology Made Easy,* which ever included any information about the history of Chaldean Numerology, about the formulas and equations, or about the processes for calculating the numbers of your name using the original Aramaean/Chaldean/Sumerian Sacred Alphabet. (Note: Because of the close relationship in time and place, between Aramaea, Chaldee, and Sumeria, these names will be used interchangeably or in combination with each other throughout the book.) *Numerology Made Easy's* discourse on the history of Chaldean Numerology was well-intentioned and on the right track, but provided only a brief overview of its true depth and significance. The formulas and equations were introduced and discussed and the calculation processes were shown and addressed, but only a basic mathematical approach was presented without the necessary detailed step-by-step instructions.

However, this book, *Numbers–The Powerful Bridge Beyond,* will provide an in-depth, detailed expansion on both the history and development of Numerology and Chaldean Numerology which are in fact one and the same, and an easy to follow step-by-step understanding of all calculation processes. This book, in no uncertain terms, will completely change the perception and understanding of the science of Numerology, particularly Chaldean Numerology, forever.

Numbers–The Powerful Bridge Beyond is the true story of Numerology and will become the recognized authority on Chaldean Numerology. It will not only contain clearly defined and prescribed formulas, methods, techniques, and applications, but will give you access to information that will describe the design and blueprint of your life—past, present, and future— and introduce you to options and alternatives that will take you beyond Numerology. *Numbers–The Powerful Bridge Beyond* will also be known as the most definitive work ever compiled and written about Numerology. And ultimately, it will be saluted for recognized excellence that will be second to none, without exception.

Chaldean Numerology was the ancestor of and basis for the spiritual sciences of the Hebrew Kabbalah mystics, their Sacred Alphabet, and their science of numbers. What will be made clear later is the fact that the Hebrew Kabbalah mystics were not numerologists, but rather spiritual scientists engaged in the unveiling of the relationship between numbers, sound-syllables, and the creative power and energy that resonates and flows out from their "Sacred" Names and the "Flame Letters" of the Hebraic Sacred Alphabet.

Chaldean Numerology was also the forerunner of the language, science, and philosophy of the Greeks, and was invaluable to scholars such as Pythagoras, who seriously and intensely studied the spirituality, metaphysics, numerology, and astronomy of the Chaldean priest-scientists. As the languages of Asia Minor, the Near East, and the Middle East, including Hebrew and Arabic, were "children," if you will, of the original Chaldean/Sumerian language, so were (are) all of the languages of the world. There is historical evidence that the Chaldean/Sumerian language is now considered by many scholars as the "Mother Tongue" of the world's diverse languages. Also, it is a historical fact that the impact and influence of the Chaldean sciences was the basis of and the foundation upon which all Western sciences evolved.

Chaldean Numerology will lead you into the new millennium as a powerful bridge that will take you beyond anything that you could have wished to understand and dared to know. It is a bridge that will take you beyond uncertainty to assurance, beyond denial to acknowledgement, beyond confusion to clarity, beyond rejection to acceptance, and beyond the statement "there's nothing new under the sun" to the reality that "everything under the sun is new." This powerful bridge will lead you to a place within yourselves where you will find the wisdom and courage to become both an observer of and a participant in your life experiences, on a path of self-acceptance and self-advocacy.

Another reason *Numbers–The Powerful Bridge Beyond* is so unique is because, based on years of collective experience, we as Master Chaldean Numerologists have made major contributions in our own right in taking Numerology to the next level. Because of the magnitude of our discoveries, this book is slated to become the "only" true story of Chaldean Numerology. *Numbers–The Powerful Bridge Beyond* will present an in-depth description, critique, and comparison of the major systems of Numerology that predominate today. As never before, this book will reveal the basis of each, or the lack thereof, as a result of extensive historical research and new surprising discoveries that were either ignored or overlooked by traditional numerologists.

The benefits of Chaldean Numerology are discussed in *Numbers–The Powerful Bridge Beyond*, as well as the demonstration of the uncanny accuracy of the results generated in Numerology charts which are your life's design and blueprint. The accuracy of the original science of Chaldean Numerology will surprise and amaze you as you witness the depth of information revealed in the numbers of your name and birthdate. The different characteristics of the Numerology chart are interconnected, and become integrated into the "story" of your life. The information in this book will lead you to alternatives and options that you can use to live a smarter and better life. Your design and blueprint is described and explained such that you can put your life (and any outcomes) into your own hands.

Numbers–The Powerful Bridge Beyond will also present a detailed comparison between the science of Chaldean Numerology, the "correct" science of numbers, and the so-called Modern (Western) number system. This comparison will reveal the false contentions of Modern Numerology, the fallacies in the origin and history of Modern Numerology, the inaccuracies in the calculation of name numbers, and the misidentification of the vibrational patterns of your name, names for your baby, names of the people around you, business names, pet's names, and so on.

This first-of-a-kind book is intentionally written as a story that's easily understood, but yet developed to be used as an "owner's" manual so that the reader can be the beneficiary of an amazing new presentation of secrets, advanced techniques, sample numerology charts, formula calculations, case studies, and much, much more. *Numbers–The Powerful Bridge Beyond* will tell you how to generate the unique design and blueprint of your life and how to use this design to better understand the personal "story" of potential unfolding events and experiences in your life. Your story becomes an owner's manual filled with information, tips, and alternatives for building and maintaining a lifetime of good choices and decisions, and right action, allowing you to effect successful change throughout your life.

Before you begin this journey of self-discovery through numbers, it's important to know there are basically three formal versions of Numerology that predominate today. They are (1) the science of Chaldean Numerology (Asia Minor/Middle and Near East/Western cultures), based on the world's original root language Chaldean/Sumerian, (2) Vedic Numerology, which was adapted to the Sanskrit/Tibetan/Hindi language grouping (India), and (3) the so-called Modern (Western) number system (whose basis is indeterminate and unverifiable).

The Chaldean Science of Numbers

This ancient science of numbers gradually became known as "Numerology," which comes from the Latin word "numerus," which means number, and the Greek word "logos," which means intelligence, divine reason, and wisdom, among other expressions. This science of numbers (Chaldean Numerology) says that each of us has a set of numbers based on our name and birthdate. It is based on the truth that those numbers represent vibrations which can be described, and from those descriptions we can determine our purpose and destiny, the sense of our personality, who we are compatible with, and more. Another way of saying this is that numbers give off a sound resonance (vibrational energy) that generates unique patterns which define and describe our lives and the world around us. The understanding of these vibrational patterns was made visible through the unlocking of ancient secret codes by Chaldean priest-scientists that revealed the interpretive language of numbers.

Chaldean Numerology is based on "sound-syllables" (sound frequencies/resonance) for identifying and interpreting the vibrational patterns of our "names." It is the predecessor to the science of the Hebrew Kabbalah mystics called Gematria, a science of numbers (but not a science of Numerology) that only concerns itself with the meaning and understanding of the sound-syllables of their "Sacred" names and the power of their Sacred Alphabet through interpreting the language of specific numerical values. The Hebrew mystics developed their interpretations based on the language of the Chaldean/Sumerian Sacred Alphabet. Chaldean Numerology, as a matter of recorded history, has been considered a science for at least 6,000 years, if not longer, and was developed to include the potential variations of the structures of all languages. Chaldean Numerology clearly and accurately interprets both the numbers of your Name and your Birthdate. *Numbers–The Powerful Bridge Beyond* will tell you the unusual and fascinating story of Chaldean Numerology and its legacy to humanity.

The Vedic Science of Numerology (India)

The Vedic version is also based on sound-syllables (sound vibrations/resonance) for identifying and interpreting the vibrational patterns of names. These sound-syllables are based on the Sanskrit/Tibetan derived Sacred Alphabet. The results reveal very accurate information, but only for those names which are directly derived from the Sanskrit/Tibetan/Hindi language grouping, or can be translated into the sound-syllables of Sanskrit/Tibetan/Hindi. *Numbers–The Powerful Bridge Beyond* recognizes Vedic Numerology as valid without challenge for names of Sanskrit/Tibetan/Hindi origin or derived languages. Additionally, Chaldean priest-scientists were well familiar with Vedic Numerology since it was developed from this same truth—numbers represent the energy of creation which is perpetually in flux, and responds to the natural order of the Universe. Since Chaldean Numerology and this book are focused on those cultures and languages which are derived or descended from the Aramaean/Chaldean Sacred Alphabets, including the English, the Vedic system is not in conflict with the Chaldean system and will not be a part of this book's scope, but perhaps another.

The Modern Number System

Two of the greatest mistakes ever made in the history of Numerology occurred with two false assumptions by modern numerologists. These were, first, the presumptuous and blatant misidentification of Pythagoras (the famous Greek mathematician, philosopher, and mystic) as the "Father" of Modern Numerology, which he was not, and secondly, an erroneous declaration that the so-called Modern number system (supposedly developed by Pythagoras) was the original system of Numerology for the West, which it was not. These false assumptions caused the introduction of that system of numbers with incorrect formulas and equations that has led, not only to the perpetuation of inappropriate and inaccurate calculations of the numbers of your name, but to misinterpretations of the vibrational patterns of your life's design and blueprint.

The so-called Modern version of Numerology is not based on the vibrational patterns of sound-syllables, but a simplistic assignment of numbers to the letters of the ancient Latin Alphabet (500–450 BCE), an alphabet which, by the way, had only 22 letters. The so-called Modern version had supposedly originated circa 450 BCE as claimed by of one of Pythagoras' disciples. How this claim was ever considered valid is beyond all reason, because this "disciple" was never a student of Pythagoras, since he was not born until after Pythagoras died in 475 BCE. This disciple invented a system of numbers without understanding or even knowing the Chaldean science of numbers as Pythagoras did, since all records of Pythagoras' "mystery sciences" were destroyed when his school was burned down by the residents of Crotona (southern Italy) where his school was founded. This "invented" system of numbers was not created until after Pythagoras died and was erroneously called Pythagorean Numerology (Western Numerology). This false claim rests solely on the word of this disciple—simply because he "said" so. Twenty-five hundred years ago an unsubstantiated claim was forced upon humanity, without warrant, falsely declaring that Pythagoras had developed the so-called Modern system of numbers in addition to being falsely portrayed as the Father of Modern Numerology. This was done without verifiable credentials or proof of evidence that Pythagoras had ever known about or even acknowledged this so-called Modern system of numbers.

As far as anyone knows, the Modern version of Numerology was neither developed nor sanctioned by Pythagoras. As if to confirm the questionable contentions of these unreasoned fallacies, we reference a statement from the Encyclopedia Britannica concerning the life and teachings of Pythagoras.

> *"Few schools of thought have professed such reverence for its founder's authority as the Pythagoreans. 'The Master said so' was their watchword. However, it is difficult to distinguish Pythagoras' teachings from those of his disciples. None of his writings has survived, and* ***Pythagoreans invariably supported their doctrines by indiscriminately citing their master's authority."***

The full story about the so-called Modern number system, which will reveal even greater fallacies than addressed here, is discussed in detail in chapter 4. Chapter 4 will also include the real story of Pythagoras' life.

Numbers–The Powerful Bridge Beyond

Chaldean Numerology for the New Millennium

Chaldean Numerology–The "Correct" Number System

Everything in the Universe is named, numbered, and influenced by mathematical equations. However, very few people are aware that our names and birthdates reveal information about our purpose in life and the experiences we will attract during our lifetime. Have you ever noticed how much of your life is influenced by numbers? The list is almost endless. You are issued your driver's license number, social security number, bank account numbers, phone numbers, credit card numbers, etc., etc., etc. Have you ever noticed how much you are attracted to certain numbers? What would you say if you knew the spelling of your name and your birthdate has a numerical value that reveals the patterns of your life and sets the stage for your experiences? That is exactly what Chaldean Numerology will show you.

Chaldean Numerology is an ancient science of numbers which says that you are born with a set of unique numerical values that represent vibrational patterns which have definable and describable meanings. The numbers of your name and birthdate can show you a design and blueprint that reveal the potential your life holds, and describe both the possibilities that are available to you and the choices that can lead to your greatest success. It is a concept that confirms a very simply stated fact that "everything doesn't just happen,"—nothing happens by accident or chance. Discover how the Numerology chart, which is developed based on the numbers and patterns of your name and birthdate, reveals the design and blueprint of your life, affects your destiny, gives you options for controlling changes in your life, and helps you gain insight into various areas of your life, whether personal or business.

There are nine basic characteristics calculated in the Basic Numerology Master Chart. The combination of these unique characteristics provides you with a complete character analysis. They also provide the information that describes the story of your life as revealed by the language of your numbers and distinctive vibrational patterns, and will include information which will guide your choices and decisions, prevent potential roadblocks along the way, and provide caveats (cautions) about certain areas and times of your life. The information you get from the design and blueprint of your life will help you review alternatives and options you can choose to put into action or not. In other words, it will better help you put your choices under your control. The Chaldean science of numbers combined with your right to choose is "the" key that will open the doors of the world around you and lead you to unlimited opportunities. If you seek to know beyond what you have been taught, then you can discover the unique and personal blueprint that lays hidden within your name and birthdate.

Conclusion

Numbers–The Powerful Bridge Beyond will make the world aware of a straightforward, mathematical approach to utilizing Numerology. Our intent is to promote an increased awareness of Chaldean Numerology on a global basis showing that it still flourishes, there are unlimited benefits to be gained, there exists a reasonable and accurate alternative for attaining self-knowledge, and it is available now. It is an approach that offers you a way to enhance your life through information about your purpose, personality, strengths and weaknesses, inner needs, emotional reactions, and much, much more. *Numbers–The Powerful Bridge Beyond* will take you beyond Numerology to self-healing and self-advocacy, give you a greater perspective on life, and prepare you for today and tomorrow, keeping in mind that ultimately you must make the final choices.

###

Numbers–The Powerful Bridge Beyond

Chaldean Numerology for the New Millennium

Chapter 2:
Chaldean Numerology History and Development

General Information

Before we discuss the history of the original science of Numerology which is still valid today, we would like our readers to understand that we did not create or invent Chaldean Numerology. It has been around a very long time. We have studied it, investigated it, applied it, and recognize both the power and value of the original science in living our lives. The story of the original science of Chaldean Numerology (which is "the" story of Numerology) is derived from historical biographies, documentaries, and archaeological translations of tablets found in ancient libraries, with referenced information about the ancient "*Chaldean Book of Numbers*," which contains the basis for and descriptions of the sciences of the Chaldean priest-scientists.

History, since approximately 4000 BCE (over 6,000 years ago), indicates that the ancient Chaldean priest-scientists believed in one impersonal, universal deific Principle as the source of creation and all that is known. The basis of their science was derived from the inner powers of human soul, and by the discernment in understanding the profound knowledge of the power of nature. The Chaldeans were the savants (scholars), the magians (magicians) of Babylonia, astrologers, mathematicians, astronomers, and diviners of ancient Mesopotamia and Sumeria.

Our purpose in writing *Numbers–The Powerful Bridge Beyond* is to initiate a renaissance, a revitalization, if you will, of Chaldean Numerology. We wish to increase people's awareness of Chaldean Numerology, from its beginnings, and to transform the modern perception of Chaldean Numerology as an ancient science into the understanding that Chaldean Numerology is a scientific process, and is as appropriate today as any other scientific endeavor. It will show people, that when faced with confusion and uncertainty, with questions that need answered, and with decisions and choices that must be made, they now have a no-nonsense source of information available to them. Chaldean Numerology will provide you with amazingly reliable, accurate, and revealing information to help you make better decisions for taking the action when faced with rapidly changing experiences. What is unusually fascinating is that many, if not most, Modern numerologists have no idea that there is such a thing as Chaldean Numerology. And we know that they "know" of the inaccuracies of the Modern system which they cannot resolve. Now, Modern numerologists will have an opportunity to become aware of the existence, the viability, and the accuracy of the original, and only correct, number system—Chaldean Numerology.

The Aramaeans/Chaldeans/Sumerians were a unique nation of people, seemingly unrelated as to race, color, creed, or culture to any the other known civilized areas of the world. The Chaldean/Sumerian language was the original language of the world, and is the progenitor, the direct ancestor, of all of the languages of the world. This unique nation of people originated in the area of the world known as the "Fertile Crescent" and occupied the upper and middle portions of the land through which the Tigris and Euphrates flowed, known by various names such as Sumeria, Mesopotamia, and Babylonia. This area of the world is also known as the Cradle of Western Civilization. To the Chaldean priest-scientists, spirituality, Numerology, and physical sciences, including medicine, were all a part of the same branch of knowledge that came from a single, ancient divine source. To the Chaldeans, there was no such thing as spiritual science versus physical science.

In Chaldea, all of their environments and life experiences were invariably linked to numbers. Not only was this true mathematically, but also metaphysically. In many references to the *Chaldean Book of Numbers*, numbers are shown to represent the energy of creation which is perpetually in flux, and respond to the natural order of the Universe. Based on this truth, Numerology was used to identify all natural environments as well as the design and blueprint of the lives of individuals, cultures, communities, and tribes. Out of this area of the ancient world, the nations of humanity grew in number, and took this original knowledge with them. This knowledge was preserved and used in all the different languages and cultures as humanity spread out upon the face of our planet.

We know that the science of Chaldean Numerology has been around for at least 6,000 years, as chronicled since the beginning of recorded history. The exact origin of this science is elusive. It may be difficult to trace the exact "starting" point in antiquity, but it is not difficult to trace the basis and development of this ancient science and its interpretive essence. You will be able to experience, firsthand, the validity and truth of Chaldean Numerology and the uncanny accuracy of the information and results. That information and those results are right on target and very, very appropriate to living in today's world. And, you can be given insight to the ever-changing patterns of our environment, our lives, and our unfolding experiences.

The Science of Numbers

As stated before, Numerology is known as the Science of Numbers. It reveals the true value of "numbers" in all areas of your life through the very accurate and descriptive information about your life's design and blueprint. It can reveal past, present, and future events, and opens the doors to unveiling your own deeper nature, and more. The unique combination of numbers contained within your name and birthdate together can be translated into a personalized Numerology chart. This chart can provide insight to your life's journey by offering guidance, identifying your strengths, and understanding your challenges. You will be able to learn more about yourself and others, personal and business relationships, compatibilities, finances, career, and health. You will be able to understand yourself at a deeper level by discovering how your personal Numerology affects your destiny and your calling. You might say that Numerology is like a mirror that reflects your life's journey in the form of the numbers and the patterns that they represent. It is indisputable that the science of Chaldean Numerology has been around thousands of years. There is evidence in many spiritual texts of the near and Far East that these sciences were actively used as long ago as 4,000 BCE. *Numbers–The Powerful Bridge Beyond* is written to introduce a renaissance in the use of Chaldean Numerology. And although it is an ancient science, it is "new" by its application in the process of self-discovery and self-advocacy. Chaldean Numerology can also give you all of the answers you will need or want for your life today. This history and development of Chaldean Numerology take you back almost 3,500 years before Pythagoras and his "Mystery School" (fl. 550–530 BCE) and present you with a most revealing story about the beginnings of Chaldean Numerology and Numerology as a science. In addition, it will provide a demonstration of the validity and accuracy of the results that Chaldean Numerology brings to you.

Development of Chaldean Numerology preceded not only the establishment of functioning "civilized" (modern) communities, but the advent of written language as a means of communication. The Chaldean priest-scientists developed and advanced their system of Numerology as a "universal/integrated" system of numbers, incorporating aspects of the Chaldean Kabbalistic system which is based on the Chaldean/Sumerian Sacred Alphabet, Egyptian mysticism, and Vedic/Sanskrit spiritual sciences (all of which were "sound-based" sciences), in order to allow for the diversity of language fluctuations and to accommodate the structures of differing language systems. The "Aramaean/Chaldean/Sumerian" language is considered an "isolate" language in that it has a stand-alone, unique existence. There is no preceding language form from which it was derived. (Again, in the context of this book, the use of the words Chaldean, Aramaean, and Sumerian are interchangeable.)

In his book, *The 12th Planet: Book 1 of the Earth Chronicles*, Zecharia Sitchin, world-renowned archaeologist, states that the translation of some of the 25,000 tablets discovered at the Library of the ancient Babylonian King Ashurbanipal, located in modern day Iraq, gives the chronology of the world's oldest existing civilizations. The tablets tell about the existence of the Aramaean/Chaldean/Sumerian language and civilization around 4,000 BCE, followed by the appearance of civilizations in the Nile Valley (Egypt) around 3,450 BCE, and in the Indus Valley around 2,400 BCE. Included in the *Earth Chronicles* is a reference to Reverend Charles Forster whose conclusions in his book titled *The One Primeval Language* published in 1851, demonstrated that "the ancient languages then deciphered, including early Chinese and other Far Eastern Languages, stemmed from the one primeval source—thereafter shown as Sumerian." This claim of one primeval language by Reverend Forster is in accord with the book of Genesis, chapter 11, verse 1, which states "And the whole earth was of one language, and of one speech."

The Aramaean/Chaldean/Sumerian Alphabet, whose purpose, intent, and form are significantly different from the Western/English Alphabet letters, is centered on the power and effect of sound-syllables (vibrational resonance). Therefore, the alphabet of Chaldean Numerology allows for variations in language development and is adaptable to the alphabet of the language system from which a "Name" is derived. Although the alphabet seems to contain "letters" as seen today in our modern languages, the alphabet is in actuality a set of sound-syllables.

The power of the Sacred Alphabets of the ancients, the original being Chaldean/Sumerian, a second being Vedic (Sanskrit/Tibetan), did not flow from the meaning of written letters or the pronunciation of a single letter, but from the sounds of syllables. These sound-syllables generate energy that creates vibrational patterns which affect our body's physiology (functionality) and energy processes, and impacts an unfolding, living, changing environment that defines energy in our lives. Each of these sound-syllables resonates to certain numbers which represent specific vibrational patterns. These vibrational patterns are then translated into written form through the interpretation of the language of numbers. The meaning (interpretation) of the numerical values was taught to the ancient priest-scientists through an intuitive (not written down) process of learning, understanding, and knowing. This interpretation provides a description of each "number's" unique vibrational pattern and the influences the patterns have on our lives and the world around us. However, with the advent of "civilized" communities and written language, the descriptions of the vibrational patterns represented by the numbers and the process of interpretation were no longer learned intuitively, but rather were passed down from Master to student each succeeding generation in the form of teachings which contain this knowledge. *Numbers–The Powerful Bridge Beyond: Chaldean Numerology for the New Millennium* is a vehicle to transfer the knowledge in written form such that all who desire to know this science will have access to the formulas, calculations, and interpretations. Numerology will no longer have to be called "occult," secret, or mystical, since its knowledge will now be revealed and available.

The Number System of the Hebrew Kabbalah Mystics

The word "Kabbalah," which originated with the Chaldean priest-scientists, existed before the advent of the Hebrew Kabbalah mystics, and is translated as "knowledge that is received directly through the mind and soul" rather than through the intellectual knowledge of a human being (note: Abraham, a Patriarch of the Jewish nation, was a Chaldean Kabbalist). The Kabbalah has now come to mean any secret, esoteric system of thought which uses alphabet letter, color, symbol, sound, and number as the basis of its metaphysical/philosophical system. Although Kabbalah did not originate in Hebrew mysticism, it is used to interpret and reveal the meaning of names. The Hebrew language (derived from Chaldean/Sumerian) is a language of sound-syllables (Aleph, Beth, Gimel, Daleth, He, Vau, etc.). The Sacred Alphabet of the Hebrew mystics represents cosmic (mystical) principles and states of consciousness that were created and revealed through innate human awareness (in other words, intuition) and understanding. The Hebrew mystics were not numerologists, since the purpose of their mission was the understanding and unveiling of the knowledge of the "Flame Letters" of their

Sacred Alphabet and their "Tree of Life." (Although the science behind Chaldean Numerology may have been the basis of the number system of the Hebrew mystics, their number system, Gematria, is not Numerology.)

The Hebrew Gematria is the art of substituting a numerical value of a given word in Hebrew with a corresponding meaning. Gematria etymology has Greek roots. It is a combination of the Greek words "gramma" (letter) and "metria" (measure), i.e., the measurement of the letters composing any word, just as geometry is the measure (metria) of earth (geo). Each letter (sound-syllable) of the Hebrew Alphabet represents a cosmic principle, has a unique meaning, and has attributes directly related to a numerical value. The Gematria, which asserts an interpretive relationship between sound-syllables and names, was developed specifically in the context of Hebrew language and mysticism. The Hebrew Kabbalistic Gematria is a science dedicated to the unveiling of the secrets of the Hebrew "Sacred Alphabet," their "Divine Names," "The Tree of Life," and the "Divine Emanations," also called the Ten Sefirot (a channel of Divine energy or life-force).

Basically the intent and purpose of the Hebrew mystical science of Gematria was not Numerology, since the development of "numerological" charts for the purpose of interpreting the design and blueprint of individuals, which also uses birthdates, was never a part of their agenda, nor do we believe that Gematria was ever used or practiced as Numerology. In addition, we have never known the Hebrew Kabbalah mystics to concern themselves or their studies with the vibrational patterns of an individual's birthdate, nor to advocate the utilization of Gematria for such endeavors.

Vedic Numerology

Vedic Astrology and Numerology, which were practiced and taught in the Indus Valley (circa 2,400 BCE), were based on the spiritual truth that the Universe is birthed from pure sound. And sound, which is represented by number, generates energy that is the source of Power, and produces vibrational patterns of manifestation—creating all that is seen and unseen within our ever rapidly changing world. Sanskrit and Tibetan (a variation of Sanskrit) mantras are sacred words (sound formulas or equations) whose vibrations, let us say, create intuitive pipelines which are portals that allow this creative spiritual energy to pass into the world.

The basis of Vedic Numerology is centered on the specific characteristics of the sound-syllables contained in the Sanskrit/Tibetan Sacred Alphabet. Although, the "Eastern" numerological systems have sound-syllable based alphabets, the determination of name and number patterns is limited to using the Sanskrit/Tibetan/Hindi sound-syllable application, which requires that a name must be rooted in the Sanskrit/Tibetan/Hindi language. Or as a minimum, a name which originates in a root language not derived from Sanskrit must be converted to Sanskrit/Tibetan sound-syllables in order to begin a numerological interpretation of the name and its derived numbers. As such, the numerological charts would, as a result of the need to convert from another language structure, be less than optimally accurate. However, Vedic Numerology, which derives from the Sanskrit/Tibetan Sacred Alphabet, does in fact yield accurate and insightful information when interpreting names that are of Sanskrit/Tibetan/Hindi origin or derivation. Of this, there is no contention or conflict.

Chaldean Numerology

Chaldean Numerology is based on the Chaldean Alphabet/Formula shown in table 2–1 which assigns only "eight" root numbers (numerical values) to the sound-syllables (letters) of their alphabet. The original Chaldean Alphabet of 22 letters (sound-syllables) was expanded to 26 letters by the third millennium BCE to accommodate the variation in language structures developed as humanity expanded its environment—derived from the Aramaean/Chaldean/Sumerian original Sacred Alphabet (see table 2–2). The Chaldean Alphabet recognized and applied certain characteristics and formulas which ensured that the accuracy of the calculated numerical values and the interpretations of the patterns of our names were maintained at all times. One of those characteristics was the fact that the Number 9 was considered to be "Sacred" in and of itself. It was sacred not only because it was symbolic of the highest level of spiritual attainment, but also because its level of creative energy was higher than all numbers. Therefore, the Number 9 could never be assigned to represent a single "letter" (sound-syllable) of the alphabet, although it can represent the number of a name, the sum of single letters/sound-syllables. As a consequence, the Number 9 is not included in the number assignment of the letters (sound-syllables) of the Chaldean Alphabet.

Chaldean Alphabet/Formula
Numerical Values with Letters Assigned

1	2	3	4	5	6	7	8
A	B	C	D	E [1]	U	O	F [2]
I	K	G	M	H	V	Z	P
J [3]	R	L	T	N	W [4]		
Q		S		X			
Y							

Table 2–1

[1]The **"E"** (with the Number value of 5) comes from the Proto-Greek (3rd millennium BCE) letter epsilon which is a sound-syllable variation of (derived from) the Aramaic/Chaldean/Hebraic *hê* (pronounced "hey").

[2]The letter **"F"** (with a Number value of 8) is a variation derived from the Aramaic/Chaldean/Hebraic letter *pê* (pronounced "pey"), which became "ph" (pronounced "eph") when incorporated into languages other than Aramaean/Chaldean/Hebrew.

[3]The **"J"** (with a Number value of 1) has multiple origins, one as a later addition to the 22 basic letters of the Hebraic Sacred Alphabet (variation of the Hebrew Sacred Letter "I").

[4]The **"W"** (with a Number value of 6), is also a later addition to the Hebraic Sacred Alphabet and is a transliteration of the Aramaic/Chaldean/Hebraic Alphabet letter (pronounced "*wâw*").

See appendix A for additional information about the make up of the Chaldean Alphabet.

Original Sacred Alphabet
Numerical Values with Letters Assigned

1	2	3	4	5	6	7	8
(A) aleph	(B) beth	(C) chaf	(D) daleth	~~(E)~~ Not Original	(U) vau	(O) ayin	~~(F)~~ Not Original
(I) yod	(K) kaph	(G) gimel	(M) mem	(H) he	(V) vau	(Z) zain	(P) pe
~~(J)~~ Not Original	(R) resh	(L) lamed	(T) teth	(N) nun	~~(W)~~ Not Original		
(Q) qoph		(S) semakh		(X) tzaddi			
(Y) yod							

Table 2–2

Our knowledge, as authors, relative to ancient languages, linguistics, phonetics, or phonology is not derived from a formal university education, but rather from what we have gained through extensive study, use, and application of these areas as they relate to the science of Chaldean Numerology. It is knowledge that has come about through years of research into the origins of a well-developed and highly advanced Chaldean science of Numerology and into the understanding of the application of the language of numbers. However, one does not need to understand Egyptian mysticism, the Hebrew mystic Gematria, or Vedic system of Numerology, in order to demonstrate Chaldean Numerology's validity. If one obtains a knowledge and understanding of the nature, purpose, application, and results of the numerological equations, formulas and processes, and the appropriate interpretation of the language of numbers, then the validity and verification of the truth about Chaldean Numerology and all its principles will follow. We don't profess to have a direct knowledge about the original scientific investigations and application of the four additional sound-syllable "letters" that were included in the alphabet used in Chaldean Numerology, since we weren't there and do not know anyone who was!

The fact still remains that the Latin/Roman Alphabet, the Romance languages, Eastern European languages (Germanic, Balkan, Polish, Armenian, Cyrillic, etc.), Mediterranean languages (Egyptian, Greek, Phoenician, Arabic), languages of the Near East (Aramaean/Sumerian/Chaldean, Hebrew, Persian, Turkish, etc.), languages of the Far East (Early Chinese, Indo-Aryan, etc.), and the English language either were derived from or incorporated aspects of the variations addressed under The Science of Numbers into the structure of their languages. These variations came about as a natural result of the development of differing, but related, language systems that followed the expansion and diversification of the human family from the lands of the Fertile Crescent (Ancient Aramaea, Chaldea, Sumeria, Mesopotamia, and western Persia)—now an area containing Eastern Syria, Southeastern Turkey, Southern Armenia, Iraq, and Western Iran). These language (sound-syllable) variations became necessary to describe certain patterns of the "new" paradigm that was being encountered by each clan, culture, tribe, etc. In other words, certain vibrational patterns that were unfolding in the new experience could not be described by the strict application of the original Aramaean/Chaldean/Sumerian Sacred Alphabet.

In modern times, most are not aware of, or have forgotten, what the Chaldean priest-scientists knew to be a reality about the developing languages of the ever more divergent clans, tribes, and cultures in the known and not so known world of their times. All of these developing languages were offshoots of the Aramaean/Chaldean/Sumerian language, with very similar but slightly differing forms and sound combinations.

The divisions of the human family were spreading outward into other lands and strange environments, toward far-distanced unknown lands of the world that encircled the "Cradle of Civilization" in the Middle East. The Chaldean priest-scientists knew this and they were aware of the need for their science to be responsive to the eventuality of variant sound combinations existing in the spoken and written word of these societies. They also knew there was a limit on how many differing language variations could eventually be created. Again, what many modern texts do not reference, and fail to make clear, is the fact that the English Alphabet evolved directly from the sound-syllable based language of the ancients.

The Chaldean priest-scientists developed their system of Numerology as a "universal and integrated" system of numbers in order to allow for the diversity of language fluctuations and to accommodate the structures of differing language systems. As a result, the alphabet (sound-syllables) of Chaldean Numerology was developed to allow for these variations to be adaptable to the alphabet of the language system in which a name originated.

Sound (spoken language) preceded written language, of this there can be no doubt. From the beginning of time until now, sound was and is the "primary" vehicle for communication—and more. It is also a central motivating force for the development and pursuit of scientific discovery and technological advances.

In the book of Genesis in the Hebrew Bible and the Old Testament in the Christian Bible, importance of the power of "sound" in the creative process is revealed. These excerpts from Genesis, chapter 1, verses 3–6, convey that importance—And God said, "Let there be light." And there was light. And God saw the light, that it was good; and God divided the light from the darkness. And God called the light Day, and the darkness he called Night. And there was evening and there was morning, one day. And God said, "Let there be a firmament in the midst of the waters, and let it divide the waters from the waters."

Numbers–The Powerful Bridge Beyond

Chaldean Numerology for the New Millennium

Although many do not accept the story of Genesis as the "literal" creation or a provable scientific explanation of creation, the inference is abundantly clear. Also, the inference to a creative process has been passed down in the spoken word of ancient mystics and scholars, and in the written spiritual texts of the major religions of the world. First, there was sound which generated vibrational resonance (energy patterns), and then there was creation (a physical world filled with life in all forms).

The existence of vibrational patterns represented by assigned numerical values was evident long before written language came into common use. In fact, the science used by the "ancients" did not require written language, since a written language was not needed in the environment of the ancients prior to the use of language by the human race for communication. How long ago was that? We may never know exactly in terms of the recorded history. Historical and archaeological evidence indicates recorded history started around 4,000 BCE.

Only recently, in the history of man, have scientific advancement in the world and innate Divine Power been treated as separate forms of creation. This separation (a "dual" view of the world) has caused us (humanity) to believe that our experiences were either material or spiritual (e.g., "God versus Mammon"). When, in fact, this dual view of the world is a modern concept and not a precept of truth, i.e., this "dualistic" view of our world has no basis in fact or "reality," but only in the minds and imagination of human beings. Prior to the concept of duality, "everything was connected"—all life and form was permeated (thoroughly filled) with spirit (Divine Power). To the ancients, science and spirit were not considered a separate or different realm of endeavor. And in the experience of the world before the advent of recorded history, the ancients weren't scientists versus priests. They were priest-scientists concerned about the "whole" body, the spirit of evolving mankind, and the unfolding environment that was the world around them.

The advent of so-called modern recorded history was caused by the necessity for the human race to use written language as the vehicle for communication and community. Previously, all science, whether spiritual, mathematical, physical, technical, astrological, or numerological, was developed based on number, vibration, form, equation, and formula and process without the need for a written language. Sound was the key, since it produced energy which, in turn, created vibrational patterns. Only in "modern times," when science was applied to community, was the use of written language required for interpretation.

Conclusion

The Chaldean priest-scientists developed an amazingly brilliant numerological system of interpretation that required only minimal sound-syllable additions to the Aramaean/Chaldean/Sumerian language structure to accommodate the whole family of diverse languages which has spread throughout the world. The demonstrated accuracy of the interpretations, bar none, of Chaldean

Numbers–The Powerful Bridge Beyond

Chaldean Numerology for the New Millennium

Numerology gives us the most exact and definitive understanding of the patterns unfolding before us in our world, including added knowledge, straight answers, viable choices, and the ability to make decisions that clarify and enhance our lives. The utilization of the science of Numerology goes back long, long before the recorded history of the Human society.

Chaldean Numerology first appeared as a "formalized" system in Ancient Babylon, and combines aspects of Chaldean Astrology, mathematics, physical sciences, and "spiritual" sciences. It integrates the interpretive elements of the Chaldean esoteric system of thought with elements of the Chaldean science of Astrology. Most importantly, we must be able to logically understand and intuitively accept the relationship of the interpretive language associated with the "vibrational patterns" of specifically assigned numerical values. To fully understand and appreciate the incredible insight and information available from the science of Chaldean Numerology, you need only be aware of the accuracy of the results. The efficacy and accuracy of Chaldean Numerology can also be demonstrated through the scientific principle of validation. (See chapter 4; see section titled *On Demonstrating the Validity of Chaldean Numerology*.)

The Chaldeans were consummate priest-scientists and were responsible for many worldly scientific and technological developments and advances, as well as the development and application of techniques and processes which were beyond what is understood as physical science. Chaldean Numerology was only one of many revelatory sciences commonly used by the ancients to understand the ever unfolding, renewing world around them. Chaldean Numerology is an extension of the concept of sound-syllables being assigned specific numerical values representing vibrational patterns. These vibrational patterns through the interpretation of the language of numbers (*Numerolinguistics*), define, affect, and impact the design and blueprint of your environment and life and, in truth, have answers that can reveal the path toward your greatest good. Chaldean Numerology, whose history traces back to the beginnings of the world's original civilization, is not the only valid system of numbers in existence today, but, the only fully accurate system of calculation and interpretation.

###

Chapter 3:
Benefits of Numerology

Introduction

As we indicated in chapter 2, although the science of Chaldean Numerology may have originated in antiquity, the methods, techniques, and formulas revealed by that science are even more important to us today, for becoming and staying informed about ourselves and the world around us. The results of Chaldean Numerology create a powerful bridge that will take you beyond the information received and beyond the interpretation of the numbers in your Numerology chart to the activation of a process of self-awareness and self-healing, which includes self-acceptance and self-advocacy.

By crossing this bridge, you will be able to arrive at an understanding of and have access to knowledge that will bring you insight and clarity. This knowledge will be available to you when you are faced with uncertainty, have pressing questions that need to be answered, have a need to resolve dilemmas that could disrupt your life, and/or are forced to make life-changing decisions and choices. *Numbers–The Powerful Bridge Beyond* will give you access to knowledge and information not previously available to you by other means. It will provide you with the opportunity to become aware of important things about your life, including events, experiences, conditions, and situations that may have been forgotten, hidden, or blocked by you unconsciously, or deliberately withheld from you by others.

In truth, you will now have available to you a book of instructions that will include techniques, methods, and alternatives for your use. For you, it will be a personal, one-of-a-kind "owner's manual" tailored to you, your life, and the ever-changing environment that is the world you live in. In this personal manual, you will learn about the potential of step-by-step guidance and advice available to help you fix, repair, modify, or change your life, your view of yourself, and your attitude toward people, success, and abundance. This "manual" becomes a very unique and special handbook that is about you and you alone, where you will find information that is real and to the point. You will have available, at your fingertips, accurate information and revealed knowledge that will actually make sense to you. It will show you discoveries that will allow you to take actions leading to a successful life, in harmony with your hopes, dreams, and desires. You will experience, firsthand, the ultimate truths about Chaldean Numerology which gives you unbelievably startling and uncanny results, results that are on target and surprisingly appropriate and correct to living in today's world. And, it will increase your insight to the ever-changing patterns of your environment, your life, and your unfolding experiences.

Do you want to realize the possibility of walking through your life unafraid for the first time? Do you want to look into a mirror and see a pair of accepting and approving eyes looking back? Do you want to finally see yourself for who you are, and know that you are truly worthy of having love, peace of mind, success, and abundance? Do you want to step upon a path in life where you can finally begin your walk toward becoming a fulfilled, complete, alive person capable of having it all—love, career, family, responsibility, success, joy, and much, much more? Do you want to know, without any doubts, with no uncertainty, that you can handle anything that comes your way—with courage and confidence?

The science of Chaldean Numerology is more than equations, formulas, sound-syllables, numerical values, and vibrational patterns. Although it may be ancient in origin, it is a new and exciting way for you to discover who you truly are, learn self-acceptance, make the most of your life, and find the best ways to be successful. *Numbers–The Powerful Bridge Beyond* will give you the opportunity to search for the answers you need and want for your life today. The almost unbelievable accuracy of Chaldean Numerology gives you an exact and definitive understanding of your life and the world unfolding before you, including knowledge, information, straight answers, and workable choices and options, as well as the ability to make decisions that clarify and enhance your life.

As you read this book, you will discover, more and more, the many additional benefits that will come to you through the use of Chaldean Numerology. This book contains results of actual representative case studies (stories within stories of many lives), and consultation sessions to provide you with an understanding of the variety and uniqueness of the stories and outcomes based on individual Numerological chart readings. The authors, with years of intense and disciplined study and investigation, with an ever-expanding professional practice, with an intimate and thorough knowledge of Chaldean Numerology, have been blessed with the opportunity to pass on this incredible system of numbers and all that it can reveal to you.

The accuracy of the interpretive power, the insight, and the understanding brought about through the use of Chaldean Numerology is both amazing and revealing. Clear, concise, and no-nonsense answers have been provided to thousands of people who have taken the challenge of receiving and accepting very specific and personal information about their lives and their dreams. Chaldean Numerology profiles are developed to represent not only the design and blueprint of your unfolding environment, experiences, and life patterns, but to provide you information and knowledge that will help you plan, direct, and shape the events unfolding before you. These profiles are, have been, and shall continue to be exceptionally accurate, staying right on the mark and to the point, showing you options for taking action, pointing out times of decision coming up in your life, and offering choices that are on the table before you. Through the interpretive language of Chaldean Numerology, you will be able to understand the information and options that will give you the best chance of fulfilling your hopes and dreams and succeeding in all your endeavors.

Chaldean Numerology is the oldest number system in existence, dating back to at least 4,000 BCE. The basis of this ancient science is that we are born with a set of unique numbers whose vibrational patterns have specific meanings from which we can derive a design and blueprint of our lives. Knowing this personal information upfront allows you to make the best and wisest choices possible, thus eliminating the "risk" in making a decision based upon impulse, unwanted pressure, or lack of facts.

The selected case studies presented depict just a few of the Chaldean Numerology charts and readings that have been performed by Chaldean Numerologists over the years. These case studies will show you the very real benefits of the information revealed by the science of Chaldean Numerology, the stories of "real people wanting to live their lives smarter and better." The information from Numerology charts can provide you with enough clarity and understanding of yourself and others, places, situations, confusing issues, and misunderstood intentions that you will be able to make informed choices, instead of guessing or judging incorrectly.

All the case studies and stories shared in this book are true. However, we have changed the names and identifying details to protect our clients' anonymity. Everyone comes with at least one or more stories and is generally looking for to questions related to career and finances, relationship issues (personal and business), health and well-being, troubling situations, feelings of low self-worth, and confusion about the direction of their lives.

Personal Case Studies

1. Personal Relationships

a. Single Man Researches Two Dating Prospects

A CEO dating two eligible candidates for marriage wanted to eliminate one candidate. However, both women were similar in nature, so he needed help in making the right choice. We ran two sets of Numerology charts and then we compared each woman's chart to his. Both women had similar characteristics, but one clearly had a more dominant personality than the other. "Dominant" was not a good thing in this case because the woman was stubborn and opinionated, which in time would clash with her partner's joyful personality. This would especially be risky, once they started a family. The information from the readings provided him a very clear and logical way of making his decision. He could now make an informed decision based on the thoroughly presented detail about each woman and her compatibility with him.

b. Single Woman Wanting Ambitious and Successful Partner

A client wanted to make sure the man she was dating was as ambitious as she was. A character analysis confirmed this was a good match for both of them because they are power people with compatible personalities that matched up in their drive and ambition. He definitely turned out to be a "keeper" which was confirmation she had made the right decision.

c. Single Man Wanted Compatibility Chart on New Girlfriend

A wealthy client wanted to know more about the woman he was dating because this woman was playing cat and mouse with him and it was driving him crazy. Being an intellectual, the roller coaster ride was not going to work so he wanted to know more about her. When the two charts were compared, it was clear that she was exciting but would probably never settle down. If he caught her sometime in the near future, he would be lucky as her freedom was actually her lover and therefore would not give up her freedom for a lasting relationship. He had tried to stretch the relationship to make it work because they seemed so compatible in other areas. During the reading he learned just why this was not a good match but knowing what he was told, he pursued her anyway. Two weeks later, he called to say that the reading was dead on and that he ended the relationship due to the reasons that were stated during the reading.

d. Reading for Mother, Father, and Two Sons, Aged 12 and 18

The Mother, who was very intuitive, ordered a family consultation because she wanted to know more about her family and how she could motivate one of her sons who had a learning disability, but first wanted to get a handle on all of the personalities in her family. All members were present during the reading where it was discovered that each family member was highly "sensitive." As a result of their sensitivity, each was easily hurt, would retreat, and would not fully communicate what they were really feeling, hence, poor communications and disappointments. That was a very important discovery.

At that point in the reading, each member was given a complete character analysis. During this process of learning about each other, a surprising thing happened. The family experienced an eye-opening discovery of a totally new appreciation and respect for each other. Each had special gifts which became very apparent.

The older boy was very intellectual and during the course of his reading, he received insight and clarity on what direction he wanted to go in and to start his own business. His dilemma for moving forward was that he wasn't sure if he had the right business partner. We soon discovered that his intuition was correct and that this partner was not the best choice. This knowledge allowed him to make new decisions surrounding his future where prior to the reading he was unsure of what to do, which held him back.

What was most surprising was that the younger boy, who had a learning disability, was given his reading last, and there was a question as to whether or not he would understand what was being presented to him. However, time would shed new and interesting results from this family's consultation. We are happy to report that this family is happier than ever, and all understand each other in a whole new light. The older son started his business. The younger brother got motivated to help his brother, and to take up new hobbies that he felt his disabilities in the past prevented him from achieving. His desire to make a change boosted his confidence to overcome his fears. Because of a mother's desire to understand the dynamics of her family and to fix some family problems and not knowing where exactly to find the information she was seeking, she felt very fortunate to have been introduced to Numerology at a time when there were no other resources available to her that would have produced the type of information received from the readings on each of her family members.

2. Marriage Relationships

a. Woman Tired of Husband Who Could Not Make Decisions

A client wanted to end her long-term marriage because she grew tired of making all the family decisions and being in the driver's seat after so many years of wanting her husband to take charge—which he never did. Their children were raised so it was nearing time to think about their retirement but her husband was not taking an active role in their plans. As always, he deferred the decisions to his wife. We determined both had different interests and most of the activities she planned were around what she wanted. Earlier on he decided that it was not worth fighting over so he went along with her program for the sake of keeping the peace in the family.

To solve this dilemma, we ran both their charts so we could get a better understanding of how each was "designed" and to see what each other's strengths and weaknesses were. What we discovered in the process was that she had strong leadership qualities and powerful numbers in addition to being ambitious. He, on the other hand, had no leadership numbers in his chart but he did have the lover numbers, thus his make up was more domestic, gentle, kind, and non-aggressive. After reading the charts and explaining that her husband was not "designed," so to speak, to be a leader but, that she was a leader, and therefore it was natural for her to step up and take charge. In this particular case, she had really overshadowed him into submission.

The charts provided the reality of what was actually going on behind the scenes in their marriage. Either she had to accept her husband the way he was, or divorce him, start over, and find a man who was a take charge kind of person. The only problem with the latter scenario was that she would run the risk that her new partner would not be as good of a lover as her husband and the new partner could possibly become too controlling, causing conflict between the two. We are happy to report as a result of the reading, the client was finally able to understand why her husband had a difficult time making decisions, which she could now accept. And having a great lover was better than risking the other outcome.

b. Husband Filed for Divorce After 18 Years, Shocking Wife

A professional couple worked together to build a sound financial portfolio for years so one day she could stay home to start a family. Both left for work one day and when she returned home found a note on the counter from her husband. The note read: "I have filed for divorce, moved out, and I recommend that you get an attorney as soon as possible." This came as a total shock even though they lacked communications skills, as both had a hard time confronting and discussing personal problems in the marriage. Clearly the marriage had been in trouble for some time. The husband just would not confront his wife with his true feelings, so he deceptively planned his escape and filed for divorce.

With nowhere to turn and in total distress, a friend suggested that she get a Numerology reading which might shed some light on the entire situation with the hope of putting the pieces together or at least to make better sense of what just happened. The client showed up severely depressed and almost motionless. The first question asked of her was if she wanted to save her marriage or actually wanted the divorce. Her answer was naturally to save her marriage. During the reading, it was learned that her husband had emptied their bank accounts by taking all their liquid cash, which left her with a zero balance. When asked if she thought she could ever trust him again, the answer was clearly no, but yet she still wanted to save the marriage. Further along in the reading, the chart indicated that she had a joyful and magnetic personality. But there was definitely something wrong, since this woman did not socialize at all nor did she have any friends. Knowing that the information provided by the chart was correct, the only logical explanation had to be that something was wrong at home to suppress this normally beautiful personality.

During the reading, the truth came to the surface, and she could now see why she had become so depressed and lonely, and lost the ability to express herself naturally. She realized it was a result of allowing her husband to dominate and control her life and her choices. His demands became so great that she was not even allowed to have family or friends come over to the house, and became a virtual prisoner in her own home.

Next, following this understanding, she was given a simple exercise to do where she was asked to list all the qualities she wanted in her perfect partner, and then was asked to list the qualities of her husband. The exercise revealed startling information to her, as well as a life shock about what led to her present situation. By the time she had completed this assignment, she knew now that she wanted the divorce more than he did, and that he was not good enough to be the father of her children. She discovered that he as mean-spirited, and had dishonored and disrespected her by what he had done to her. She was now ready to get the best attorney possible to protect her rights and her home, in hopes of bringing some balance back into her life after so much grief and pain.

The reading also provided a holistic look at her entire life, which made perfect sense to her once the details were put on the table and discussed. The best part of this story was that she reclaimed her power, was now ready to go forth to start a new life, and to meet a new partner. This woman gave off a strong and determined sense of relief after the reading that from this point forward, she would be paying closer attention to managing her life and affairs differently.

c. Husband and Wife–Marriage on the Rocks

A client wanted to know more about herself, and get a better understanding of her husband, since they were close to a divorce. She wanted to save the marriage, but did not know how to go about this in their current state of affairs, living together but not communicating at all. They were actually living two separate lives while living under the same roof. In order to help this client, two Basic Charts (blueprints) had to be generated, a complete character analysis on the client and one on her husband. The information provided from these readings also included their strengths and weaknesses.

After the two charts were run and compared, a startling discovery was made. Both had the same Destiny, Soul/Heart's Desire, Personality, Purpose, and Life Goal numbers which meant they were competing with each other on all levels. Because of one set of numbers on the Soul/Heart's Desire, both wanted to be in charge. And since both were very stubborn and opinionated anyway, the friction and disruption mounted up over time to the point where their marriage was on the rocks.

After explaining what her journey in this lifetime was and how she was designed, and learning about her husband's path, she was surprised to learn how great an amount of information could be extracted from their charts. The one problem that always kept them at a distance was the fact that she was forced to sign a prenuptial agreement when they married. She had to sign this agreement even though she had helped him grow his successful business. The prenuptial agreement had created an underlying resentment that continued to grow over the years.

After the readings, we came up with a game plan for how to save her marriage which turned out to be simple and straightforward. Her lack of attention and affection led her husband to believe that she did not love nor need him, so he had withdrawn altogether. The first part of the plan was to put him back in the driver's seat so that he could be in charge, and she could coast. Next, she greatly altered her routine. She would come home early, prepare a nice dinner and ask him to fix those things around the house that she typically took care of. Then she started planting romantic cards in his coat pockets and around their home to surprise him. In addition, she now wanted to give him massages and become close again. She hadn't done this for so long that she almost forgot how easy it was to rekindle their romance based on making their relationship fun, interesting, and loving again.

This story had a happy ending. Within two months, they were watching TV together, sleeping together, and enjoying each other's company again. The competition between the two had forced them apart, but when she decided that she no longer needed to be in control, everything changed. He came home one night and planned a romantic evening to surprise her. Part of the surprise was tearing up the prenuptial agreement she was forced to sign, as he felt that she no longer was a threat to his income and they were to remain partners. The information from the charts brought insight, clarity, understanding, acceptance, and the desire to make better choices in their marriage once they first had an understanding of themselves.

d. Husband and Wife–Better Understanding of Long-Term Marriage

A client told her husband that she wanted a Numerology reading since she had tried many different venues before and failed to get an accurate account of what was going on in her life. She also wanted to have a better understanding about what made her husband tick or how he was designed—since she was much more aggressive, felt he was not doing his part to contribute, and because she wanted him to assume more responsibility. She knew this would lessen the stress and frustration on her, since she had carried the majority of the responsibility in raising their family while working to grow their business.

Upon evaluating their charts, we discovered she had "Leader/Lover" numbers and naturally assumed her husband only had the "Lover" numbers, which would account for why he was not as aggressive. To our surprise, her husband also had the Leader/Lover numbers. However, because she had a more aggressive destiny and he had a non-aggressive destiny of a peacemaker/diplomat, he was not driven to take the lead (if he didn't have to). With this understanding, and knowing that he was designed to be more aggressive than what he demonstrated in the past, it was now clear that it was time for him to step up and assume more responsibility to give his wife a rest. After comparing their two charts, he now had a clear understanding of why he remained non-aggressive—his wife always assumed the lead. Had he challenged her, he felt, there would have been friction. So he decided to assume the partnership support role and back her up, not realizing the pressure she was under all this time, that is, until she said she had enough. The reading brought the clarity and understanding that was needed in this relationship. The end result was that he was ready to step up to assume more control and work together, since they wanted to expand their business. By using their talents collectively and with a refreshed desire to incorporate more creativity into their lives, they revived a loving marriage that became off target.

3. Other More Complicated Relationship Issues

a. Long-Term Marriage, Lover, Wrong Business Partner

This client was in a long-term marriage primarily as a caregiver to her dying husband, and had a lover for moral support during this trying time. Unfortunately, while letting her business affairs slip, she discovered her partner was embezzling from her software company. Not knowing what to do about her business partner, she chose not to do anything at all knowing that she was personally liable for any wrongdoings that may surface but since she had her hands full, she hoped the problem would resolve itself. The woman was in complete denial about what was happening around her business since her husband's illness had totally consumed her. Although she knew he had only a couple of months left to live, she started to resent his presence.

A close friend shared her Numerology reading with her and the difference it had made in her life. On an impulse and out of desperation for seeking insight, clarity, understanding, and acceptance for the chaos in her life, she booked the appointment. Secretly she wished for a plan of action to help her take control of her life so she could get back on track, now greatly concerned that she could lose all of her assets should she be sued as a result of the actions by her business partner.

During the reading, we had to run multiple charts that included hers, her lover's, and her husband's. When all the details of her entire life were placed on the table, we were able to put the pieces that made sense back into the puzzle, thus allowing us to concentrate on how to resolve the rest of her dilemmas and then to come up with a strategy for moving her forward. The information extracted from the charts was way beyond her expectation. Her Destiny is that of the diplomat/peacemaker and is non-aggressive so she did not have the ability to deal with her business partner nor confront her lover with needing more attention from him. Her lover had similar non-aggressive numbers so he was more passive and was withdrawing from their relationship because she was not meeting his needs, a total misunderstanding altogether.

We were able to come up with a game plan that resolved all of her issues. First, she was going to see to the affairs of her husband and to be with him his remaining days. She would then resolve the issues with her lover and commit to putting more energy and fun back into her relationship which had become boring and stale. Next, she was going to hire a trusted business associate/attorney who was a strong leader and very aggressive to clean up her affairs at work, since she was not designed to take charge or truly manage a company the way it needed to be. By offering him a part ownership in the business, he was eager to jump in and clean up things so the arrangement became a win/win for both of them.

Without the information gleaned from all three charts, it would not have been possible to provide the magnitude of information that was given through this reading. By understanding each of the characteristics of the individuals involved and each of their strengths and weaknesses, it was then easy to see the whole picture and to choose the right people based on their skill sets and characteristics.

b. Long-Term Marriage that Included a Lover on the Side

A client who was married for 24 years found herself in an emotional state when she learned from her lover of 10 years that he had decided to end their relationship, since he grew tired of her not making a commitment to him or filing for divorce. The woman hadn't loved her husband for many years but he was wealthy and a good provider. Her lover was much younger than her and deep down inside she feared that eventually he would grow tired of her as she got older; therefore, she decided not to deal with the situation since she figured her lover would always be there.

In order to fully understand what was going on in the lives of three people—hers, her lover's, and her husband's—all three charts had to be generated in order to provide the answers to her questions, and to determine the emotional state of each by taking a holistic view of their lives and then running their charts to get the basic information as to what cycles they were in or going into. Interesting enough, now that she knew her lover was serious about wanting a permanent partner, it was too little, too late. She wanted him, but tired of waiting for her to make a decision, he found a replacement in his area and was ready to settle down to a normal relationship and environment.

What we learned from generating all the charts and extracting information from them was that all three individuals were in a year of emotions, completions, and endings—all at the same time and the story finally had played out. Come to find out that her husband filed for divorce shortly thereafter which was totally unexpected, the lover left, and she was in turmoil over what to do with her life and how to start over again.

4. Personal Issues

a. Illness That Stemmed from Moving into the Wrong Home

A client who purchased a home became ill right after she had moved in. Shortly afterwards, in addition to feeling ill, she developed fungus on her legs. After seeking medical attention that turned up no answers as to what could have caused this, a friend of hers suggested she investigate if a Numerology reading would reveal something about her home in general that would explain what no one else could. So now she wanted to know whether or not the illness was a result of moving into the home.

We ran the street numbers and then the street numbers and street name together so we would know what the vibration was coming from the home and then the area. It turned out that the home vibration for this particular individual was highly emotional and electrically charged, and that the home was in a disruptive location. The vibration of the home was working against her body make up and therefore it was assumed that her body started to deteriorate due to this environment. Six months later the woman moved into another home in another location and reported back that the fungus on her legs had healed and that she felt so much happier living in her new residence.

Although this type of situation is difficult to understand (and even more difficult to prove that the medical condition was a result of moving into a particular home), medical doctors could not explain how this woman developed the fungus on her legs, which did not heal until after she moved. It was confirmed that after running her chart based on the numbers of her new home that the vibrational patterns of the new location were in complete harmony with her.

b. Brilliant, Gifted Teenage Child, Trapped in a Crippled Body

A client wanted a reading on herself and her daughter so she could understand and make sense out of all the bad experiences she attracted in her life and how to better help her daughter, now a teenager, to cope with all her medical problems. Her daughter was trapped in a crippled body due to deformities believed to be the result of her mother being a drug addict during her pregnancy, and of course, there are guilt feelings over her daughter not being normal.

Her daughter was constantly teased at school and not only felt ugly but was unpopular. She struggled with her physical appearance, but realized she had the talent to foresee the future. She had been born psychic and intuitive, and had some magic talent to forewarning of unwanted events. She was so accurate that it spooked most people. Feeling odd and alone, she wanted to retreat from the world.

We generated both charts and discovered that her mother is a Light Worker or Child of the Light who had come into this lifetime to help mankind on a spiritual level. As it turned out, her daughter has all Master Numbers in her chart and is a very powerful human being that's been trapped in a crippled body. After her reading, the girl realized that her oddness separated her from mainstream, which really protected her talent. And after having an understanding of how she came into this lifetime to provide clarity, something happened that made the girl feel that her gift was worth anything she would have to deal with.

Her mother's dream was to open up a healing center, which she finally did, with the intent of having her daughter partner up with her when she was old enough, so she too could use her gifts to serve mankind in a safe environment amongst other healers. The reading confirmed what a special girl she is because of her unique gifts and that she was sent here on a special mission—and to date, we have only seen one other blueprint similar to hers with all Master Numbers.

Business Case Studies

1. Selecting Business Partners

a. Business Owner Selects Business Partner from Three Candidates

Three candidates were interviewed for a partnership opportunity. The owner wanted to make sure that whoever he hired would be an equal to him, complimenting his strengths and weaknesses. Out of the three candidates interviewed, only one had the power and ambition numbers and wanted to serve mankind. The second man, in contrast, was very intellectual but lacked the personality needed to be in the public arena, while the third candidate was more creative but did not have the business savvy. By generating Numerology charts on each of these candidates, we were able to quickly cut through the chase by presenting the business owner with valid information on each, which allowed this man to make his choice based on a character analysis of what he was seeking, thereby saving him time and money in the long run.

b. Legal Notice Given to Change Company Name

The owner of a company was notified after doing business for three years that the name they chose for their business had already been taken by a company doing business for well over 20 years. They were formally notified to change their name within 30 days or face legal action. Of course the owner was upset since not only was this going to be a financial hit but they spent a lot of money advertising and changing the name meant a huge impact on the company's image. It is interesting to note that this company was not thriving or doing well in the first place and the owner could not figure out why. As it turned out, the name carried a "Karmic" and disruptive vibration with it. After changing the name to a more unique name tailored to the type of business this was, virtually overnight the business picked up strictly by referrals. Out of this upset came a new opportunity for this business owner since the new name was a better fit as opposed to the other name that was picked in a hurry at that time without knowing the vibrational patterns assigned to it.

Name Changes

1. Personal Name Change

a. Choosing a "New" Name Following a Divorce

This client wanted to change her name after her divorce and was clear that she did not want to reclaim her maiden name since she was in an abusive environment growing up and did not like her name for that reason. She provided four names and wanted to know which of the four names would give her a more spiritual vibration since she had transitioned into the metaphysical world. We ran charts on all four names and although each was unique, there was one name that stood out amongst all of them, and it happened to be her favorite one. It was the perfect fit for her as it was the vibration of the compassionate humanitarian which she was. The charts were laid out side by side so she could see the differences that each name would bring. She then realized just how important it was to choose a name that she could resonate with, and how powerful names really are. The name she selected combined all of the vibrations this client wanted, in addition to the fact the new name made her feel more spiritual, beautiful, magical, and confident than any name she had prior. The vibration from her "new" name was such a perfect match that she immediately resonated to it.

b. Deciding What Name to Go by Prior to Marriage

A client was getting married and needed to decide if she would assume her husband's name after marriage or keep her current name. Actually, there were four names to choose from; her maiden name (that she never used), the name given to her by her grandmother (that she has gone by for years), a former married name or her husband's name which is one of those names that has a negative connotation to it. The problem is her husband wanted her to take his name but he understood her dilemma because the name she goes by is the name she resonates with out of all the names and was having a hard time emotionally giving up that name.

Charts were generated for all of the name options only to find out that the name she goes by is absolutely the perfect fit and any of the other names would have drastically changed her current characteristics over time. A decision was made to keep the name she goes by which she loves and will introduce herself as his wife at social events taking his name for social purposes only. This was a good compromise because they both got what they wanted.

Conclusion

Because of the accuracy of the science of Chaldean Numerology—the only correct system of Numerology—the charts and readings are so unique and powerful that regardless of the reason for ordering a chart, each individual will absolutely walk away with insight, clarity, understanding, and acceptance to their experiences in addition to getting the inside scoop of what they came into this lifetime to experience, and how their design characteristics affect all relationships.

In addition, each individual will experience a number of reactions as a result of the reading, regardless of their story. What is consistently evident is that all of the reactions are positive. The two most predominant reactions are: either they walk away with confidence, or they are ready to kick-start their life as shown in table 3–1 on the following page.

Reaction to a Reading

Reaction #1 Walk Away with Confidence	Reaction #2 Ready to Kick-Start Life
The client walks away feeling very confident that the decisions they have made and the direction they have embarked on is in fact "the" right choice or path, which serves as a confirmation that they are on target and have their life in order. The client feels comforted and reassured that they can now forge ahead in fulfilling their life with confidence.	The individual learns new information about themselves, their life, and others in their life, and can now take charge and make better decisions and choices based on what they just learned. This becomes a "reality" check when an intuitive Numerologist interprets their chart or blueprint and then spins the data in such a way that the individual can actually connect the dots and see clearly what they could not see prior to the reading about their life. The reading actually sparks a new type of excitement, desire, and drive from within that overshadows old fears, to get their life back on track, and to have the courage to move forward with confidence. This type of reading helps the individual to transition from fear to courage, providing a new lease on life.

Table 3–1

The numerologist facilitates the extraction of personal information from a chart and through a question and answer process that will interpret the story about the individual. It should be noted that each numerologist will have their own style in how they develop their charts and likewise, their technique for how they interpret them. It is best to seek references and to do research before selecting just any numerologist, because after all, you deserve to have an accurate reading.

From its beginning, Chaldean Numerology has been a respected and appreciated source of knowledge and wisdom, used by people from all walks of life—farmers, artisans, scholars, priests, kings, warriors, and many others. Throughout the ages, it has been used as a matter of course in people's lives because of the demonstrated truth of the information and knowledge that is always revealed. Chaldean Numerology is an ancient, but new science that has survived the test of time as well as the skepticism of so-called modern scientists, and will continue to bring you the gift of knowledge about your character, your inner desires, your path to prosperity, and the world and people around you.

###

Numbers–The Powerful Bridge Beyond

Chaldean Numerology for the New Millennium

Chapter 4:
Chaldean Numerology Versus the So-Called Modern Number System

General Overview

In order to address the differences between the science of Chaldean Numerology and the so-called Modern (Western) number system, certain information must first be conveyed to the reader in order to explain the reason that such a comparison is even necessary. First, the Modern number system is an existing portrayal of Numerology that has never been investigated or validated as a viable and functioning process. It is vastly incorrect in its premises and formulas for calculating the patterns of our name which determines our Purpose (calling), our Soul/Heart's Desire (what drives us), our Personality (the way that others see us), and our Soul Qualities (lessons to be learned), and is used to determine our final Life Goal number. Modern Numerology has surreptitiously predominated in the West for decades due to the fact that Modern numerologists have refused to acknowledge the existence of Chaldean Numerology, either out of ignorance (lack of knowledge) or out of fear (admitting the inaccuracies of a system that they embrace). Chaldean Numerology (the original science) has, for the most part, been ignored and discounted. But that will no longer be the case. *Numbers–The Powerful Bridge Beyond* will now dispel the misconceptions of Modern Numerology and unlock the true process of Numerology by revealing the only correct number system, the science of Chaldean Numerology.

The contention here is there has never been any basis whatsoever for so-called Modern Numerology. These areas of contention will be discussed prior to addressing the basis for the development of the Chaldean and Modern number systems. First, we will address the fallacies and false assumptions of Modern Numerology. Next, we will tell the real story of the life and travels of Pythagoras, a brilliant Greek mathematician and philosopher, as gleaned from several biographical histories. Then, the basis for the development of Chaldean Numerology will be discussed at length, followed by the history of so-called Modern Numerology and its failure. Prior to concluding this chapter, we will address the validity of accuracy of Chaldean Numerology and its place as the only "correct" system of numbers.

Fallacies of So-Called Modern Numerology

As we stated in chapter 1, one of the greatest mistakes in the history of Numerology was the presumptuous and blatant misidentification of Pythagoras as the "Father" of Modern Numerology, which he was not. As previously mentioned in chapter 1, the supposed origin of the Modern system came about when a disciple of Pythagoras, without proof of authority or authentication, falsely "claimed" that Pythagoras had developed such a system. This is so far from the truth as to be unconscionable at a minimum. There is no evidence that Pythagoras was the Father of so-called Modern Numerology by any known process of verification. Historical biographies show that this false claim was made long after the death of Pythagoras, who, obviously, could not acknowledge Modern Numerology, let alone validate it. This has lead to the general unsubstantiated belief that so-called Modern Numerology was the original system of Numerology for the West. This is a false statement in that it's based on an unwarranted, unverified claim that Pythagoras "created" Modern Numerology, a fact which has never been established as truth. This belief and claim has persisted among Modern numerologists even though Chaldean Numerology has been in use in the East <u>and</u> West for over 6,000 years, and has continuously been proven, down to the world today, to exhibit uncanny accuracy, while providing an in-depth story of our life's design and blueprint.

There has never been a demonstration of the validity or accuracy of the so-called Modern system. To our knowledge, no Modern numerologist or Numerology text (or historical text) has ever discussed anything that would be remotely considered as a logical basis for the equations and formulas, design, development, or application of the Modern number system. In fact, any implied authenticity and validity is conspicuous by its absence from most, if not all, discussions of the so-called Modern number system. Its only claim to existence is that a disciple of Pythagoras had "said" so. No records, letters, or historical documents exist that even infer, let alone declare, that Pythagoras ever endorsed the so-called Modern system of numbers.

Other fallacies in the Modern number system include the inappropriate and inaccurate calculation of numerical values of your name, the misidentification of the correct vibrational patterns, and the misinterpretation of the most important parts of your life's design and blueprint. These fallacies alone cause major distortions in the underlying truths about Numerology and your right to understand what Numerology offers. It would be like mistakenly receiving an owner's manual for a microwave oven when you ordered a manual for a refrigerator. Modern numerologists erroneously deviated from the Chaldean Alphabet and assignment of numerical values, either through ignorance or choice. However, the final area of questionable validity is the baseless presumption of Modern Numerology that it is acceptable for them to use, as they currently do, the interpretive language of the Chaldean number system which describes the vibrational patterns of the numbers (numerical values) calculated from the sound-syllables of our names, while rejecting the basis (formulas and equations) of calculating those numbers—the Chaldean science of Numerology. This seems, in the most basic form, to be illogically irresponsible—rejecting the Chaldean Science of Numbers, while accepting the Chaldean process of interpretation and the only source of a descriptive interpretive language of numbers—a language of numbers which was in use at least 3,500 years before the supposed origin of the Modern number system. Modern numerologists fail to understand that the Chaldean priest-scientists used a process of interpretation and a language of numbers which were a direct result of the creation of their sound-syllable based science of Numerology.

Numbers–The Powerful Bridge Beyond

Chaldean Numerology for the New Millennium

For some 2,500 years, people have accepted Modern Numerology's unjustified declaration of being valid without any evidence of its truth because no other numerologist has ever stepped forward to challenge its validity, that is, not until now. However, we do not and can not in good conscience allow the assertions of so-called Modern Numerology to go unchallenged in light of the evidence of history, or, as it really is, the lack of evidence which is nowhere to be found— not in memoirs, not in historical documents, and not in biographies. The Modern number system uses an alphabet that was not even in existence at the time of Pythagoras (6th century BCE) and did not come into use until almost 400 years later. It discounts the very basis of Numerology—sound-syllables of your name, vibrational resonance, and assignment of numerical values and meaning to the "letters" of the Sacred Alphabet. Modern Numerology uses number formulas and equations that fail to tell you the correct meaning of the numbers of your name—the keystone of the design and blueprint of your life.

The Story of Pythagoras

Pythagoras (570–475 BCE) was a Greek mathematician-philosopher, was initiated into the "mysteries" of the Eastern mystics, and was the catalyst for bringing the science of Chaldean Numerology to lands north and west of Egypt, Chaldea, Sumeria, and Persia. He had a brilliant mathematical mind and profound spiritual nature. This story relates the true nature of the life of Pythagoras as it has been recorded in historical and biographical references. It attests to his involvement in the spiritual sciences of the Chaldean/Kabbalah scientist-mystics, Egyptian and Persian mystery schools, and the Vedic teachers of western India. Pythagoras established his "mystery" school, based on mathematics, astronomy, philosophy, and mystical sciences of the "East," in southern Italy (circa 550–530 BCE) to pass on the mystical sciences to Western students. He was one of the foremost spiritual and scientific leaders of his time and was considered to be the first "true" mathematician.

He studied the phenomenon of sound resonance (notes) that was produced by vibrating strings and their mathematical relationship to numbers. Pythagoras believed that numbers had personalities and identities, and designated odd numbers as male and even numbers as female. Many may know about Pythagoras (or at least heard of his name) from Geometry and the Pythagorean Theorem. Pythagoras was known as the "Father of Numbers" (not the Father of Modern Numerology) by future generations because of his genius in mathematics.

Pythagoras was born on the island of Samos in the Aegean Sea, off the coast of Asia Minor (modern Turkey), where he lived with his father who was from Phoenicia (once a part of ancient Aramaea) and his Greek mother. History indicates that Pythagoras traveled throughout Egypt, Chaldea, Persia, and India, where he met and studied with Chaldean priest-scientists, the Magians (magicians), and Egyptian and Vedic (India) mystics. This occurred at the time of Cyrus the Great of Persia who was creating a vast empire to the East. The advent of Cyrus is noted here, because it was the very nature of his Empire that allowed Pythagoras to travel throughout the Persian Empire and study in Egypt, Chaldee, Judea, and India. Cyrus allowed freedom of travel, freedom in the arts, and freedom of religion throughout his empire. As a result, Pythagoras had a unique opportunity to visit to many lands where he was able to not only study under the tutelage of Chaldean priest-scientists, Hebrew mystics, and Magians from the East, but had the opportunity to visit and observe the mystics of India, Persia, Babylon, and Egypt over those years.

There is little doubt from historical records that Pythagoras studied, investigated, and understood the basis of the Eastern systems of Numerology which included a mathematical and philosophical integration of the science of Chaldean Numerology. His understanding of sound resonance and the relationship to mathematical numerical values would have made him a "natural" in the use of the Chaldean science of Numerology where every letter (sound-syllable) had a unique vibrational pattern, with numerical values assigned to the alphabetic sound-syllables based on the vibrational resonance. Pythagoras had been initiated into, and became a "Master" of, many of the mysteries of the Chaldean priest-scientists and spiritual teachers of Egypt, the Near East, and India.

Numbers–The Powerful Bridge Beyond

Chaldean Numerology for the New Millennium

Pythagoras

Believing humanity to be under divine guidance at all times, Pythagoras was an intuitive being, counseling that no human should ever accept that they had been passed by or abandoned by the Universe and the Architect of the Universe. Life itself was the big show, the proving ground, if you will, for humanity to fulfill their mission and destiny. Pythagoras taught that there was a definite relationship of numbers to one's total life experience.

When Pythagoras returned to the "West" and established his school in southern Italy, he introduced many of the "Eastern mysteries," including the Chaldean number system. This Numerological science was based on the understanding and interpretation of the sound-syllables of the "name" at birth. These sound-syllables represented vibrational patterns identified through their assigned numerical values. And through the use of the language of numbers, the patterns were interpreted (translated) into meaningful descriptions. Pythagoras divined fortunes and analyzed personalities using these mystical sciences. He believed in the divine significance of numbers, whereby each number created patterns of living derived from the vibrational essence of the number.

Chaldean Numerology–The Basis of Its Development

As stated in chapter 2, the precise origin of Chaldean Numerology is elusive. However, it isn't difficult to trace and understand the development and application of this ancient science. The development and application is based on assigning the proper numerical values to sound-syllables (which present themselves as "letters") or combination of letters as in a name (see table 4–1). [Note: As discussed in chapter 2, the Number 9 was considered "Sacred" in and of itself, was symbolic of the highest level of spiritual attainment, and had an energy level greater than any other number. Although a "name" could be identified with the pattern of the Number 9, a single "letter" (sound-syllable) of the alphabet could not.] These sound-syllables, in turn, generate vibrational patterns that can be described and interpreted into meaningful information through the use of the "language" of numbers (Numerolinguistics). This ancient science of Chaldean Numerology has been demonstrated to be continually consistent, accurate, and clear, as a matter of course.

Chaldean Alphabet/Numerical Value Assignment

1	2	3	4	5	6	7	8
A	B	C	D	E	U	O	F
I	K	G	M	H	V	Z	P
J	R	L	T	N	W		
Q		S		X			
Y							

Table 4–1

The Chaldean priest-scientists amazingly and brilliantly developed a numerological system of interpretation that required only minimal sound-syllable additions to the Chaldean Sacred Alphabet structure to accommodate the whole family of diverse languages which has spread throughout the modern world. The demonstrated accuracy of the interpretations of Chaldean Numerology, bar none, gives us the most exact and definitive understanding of the patterns unfolding before us in our world, including added knowledge, straight answers, viable choices, and the ability to make decisions that clarify and enhance our lives.

Numbers–The Powerful Bridge Beyond

Chaldean Numerology for the New Millennium

Modern Numerology

Most Modern numerologists have a misconception in regard to the difference between the modern disciplines of linguistics (study of written language/spelling), phonetics (vocal sounds/speech processes), and phonics (sound of letters of the modern alphabet), and the sound-syllable/vibrational resonance-based science of Chaldean Numerology. They appear to confuse the disciplines of modern language usage with the science of Numerology whose origin goes back almost 3,500 years before the beginning of so-called Modern Numerology. Modern numerologists appear to rely on their own interpretations, opinions, and guesses, as if these give them the right to declare something proven simply based on the fact that they say it's so. They rely on the hope and expectation that people will accept their word at face value and assume that what they say is valid because it is said to be valid. As a result, the words of Modern numerologists detract from the truth in that they do not really know what it is that they embrace or practice. They pick and choose unrelated rules of modern language disciplines (even if they are out of context) to justify what they don't know and can't understand about the underlying basis of Numerology.

Modern Numerology also discounts the highly Sacred and Spiritual reverence placed upon the Number 9. The spiritual scientists and mystics of all ages have considered the energy of the Number 9 to be too powerful to be assigned to the level of a *letter* or a *sound-syllable*. The so-called Modern system assigns the Numbers 1 through 9 to the first 9 letters of the Western Alphabet (a descendant of Old Latin Alphabet circa 700–500 BCE which had only 22 letters), and then repeats the sequence of assigning the numbers 1 through 9 to letters without any basis or scientific rhyme or reason. There is no historical or scientific evidence as to the reason for this type of numerical value assignment. As a result, so-called Modern Numerology virtually destroys the validity of the name numbers and their meaning. What Modern Numerology fails to acknowledge is the fact that the language of the numbers of our names gives us the most important facts about the direction in which our lives are unfolding.

It appears that the so-called Modern number system failed in a number of instances of knowledge about Numerology and language. There was apparently a total lack of awareness that the Old Latin Alphabet (a pre-Roman Empire Alphabet) was derived from the Etruscan language (which originally had 26 letters in the alphabet), but only adopted 22 of the Etruscan Alphabet letters (see table 4–2). The Etruscan Alphabet evolved from the Greek Alphabet which is traceable back to the sound-syllable based Chaldean/Sumerian Sacred Alphabets used by the Chaldeans and the Hebrew mystics in ancient Sumeria. In addition, the Greek, the Etruscan, and even more so, the Old Latin Alphabet deviated from the Chaldean/Sumerian Sacred Alphabet, retaining most of the sound-syllables, but eliminating some and changing others, without any apparent reason for doing so.

The Old Latin Alphabet of Pythagoras' times, which the Modern system swears by, did not have 26 letters. The Latin Alphabet that the Modern numerologists believe to be the basis of the Modern system did not reach 26 letters until 100 BCE, almost 400 years after the so-called Modern system was supposed to have come into being. This fact in itself should have caused Modern numerologists to question and examine its validity. The failure of the so-called Modern system of numbers and its advocates to demonstrate any verification of its origin or development is obvious by the glaring inaccuracies caused by the Modern Numerology basic alphabet/numerical assignment (shown in table 4–3) which did not even exist until almost 400 years *after* Pythagoras had died. And, to this day, there has not been an accounting for the use of this invalid alphabet/number assignment table. The pressing issue about this, relative to the fallacies inherent in the Modern system, is that it cannot be ascertained whether Pythagoras' disciple even had any scientific understanding in "creating" the so-called Modern system. The fallacies in the Modern system guarantee that it cannot accurately determine the correct numbers and meaning of your name. One of the only things known for sure is that all of the letters now included in the English (Western) Alphabet did not exist in Pythagoras' time.

Old Latin Alphabet/Number Assignment

1	2	3	4	5	6	7	8	9
A	B	C	D	E	F	G	H	I
	K	L	M	N	O	P	Q	R
	T		V		X	Y		

Table 4–2

There has never been a demonstration of the validity or viability of the so-called Modern number system and the specific basis for its development, only that a disciple of Pythagoras "said" that Pythagoras had developed it—with no proof, no logical premises, and no description of the development of this particular approach. There are no historical documents that even hint that Pythagoras was in any way a part of the so-called Modern system of numbers or acknowledged it. The use of the Modern number system has since caused a major distortion in the accuracy of one's name interpretation—an inaccuracy which fails in providing anyone with the appropriate and correct meaning and interpretation of the most important part of their life's design and blueprint—their name.

The origin of the Modern system of numbers was falsely attributed to Pythagoras. This pronouncement and claim is questionable at best, since there is no evidence that Pythagoras ever developed or advocated such a system. The advent of the Modern system was an extremely unfortunate development which led to an application of a system of numbers that was not developed or demonstrated through any scientific process of validity. It is now called

Modern Numerology and inappropriately calculates the numbers of a person's name at birth through a sequential assignment of "Numbers" (1 through 9) to the letters of the English (Western) Alphabet (see table 4–3) instead of assigning the proper numerical values to sound-syllables which are the basis for interpreting unfolding vibrational patterns. Modern times (since the advent of so-called Modern Numerology) have eroded the true meaning of letters of the ancient Sacred Alphabets.

At the time that so-called Modern Numerology supposedly was originated, the letters J, U, W, and Z were not a part of the Old Latin Alphabet (see table 4–2). Therefore, how can so-called Modern Numerology claim to be based on the 26–lettered English (Western Alphabet) that wasn't even around when the so-called Modern system was supposed to have been started? What modern texts do not reference is the fact that the *English Alphabet* (and the Latin Alphabet, all romantic languages and their derivatives, as well as all other languages) evolved from the sound-syllable based Chaldean language of the ancients. The accuracy of the so-called system of Modern Numerology is contradictory and inconsistent, and, at best, yields conflicting results. It is the inaccuracies of the Modern system that defeat the purpose of generating and describing the best possible design and blueprint of your life.

Modern (Western) Alphabet/Number Assignment

1	2	3	4	5	6	7	8	9
A	B	C	D	E	F	G	H	I
J	K	L	M	N	O	P	Q	R
S	T	U	V	W	X	Y	Z	

Table 4–3

On Demonstrating the Validity of Chaldean Numerology

Although this has been discussed at length in chapter 2, the following paragraph is a synopsis for the purpose of leading into the demonstration of the validity and accuracy of Chaldean Numerology. The science of Chaldean Numerology is derived from the power, energy, and effect of the *Letters* (sound-syllables) of the original Sacred Alphabet. These *Letters* are not letters in the sense of the modern alphabets which use letters for their written languages. The *Letters* of the Sacred Alphabet are sound-syllables (vibrational resonances) which give off vibrational patterns. The Chaldean number system is based on the premise that our names are made up of, not letters, but sound-syllables which lead to an in-depth description of the design and blueprint of our lives. As stated in chapter 2, these sound-syllables generate energy that creates vibrational patterns which affects our body's physiology (functionality) and energy processes, and impacts an unfolding, living, changing environment that defines our lives. (Note: Additional information in regard to sound-syllables is contained in appendix A.) The sound-syllables are assigned numbers (numerical values) that are the key to interpreting these vibrational patterns through the use of the Language of Numbers, each of which has a specific and unique interpretive description.

The sum of our name's numbers is a *Number* which has a unique vibrational pattern that can then be interpreted and described. The Language of the Numbers (Numerolinguistics), associated with the sound-syllables of the name, is not the result of an assignment of a number (and its vibrational expression) to an English dictionary letter. Also, it is not individual letters that determine the meaning of the name; it is the combination of the sound-syllables (vibrational expressions) within a name (the language of the sum of the name's numerical values) that determines the meaning of the patterns unfolding in our lives. Usually, someone wants to understand the techniques and methodology of a scientific process before being convinced that it works. The science of Chaldean Numerology can be demonstrated as valid, if someone is willing to spend the effort and time required to understand the techniques and methodology underlying the basis of Chaldean Numerology.

Or, one can demonstrate the viability and accuracy of Chaldean Numerology, not necessarily from knowing "how" the science came about or how the process is defined, but from the verifiable results yielded from the use and application of the scientific principles. Even in today's scientific atmosphere, the scientific method of proof allows for demonstrating that the "established" premises do, in fact, result in valid and true conclusions (not from demonstrating or proving the principles of Chaldean Numerology, but from the accuracy and information that you actually get from Chaldean Numerology). Or, as it is sometimes said, the proof of the pudding is in the taste! *Numbers–The Powerful Bridge Beyond* is written to do precisely that—to show you Chaldean Numerology can give you the "proof of the pudding" by demonstrating that the accuracy and depth of information, the story of your life, will continually and always be evident This book contains the results of but a few of the thousands of case studies and consultations that have been documented over the years. The accuracy of the interpretive power and insight brought about through the use of Chaldean Numerology is both amazing and uncanny. Clear, concise, and no-nonsense answers have been provided to thousands, and soon to be, many more thousands, of people who have taken or will be taking the challenge of getting very specific and personal information about their lives and their dreams. Chaldean Numerology charts are developed to represent the design and blueprint of each and everyone's unfolding environment, experiences, and life patterns. These charts are, have been, and shall continue to be exceptionally accurate, staying right on the mark and to the point of showing you options for taking action, decision points coming up in your life, and choices that are on the table before you. The interpretive language of Chaldean Numerology will provide the kind of answers which will give you the best chance of succeeding in all your endeavors and in fulfilling your dreams.

Conclusion

In order to ensure accuracy in developing this numerological "story" of anyone, you must be able to understand the relationship of the interpretive language associated with the vibrational patterns represented by name and birthdate numbers (numerical values). To fully understand and appreciate the incredible insight and information available from the application of the principles of the science of Chaldean Numerology, as with any science, one needs to investigate/study the elements presented and confirm the accuracy of the results.

The concepts and application of Chaldean Numerology used in this book, are based on certain "foundational" basics contained in the book, *Numerology Made Easy*, which discusses the definition and application of the concept of Numerolinguistics, as well as the process and application of Vibrational Interpretive Analysis (VIA). New additional information, clarifications, and the introduction of advanced techniques have been included in this book. The original Chaldean number system is the most accurate system known in Numerology, as proven consistently by the thousands of readings done for people over the past decades. Ongoing study and investigation, continuous research, and real-time consultations continue to validate the uncanny accuracy and depth of the original science of Chaldean Numerology.

###

Numbers–The Powerful Bridge Beyond

Chaldean Numerology for the New Millennium

Chapter 5:
The Importance of the Name and Birthdate

Introduction

When you understand the science of Chaldean Numerology, the only correct number system, you will learn that we come into this life with an "owner's" manual describing how our "name" and "birthdate" provide a design and blueprint for each person's life experiences. This design and blueprint is developed through the generation of a Numerology chart that contains very specific and very personal numbers which identify the vibrational patterns of your name and birthdate.

There are nine major characteristics in your Basic Numerology Master Chart. Four of those characteristics are revealed from the calculation of the numbers of your name. Four are revealed from the numbers of your birthdate. And one characteristic, called the Life Goal, is calculated from the "integration" (the sum) of the numbers of your name and birthdate. The Life Goal will manifest itself as a subtle influence that comes to the surface in the middle half of life. Its function is to give both hope and opportunity for continued purpose, and it is called the ultimate or final goal by some.

What would you say if you knew that your name and birthdate have a numerical value that can reveal to you, in writing, an in-depth character analysis of who you are, and that you could get the same information about those you know or are about to meet, from their name and birthdate? What would you say if you knew that you could determine whether you and anyone else were born to be a lover, leader, business executive, diplomat, lawyer, entrepreneur, entertainer, healer, or teacher? And by knowing this information, you could have a better understanding of relationships, behavior, compatibilities, personalities, strengths, and weaknesses? What benefits would you derive from the opportunity to make better choices and decisions in your life, particularly when selecting your soul mate, roommate, business partner, or career?

The magazine publication *Consumer Reports*® prepares us for making the best choices based on presenting us with thorough facts and information on the benefits and features of products and services. So, why not try a new approach using the avenue of Numerology charts to find information about the benefits and features of relationships, careers, places, schools, etc., and reap the rewards for making wise decisions and smarter choices, such as happiness, success, and enjoyment?

Can you imagine the advantage you would have in being able to "check out" a person in the early dating (blind or not) stages, or at the beginning of a selection process for the right business partner, without having to invest a great deal of time or money? Wouldn't this be considered a smart move to know, in advance of the time of choosing a partner, the results of researching the characteristics of the relationship you are about to experience? This can be an invaluable tool whether "checking out" a potential personal relationship or a potential business partnership.

The Importance of the Name

The language of the numbers of your name reveals important and useful information and knowledge to you about yourself and your environment. The four basic characteristics of your full Name (First, Middle, Last) are your Soul/Heart's Desire known as your emotional desire (from the Vowels of your name), your Personality, as others see you (from the Consonants of your name), your Purpose or "calling" (from your total name), and your Soul Qualities (lessons and talents you came into this lifetime to learn and develop, derived from missing numbers in your total name). In addition, your total name (Purpose) is used in conjunction with your birthdate (Destiny) to calculate your Life Goal (final opportunity) number. This chapter will first address what the four characteristics of your name will, in fact, give to you.

– The Soul/Heart's Desire represents your emotional aspect, the innermost desire of the heart calling out for you to express yourself. The vowels of your name, which determine the number of your Soul/Heart's Desire, are the reflection of your emotions, that is, the way you feel about things, people, places, and situations including yourself and your life. Emotions react to the environment in which you find yourself, interpret and express your responses to people and the world around you, and confirm your dreams.

– Your Personality is the first impression you give to others, and represents your "physical" aspect. It is the "form" or pattern of your outer self which radiates outward to others. When you walk into a room, you give off vibrations that create this first impression, which people sense and interpret. It seems to be human nature to make judgments about a person based on how they first appear, which unfortunately, seems to lead to misunderstandings and sometimes confrontation in misinterpreting the individual's true Personality. Always keep in mind the fact that your Personality is not the true representation of "you." It is only the "face" that you show when relating to others.

– Your Purpose number reveals your "calling" in life. It tells you specifically what you need to do and be to find your greatest joy and success. It does not tell what you are or what you may desire to be. It identifies the experiences that get you the most out of life. The Purpose number is a reflection of your intuitive aspect, and reveals itself to you in the form of hunches, not through your thinking process. As the intuitive aspect, it represents an inner knowing without the need of facts to reach an answer. It is your inner connection with the forces of the Universe, the part of you that knows things before you become aware of them.

– The Soul Quality numbers of your name form a picture of your strengths and weaknesses, and what areas need developing in order for you to become a more integrated individual. Strengths are specific areas where your talents and abilities have been developed, and now can be utilized for your growth and success. Weaknesses signify specific areas which have not yet been fully developed. Having a "weakness" does not mean that you are "lacking"—rather, it simply means that you will need to strengthen the abilities and talents revealed by those patterns in order to achieve your highest potential. They are identified by recognizing which vibrational patterns are missing from the letters in your name—a unique formula that determines the level of development for each of the Soul Qualities you are here to experience, unless you have already mastered that particular lesson, talent, or ability.

Since your name is paramount in providing you access to the design and blueprint of your life, it's importance is also evident in the clarity you can gain about your life, how and to what extent you can use the knowledge, where and when you can best direct your energies, and in the wisdom that you can apply in making correct choices and decisions.

Your awareness of the language of the numbers of your name becomes even more important when you realize the advantages that come to you in a world where you can change your name at anytime, even on a whim. You may change your birthname many times over your lifetime (either legally or not) through adoption, marriage, or for career purposes, or you may simply want to change your name because you do not like your birthname. So, what's in a name? Is your name really important? And, does it really matter what the name is that you are called?

A new name will gradually influence the characteristics and patterns of your life over time. As you use the new name, its effect on your experiences becomes more and more predominant. And whatever the reason for a name change, the change does, in fact, have either a positive effect or a negative effect on you. However, most people are not aware of this. Most parents spend quite a bit of time and thought in going over and sounding out baby names before finally choosing one, and then it's permanent—that is, until the name is changed!

When you change your birthname, you alter or modify your original foundational design and blueprint. Your "new" name acts as an overlaying influence on the original blueprint, and attracts a new set of experiences. Always remember that your name at birth defines your "true" calling. Your new name will channel your life into new directions, which can either enhance the characteristics of your original blueprint, or not! The name you were born with gives you the foundational design and blueprint of your life, no matter how many times you choose to change it. However, you can change your name, and if you do, the changed name will form a new design, a new blueprint, altering the characteristics that your original name revealed (Soul/Heart's Desire, Personality, Purpose, and Soul Qualities). The previous sentence about a "changed name" is the single most important truth for you to grasp and fully understand, for the altering of your name can, and will, be a major life-changing action which you will have to live with, for better or worse.

In our society, particularly for women who change their name through marriage, the changing of your name can drastically alter the way you live your life, the goals you wished to reach, and the fulfillment of your true heart's desire. You need to carry this truth with you, wherever you may go and whatever you may do, and always remember who you really are and what your real design and blueprint has shown you. Would you not want to know what these potential changes will bring before changing your name?

In time, under continued use and habit, these "new" influences and patterns, for better or worse, become the path forward for you. After seven to nine years, the name change vibrations and resulting patterns will resonate 100% with you, attracting experiences different than those planned in your foundational blueprint and may in some cases be in opposition to your original design and blueprint. The name that you accept and use will now reflect the vibrational patterns of the role that you are playing, or events or situations you are experiencing. To make things even more difficult to understand, you will probably have and use multiple names at the same time—for example, having a legal name change, a nickname, an office name, or a stage name. And, if and when this occurs, potential complications may result from using different names for different occasions at the same time—such as causing new and different experiences, choices, or opportunities to occur in your life simultaneously—sometimes overwhelming, sometimes blissfully exciting, as each name attracts unique experiences from the vibrational patterns of that particular name.

Normally, the "names" that you want to be called are the "sounds" that you feel comfortable with. As a result, certain environmental patterns, or models of living that are built up in your mind, come into your experience. When you resent or hate your birthname, it is indicative of rebellion against (1) the particular blueprint outlined for you in this life or (2) the environment in which you grew up. You may believe that you had no say so in the name chosen for you at birth and that may be true from a conscious or human perspective. However, "nothing happens by chance," even if you think so. You must take care to be very sure of the motivation for rejecting your "name,"—your calling. If you unconsciously rebel against your birthname, which represents the unfolding vibrational patterns which you signed up for in this life experience (like having a "spiritual" legal contract between you and your higher self), you then have decided at some level not to honor that contract. The result of that decision could cause a vibrational pattern spiral effect on your life. Therefore, whatever reason you use to "change" your name, understand that you are changing the nature of your life, your goals, your expectations, and possibly your greatest successes in life. Are the changes bringing you a life that you wanted or anticipated?

If the patterns of your life deviate so greatly from your original Purpose because of the name change, then startling and unsettling events may take place. After you change your name, the patterns of the "new" name will become dominant over time. And although your foundational design and blueprint will generally become dormant, the "original" vibrational patterns are still diligently on duty below the surface waiting to reassert themselves, if you let them. It is recommended that you use one legal name to avoid as much confusion in your life as possible caused by the different experiences from each multiple name. Use a nickname or stage name, but keep in mind that multiple names bring new and unexpected patterns and circumstances into your life.

The Importance of the Birthdate

The birthdate reveals information and knowledge not only about your Destiny (Life Path), but also about your Personal Year numbers, your Birthday Cycles, meeting your Challenges (to strengthen your abilities and open closed doors), and your Pinnacles (to recognize open doorways to opportunities). In addition, your total birthdate number (Destiny) is used in conjunction with your total name number (Purpose) to calculate your Life Goal (final opportunities) number. Now, with your birthdate, your understanding of the vibrational patterns that are revealed to you is especially important, since your birthdate never changes. This means that the patterns of your birthdate will always be with you. Now, wouldn't it be wise to become familiar with the characteristics of your birthdate and learn about the path upon which you are walking? Is it not better to have information that your birthdate can give about the experiences that are unfolding before you? The four basic characteristics of the numbers of your birthdate are as follows.

The Destiny or Life Path is the mental aspect of you and the controlling factor in deciding what you choose to receive from experiences in this lifetime. It is what you are born to do, and the part you are to play on the stage of life, now and in the future. We are all born with a unique design and blueprint that is derived from our name and birthdate. This blueprint also provides the discipline and the direction to fulfill the master plan. Your Destiny number and patterns remain the same throughout your entire life.

Your Personal Year is one of the most important tools in understanding and preparing for the true nature of events you are to experience during that year. The Personal Year clearly defines what can be expected, what to avoid, and the nature of your personal affairs to be experienced. This knowledge should be used in conjunction with that of the birthdate numbers, and the Universal (calendar) Years to show the correlation of all the events and responsibilities that exist between these factors.

Although the Birthdate Cycles and Challenges both influence your life in three periods of time (cycles), each period of time being similar in duration, they are considered to be two separate characteristics. The Birthdate Cycle numbers represent a combination of the final, reduced-down digit of the Birth Month (First Cycle), Day (Second Cycle), and Year (Third Cycle), divided throughout your life into three major age spans as outlined in your Basic Numerology Master Chart under Birthdate Cycles (see figure 6–1). The Cycle numbers are important because they represent how you will feel internally during each of these age spans and the nature of your life experiences. The vibration of each Cycle will last for the duration of that particular age span that you are in.

The Challenges show the strengths and weaknesses you must deal with in order to become a more integrated and harmonious person. There are two "Minor" Challenges known as Sub-Challenges, one "Main" Challenge that is felt throughout your entire life, and a Third and Last Sub-Challenge. The Sub-Challenges are determined for each of the three major age spans during your life (similar in duration to the Birthdate Cycles).

Your Pinnacles define the timing and the nature of the four major, positive change periods in your life. The Pinnacle numbers show you the "Open Doors" that lead to your greatest success. These periods of time are different for each individual since they are derived from the birthdate and year. The Pinnacles are like road maps that clearly show the path you are traveling on now or will be traveling on in your quest to find the ultimate soul fulfillment, the Apex of Life. Pinnacles are like the four seasons in life: spring, summer, autumn, and winter—but are clearly defined by an age cycle you are in or will be going into so that you have an idea during that period of time what the vibrational patterns are that you will be attracting for that Pinnacle.

Conclusion

We have discussed the importance of your name and birthdate by describing the type, nature, and scope of the information that is revealed by the characteristics of both the name and birthdate, and what you must pay attention to when making decisions and choices.

However, the most essential factor in ensuring that your name and birthdate numbers identify the "true" vibrational patterns of your design and blueprint is the absolute requirement that the information and knowledge being generated by your Numerology chart reveal the appropriate, accurate, and correct story of your life. We cannot emphasize enough the importance of this accuracy, because *this accuracy can only be validated if the science of Chaldean Numerology, the only correct number system, is used to determine the numbers and patterns of your name*

Calculating the numbers of your birthdate is relatively straightforward, since they are "numbers," and do not have to be determined from the sound-syllables of your name. The accuracy of the numbers and accompanying vibrational patterns of your birthdate is almost pre-determined, when you use the Chaldean Numerology formulas in calculating the numbers of the characteristics of the birthdate. The Chaldean System of Numbers is the only correct system for calculating the numbers of your design and blueprint.

If you use an incorrect number system for revealing the numbers and vibrational patterns of your name, you will fail to determine the correct interpretation of these essential patterns of your life's design and blueprint (Soul/Heart's Desire, Personality, Purpose, and Soul Qualities), which depends on the accuracy of the numbers of your total name. In addition, the meaning of the patterns of your name will be so far out of synchronization with the correct meaning that it will end up making your life's story sound like nonsense. Or worse, it would lead you down wrong paths and through wrong doorways, lead you to places that could cause you grief and conflict, or lead you to doors that won't open. The importance of your name and birthdate is in the value that comes through the correct information and knowledge provided to you, the insight and clarity that you get, your acknowledgement and acceptance of what's revealed, and the wisdom of action that this information and knowledge can bring you.

It is essential to reiterate the importance of knowing the "correct" name to use before generating a Numerology chart in order to get a "correct" reading. If you go by your birthname, then that is the correct name you would use (the full name that is, even if you don't typically use a middle name when you sign your name on any document). If you have had a legal name change within the last seven to nine years, then you would want to use that name as it would be a more accurate reading since your foundational blueprint would no longer represent the true identity of the characteristics that have been altered by changing your name. If you have had a legal name change within less than seven years, then you would want to use the name prior to the change since it will resonate more accurately with you.

###

Chapter 6:
Defining the Nine Major Characteristics and Development Areas of the Basic Numerology Master Chart

Introduction

The following Basic Numerology Master Chart, shown in figure 6–1, contains the nine major characteristics and development areas of a Basic Numerology Master Chart—Destiny, Soul/Heart's Desire, Personality, Purpose, Life Goal, Personal Year, Birthdate Cycles, Challenges, Pinnacles, and Soul Qualities.

It's the combination of these nine characteristics and development areas that make up the complete story about the person and is the sum total of components that form their blueprint. The definitions of the nine characteristics and development areas follow the example of the Basic Numerology Master Chart and are presented in the same order as shown in the Basic chart.

See Figure 6–1 on the Following Page.

Example of the Basic Numerology Master Chart

Name: Joanne Marie Justis **Birthdate:** 3/4/1949

The Nine Major Characteristics of the Basic Chart:

Destiny = 3
Soul Desire = 9
Personality = 1
Purpose = 1
Life Goal = 4
Personal Year (2006) = 6 (See chapter 13)

Birthdate Cycles & Challenges
Strengthen Weaknesses/Talents
Lessons in Life

(1–33) (33–60) (60 +)
3 4 23/5 (BD 3/4/1949)

(1–33)
1st Sub-Challenge
#1

(33–60)
2nd Sub-Challenge
#1

(Birth to Death)
Main Challenge
#0

(60 +)
3rd (Last) Sub-Challenge
#2

Pinnacles
Periods in Time–Like 4 Seasons
Apex of Life

(51 +)
4th Pinnacle
#8

(42–51)
3rd Pinnacle
#16/7

(1–33)
1st Pinnacle
#7

(33–42)
2nd Pinnacle
#9

Soul Qualities
(Soul Qualities 1–8, +More, –Less, 0 None)

SQ#1 = 6+ SQ#2 = 1 SQ#3 = 2- SQ#4 = 2+ SQ#5 = 4+ SQ#6 = 1 SQ#7 = 1 SQ#8 = 0-

Figure 6–1

6.A Destiny (The Numbers of the Birthdate)

The birthdate number is known as the number of your Destiny (the number of your Life Path) which describes how you perceive and look at your personal reality. Your birthdate number reveals the nature of your thinking process and the fields of knowledge and endeavor to which your thinking will lead you. It reveals your intellectual perspective, that is, what you "think" your actions need to be to fulfill your Destiny. It is the way your intellect looks at the how, what, when, where, and why of your experiences.

Since your intellect (mind) is considered the center for initiating and controlling action, the number of your Destiny determines what actions you must take in order to create an environment that will keep you on your Life Path. Everything around you in this world that supports your Destiny is perceived or sensed through the interpretation made by your intellect. Your intellect provides the discipline (or fails to) to walk upon your Life Path (achieve your Destiny). And your intellect is responsible for your ultimate choice of things—for your judgments, and for your decisions. It is the instrument which shapes your life and molds your environment, your personal reality of experiencing, and your Destiny.

Most people identify more with the language of their birthdate (Destiny, intellectual perspective), than with the language of their name (Purpose, intuitive perspective). Since your birthdate never changes and is celebrated year after year, you always pay more attention to it. You are usually less in tune with the vibrational patterns of your name numbers (i.e., birthname, nicknames, legal name changes, or different names used for whatever purpose throughout periods of time in your life). In the beginning, others changed your name for you; later, you changed your name yourself to fit your preferred situation/environment. However, your Destiny number (birthdate), which never changes, is very strongly tied to the way you think about your life, your experiences, and things in general. It is interesting to note how difficult it is to change your "mind" when it's made up, but not so difficult to change feelings, hunches, and physical tastes (which are determined and described in the patterns of our name) constantly and sometimes quickly.

Whether or not you are consciously aware of it, your mind is active for most of your life—perceiving, receiving, judging, and choosing. The unfolding patterns of your Destiny number have a decided impact on the way that you "think" about your experiences. Your Destiny vibrational patterns describe your intellectual process and show you that you can achieve through the power of your mind. Understanding the language of your birthdate number can aid you in fulfilling your Destiny.

The calculation of the number of the Destiny (total birthdate sum) is included in chapter 7, section 7.A. The description and meaning of the Destiny numbers are included in chapter 8, section 8.A.

6.B Soul/Heart's Desire (The Numbers of the Vowels of the Name)

The Soul/Heart's Desire is derived from the Vowels of your name, is a reflection of the patterns of your emotional experiences (the desires of your heart), and expresses the emotional view or perspective that unfolds in your life. These patterns reveal clues as to why you feel the way you do about important experiences. The language of the numbers behind the Vowels of your name provides you knowledge that leads you toward an understanding of how you will feel about your life, the people you meet, the things you do, the environments you encounter, the events in which you participate, and more.

Your Vowels can also be said to reflect the inner you, your psychological self, the way you see yourself and your life. But it is only a partial picture influenced by what you have experienced. You create certain models which you worship and swear by, models of things that you want to bring into your life, and models of jobs, places, and people that you feel are right for you. And sometimes, when your emotions respond, or more likely react to the environment in which you find yourself, your true emotions get buried or are hidden, because they "do not" fit in. If this happens and you begin to feel lost, you can now rely on the patterns of the Vowels of your name to lead you back to your true heart's desires.

You can know which environments feel the most comfortable for you or those in which you will feel best (your comfort zones), through the language of the numbers of your Vowels. Or, if you don't feel comfortable in any given situation or environment, you can determine why this is so. This inner you (your psychological being, if you will) is that part of you which interprets and expresses your emotional responses to the people and environment around you. The urge to go somewhere important or to do something major is almost invariably tied to the language and descriptive patterns of the numbers of your Vowels. The Vowels of your name will confirm your dreams and reflect the desires of your heart.

The calculation of the number of the Soul/Heart's Desire (vowels of your name) is included in chapter 7, section 7.B. The description and meaning of the Soul/Heart's Desire numbers are included in chapter 8, section 8.B.

6.C Personality (The Numbers of the Consonants of the Name)

The third major aspect of your name is understood through the Consonants of your name. This characteristic addresses the physical perspective which you display and also refers to the physical environment which you experience through your five senses of taste, touch, sight, sound, and smell. It's the physical appearance or impression that you make in your environment, or the outer you, as others see you; it is your Personality. And, to answer that very question, the language of the numbers of your Consonants can give you exactly that—"the gift to see yourself as others see you."

Where your total name is your intuitive response to your life and the Vowels your emotional response, your Consonants define your reflection in the physical world. The language of your Consonants provides you with clues as to the style of clothes you would look best in, the kind of car that would appeal to you, and what design you would like in a house. And again, it gives you the opportunity to see yourself as others see you. Your Consonants give you insight into understanding the nature of how you fit into your physical world.

When you walk into a room full of people, you always make a first impression. You give off specific personality vibrations which people pick up on and interpret, and you don't even have to speak a single word! The "first" impression you make is unfortunately based on how you look, your outer appearance, because that is all one has to go by until they get to know you. How many times have you heard people say, "I know that type!"? And how many times have you heard people say they always go with their first impression? What do people base a first impression on? Why, the personality. However, when you view things in this manner, you are only dealing with the outer surface or superficial aspect of other people. If you do not care to know the essence of a person, if you do not wish to go beyond the surface contact, your first impression would, of course, always be right.

Through the language of your Consonants you can discover why people react to you differently than you might expect them to or think they should. It will also allow you to stop and reconsider any first impressions that you may get, so that perhaps you can discover whether or not your first impression is really the person you see! The numbers of your Consonants represent vibrational patterns which become a part of your environment and define your personality. Each set of vibrational patterns has its own unique description or meaning.

The calculation of the number of the Personality (consonants of your name) is included in chapter 7, section 7.C. The description and meaning of the Personality numbers are included in chapter 8, section 8.C.

6.D Purpose (The Numbers of the Total Name)

The total name, the name you use, is what you are "called." Therefore, it is your "calling," your Purpose or Mission, the way you are to express yourself in the world. This Purpose is what is known as your "intuitive" perspective. It is that view of your life experiences which says "this is what you should be, what your divine self urges you to become to gain the most from living." It is a perspective which your other characteristics do not give you, the part of your total expression which gives you intuitive knowing, or hunches. This intuitional aspect within you is that part of you which watches your physical, emotional, and intellectual aspects in operation. However, it is, for the most part, left out of one's experiencing today by a significant number of men and women who believe that their minds and intellects are the final authority. Although men seem to be intent on giving their intellectual perspective dominance, it is essential that the intuitional aspect of your being be given an equal role in the conduct of your life and experiences, that is, if you wish to bring greater success and balance into your life and living. This intellectual aspect is discussed in more depth under the numbers of your birthdate (Destiny).

There is a design and blueprint of your life's experiences. There are certain general things which you will do, certain growth which you will experience, and certain value which you will pull from these experiences. Your intuition is that part of your being that knows about those things before you become aware of them. It is the link between your experiences (physical, emotional, and intellectual) and what has been called your Divine Self, super conscious, cosmic consciousness, etc. Your Purpose is only the minimum of what you can achieve and is what your higher self wants you to be, urges you to be, but only if you choose to accomplish it. It is that particular way in which you can experience your world and find your greatest satisfaction and fulfillment in it.

The name that you go by, accept and/or use, happens to reflect the vibrational patterns that are being created in your environment—events, conditions, or situations you are experiencing. You attract the experiences that fit the name. Normally, the "names" that you are called or like to be called are sounds that you like or feel comfortable with. As a result, you bring certain environmental patterns into your experiencing, or image certain models of living that you have built up inside your mind.

What about those people who literally cannot tolerate their full name at birth or only one of their names? When you resent or hate your birthname, it is a reflection of your rebellion against the particular design and blueprint outlined for you from birth, which is in conflict with who you are. You're unconsciously rebelling against the unfolding vibrational patterns which are flowing from (or trying to flow from) your name. You may just be rejecting the truth of what's best for you due to traumatic experiences that caused you to find your name distasteful. As a result, you are unconsciously denying or rejecting the story and design that is revealed by the blueprint given to you at birth.

Not liking your name may create conflict in your view of life and in your values or concepts of living. It normally shows up in a dissatisfied lifestyle—dissatisfaction with your career, an indifference as to what happens to you, a rejection of opportunities (open doors), or a failure to develop close or lasting relationships with people. Although you may be aware of rebellion or conflict, you may not be aware of the root cause of your dissatisfaction. Once people are able to "see" the truth of the matter, they have a chance to re-evaluate their lives in light of this "new" information (evidence).

However, it doesn't really matter what name you use, as long as you understand and acknowledge the vibrational patterns of your name, which give you valuable and valid information about who and what you are. When someone says to you, "Just be yourself," you no longer have to ask "How do I do that?", "How do I know what that is?", or "How do I find out?" Now, you have a way of getting in touch with who and what you are, without uncertainty, without the need for some self-awareness workshops or self-image course of instruction. When you change your name, or are given a new one, be sure that the vibrational patterns which unfold around you fit a specific role you are playing or a new situation that you are in. However, no matter what you are called, always be in tune with the truth of who you are, staying aware and taking advantage of the experiences that come to you. These vibrational patterns will develop into the experiences of your life that express naturally.

The calculation of the number of the Purpose (total name) is included in chapter 7, section 7.D. The description and meaning of the Purpose numbers are included in chapter 8, section 8.D.

6.E Life Goal (The Numbers of the Total Name Added to the Birthdate)

In the last half of your life, or midlife as it is termed (i.e., 50 if you live to be 100), the vibrational patterns of your Life Goal or Final Opportunity number begin to unfold, providing some of the predominant influences on the remaining experiences of your life. This Life Goal number is found by adding the number of your total name, your Purpose, to the number of your birthdate, your Destiny (see chapter 7, section 7.E). The combination of your name and birthdate provides you with the patterns which lead to what is known as the "integration" of your intuition and intellect. This integration provides you with the understanding of environmental patterns which are in tune with the total development of your life experiences. You can take full advantage of these unfolding patterns simply by preparing yourself for the events and situations indicated by your Life Goal number. Your Life Goal number brings together the characteristics of your intuitive perspective (name) and your intellectual perspective (birthdate) to develop for you an additional arena of experiencing, the integration of your intellect and intuition, so to speak.

If you can get in tune with these Life Goal vibrational patterns by your middle to late thirties, you will find the final half of your life to be exciting and fulfilled. You can let your life experiences help you gain knowledge, develop your talents, and align you with your patterns of success. Then you can move into the influences of this Life Goal pattern smoothly, rapidly, and naturally toward the achievement of your life goals.

If you develop both of those characteristics to their fullest, you can have a highly successful final half of life. Real freedom doesn't necessarily come during the first half of life. You can be freer and even more successful during the last half of your life. That's generally the time to shed past burdens and insecurities, and concentrate on experiencing the "finer" goals of your life.

The calculation of the number of the Life Goal (the sum of your name and birthdate) is included in chapter 7, section 7.E. The description and meaning of the Life Goal numbers are included in chapter 8, section 8.E.

6.F Birthdate Cycles (The Numbers of the Birthdate Divided into Age Spans)

The Birthdate Cycle numbers represent a combination of the final, reduced-down digit of the Month, the Day, and the Year of your birthdate divided throughout your life into three major age spans as outlined in your Basic Numerology Master Chart under Birthdate Cycles. The cycle numbers are important because they represent how you will feel internally during each of these age spans and the nature of your life experiences. The vibration of each Birthdate Cycle will last for the duration of the particular age span that you are in.

The calculation of the number of the Birthdate Cycles (month, day, and year of your birthdate) is included in chapter 7, section 7.F. The description and meaning of the Birthdate Cycle numbers are included in chapter 8, section 8.F.

6.G Challenges (The Numbers of the Challenges)

(Lessons to be Learned; Closed Doors to be Opened; Weaknesses to be Strengthened)

"*Ask, and it will be given you; seek, and you will find; knock and it will be opened to you.*" (Matt. 7:7)

Challenges represent areas in your life which you may have avoided, or talents which you failed to develop fully, because you didn't believe that you were capable of expressing these talents. These challenges can set you on a course that will let you to do something about what you consider to be shortcomings. Resolving these challenges can open many doors of opportunity for you, and all you have to do is knock. They are situations, events, circumstances, and/or people operating in your environment that present themselves to you for viewing and experiencing. Challenges can help you strengthen what you may think are weaknesses, and prepare you for the onset of greater opportunities than you may have hoped for.

There are four types of Challenges. There is the Main Challenge, whose influences will be felt throughout your entire life (birth to death), and is the "primary" or overall Challenge in your lifetime that you will need to overcome. The other three Challenges are known as Minor (or Sub-) Challenge cycles. You will feel the influences of the First Minor Challenge between the ages of 1 and 35. You then walk through this set of experiences that are designed to strengthen your abilities and open the doors previously closed to you. The age cycles/duration assigned to the First Minor Challenge and the First Pinnacle are identical and are the only Challenge and Pinnacle that share the same age spans.

At the end of the First Minor Challenge, a change usually occurs in the Second Minor Challenge number (although it may stay the same) and lasts for 27 years. The Third Minor Challenge affects the last part of your life, along with your Main Challenge.

Meeting your Challenges can strengthen your abilities and increase your chances for success. And, meeting your Challenges can very well open new and exciting doorways for you or lead you to doors already open that were ignored because you didn't feel capable of "meeting" the Challenges.

There is a saying that "God won't give you more than you can handle at any one time," and although, initially, each Challenge may seem more than you can deal with, ultimately you will understand and come to know that the experience was a "gift" or "blessing," helping you become a more complete, more integrated individual, as your weaknesses become strengths, and your talents and abilities begin to shine through you.

The calculation of the number of the Challenge is included in chapter 7, section 7.G. The description and meaning of the Challenge numbers are included in chapter 8, section 8.G.

6.H Pinnacles (The Pinnacle Numbers of the Birthdate)

Pinnacles are numbers which signal specific vibrational patterns that identify areas of opportunities that are becoming available to you, if you choose to take advantage of the information. There are criteria for determining the specific age spans, or cycle durations, that are calculated for each of the four Pinnacles. This will allow you to know how long the patterns that affect and influence each Pinnacle will last, in addition to giving you information revealed by your numbers about the potential experiences that could be attracted into your environment.

Where meeting your Challenges will open up closed doors, Pinnacles point the way to doors "already opened" and waiting for you to walk through for your greatest success. The numbers of your different Pinnacles (some of which may be repeated for you) will be described for each cycle in your life.

How many times have you felt or sensed that major changes seemed to be taking place in your life, but you couldn't define or explain precisely what that meant or felt like? How many times have you seen new opportunities unexpectedly open up to you in your current field or job? And what of those opportunities that appear that are unrelated to what's going on in your life? The change may foreshadow a total shift in your career, mental outlook, emotional attitude, and/or the direction or focus of your life's energies. How many friends, family members, or neighbors in their late twenties or early thirties have you known or been told of that have changed or questioned the direction of their lives? How many times have you thought of getting advice or counseling in order to sort through opportunities and/or options that appear in your life? If you know the numbers of your Pinnacles and understand the information that they can give you, you will be able to decide and choose what's best for you on your own. The influence of your Pinnacles has a major impact on your life and you may, indeed, feel like your life is shifting into a different gear as the prior Pinnacle ends and the next one comes into play.

The length of the First Pinnacle is 36 years. This is made up of four 9–year cycles. Your First Pinnacle ends when you are between the ages of 27 and 35. The longer length of the First Pinnacle allows for sufficient time for you to prepare your "young" self to experience and take advantage of the full effect of the Pinnacle's influence. The length of the first 9–year cycle depends on the number of your Destiny (your birthdate number). For instance, if the Destiny Number is 1, then the duration of the first 9–year cycle is 8 years (9 - 1), and the total duration of the First Pinnacle is 8 plus the remaining 27 years (the last three 9–year cycles) will be 35 years long. If the Destiny Number is 9, then the duration of the first 9–year cycle is 0 years, and the total duration will be equal to the remaining three 9–year cycles or 27 years long.

The duration of the Second Pinnacle is always 9 years. Also, the duration of the Third Pinnacle is always 9 years. The Fourth, and final, Pinnacle influences your design and blueprint for the remainder of your life. If you are able to keep your life focused on these "open doors," you will finally have an opportunity to enjoy long periods of success and accomplishment. (Note: The First Pinnacle is made up of a maximum of four 9-year cycles so that, as a child and adolescent, you will have time to learn and train and practice new skills and develop talents during the early years of your life. This lets you prepare yourself for and gives you the opportunity to find success during the latter part of the First Pinnacle.)

The calculation of the number of the Pinnacle is included in chapter 7, section 7.H. The description and meaning of the Pinnacle numbers are included in chapter 8, section 8.H.

6.I Soul Qualities (The Soul Quality Numbers of the Name)

There are eight Soul Qualities (SQ) listed in the Basic Numerology Master Chart and each is assigned a numerical value based on the formula used to calculate the Soul Qualities. To determine whether the particular Soul Quality has already been developed and to what degree, or if it is an area that must be developed in order to achieve the highest potential in this lifetime, NumbersRU.com developed in the 1980s a method of evaluating the individual's development (area/level) using a rating system for comparing the numbers in the chart that would be considered "normal" to where the individual is at the time of the reading. This rating system is an enhancement to the Science of Numbers and works like this: Soul Qualities 1, 3, and 5 will have a normal value of 3, while Soul Qualities 2, 4, 6, 7, and 8 will have a normal value of 1 and a "zero" (0) would indicate a Karmic lesson in this lifetime. By using this rating system that has become a standard for NumbersRU.com, we are able to pinpoint the areas of development the individual needs to work on in order to become a more integrated person.

A zero (0) value on any Soul Quality means the person has a Karmic lesson to learn. A Soul Quality assigned a number value with a plus (+) means that the person has been developing this quality and exceeds the normal value indicated. A Soul Quality assigned a number value followed by a minus (–) means the person has not yet reached the particular level of understanding for that Soul Quality and has more work to do in that area in order to achieve balance and full potential.

The calculation of the number of the Soul Quality is included in chapter 7, section 7.I. The description and meaning of the Soul Quality numbers are included in chapter 8, section 8.I.

Conclusion

As a final note about the characteristics of your Basic Numerology Master Chart, we would like to give a brief definition and explanation of the importance of the Personal Year and why it's included as one of the characteristics listed in the Basic Chart even though it is not a characteristic.

The Personal Year will play a very important role in the design and blueprint of your major numbers so you will want to look at the events that are happening or about to happen in your life stemming from the experiences this year or future years will bring. Each Personal Year number is derived from your birthdate—using your Birth Month and Day only and the Universal (calendar) Year in which you are interested. The vibrational patterns of the Personal Year will show you potential events, situations, and conditions that are unfolding within the environment defined by the Personal Year patterns. By knowing the possibilities that the year may have in store for you, you can use your resources to your greatest advantage.

We, as humans, seem to have an inordinate interest in the upcoming years, with our rituals in celebrating the end of the old year and the beginning of the "New Year." Many cultures have their own rituals for celebrating the going out of the old and the welcoming in of the new, with hopes and dreams of better things, and of course, for the very popular making of resolutions for the coming year. Instead of hoping or guessing what you may be faced with, you now have a source of important information about the "new" year that is revealed in the numbers of your Personal Year and the description of the patterns generated by those numbers.

The language of numbers gives you information that helps prepare you for experiencing the potential of each Personal Year. Each Personal Year's vibrational patterns are a snapshot in "time" within the patterns of your design and blueprint, for a year from now or ten years from now. The more aware you are of events coming up, the easier it is to work with them, and the more successful you can be.

A more thorough discussion of the meaning and calculation of the Personal Year numbers is included in chapter 13.

###

Chapter 7: Calculating the Numbers of the Nine Major Characteristics and Development Areas of the Basic Numerology Master Chart

Introduction

In this chapter you will be given step-by-step instructions on how to calculate the nine major characteristics and development areas that you came into this lifetime to experience. Each has its own unique formula and calculation. In chapter 6, we provided you with a sample of a Basic Numerology Master Chart (figure 6–1). This allows you to see what a complete chart looks like and the characteristics and development areas included in it. It gives you an opportunity to understand how the parts form the whole picture before we define the characteristics and development areas individually, calculate the numbers of each trait, and describe and explain the meaning of the language of their numbers. Here in chapter 7, the calculations will be shown using the name and birthdate of "William Michaels" as the example for applying the Chaldean numerical assignment formula that turns a name into numbers (see figure 7–1). Using this name and birthdate, we generated another Basic Numerology Master Chart example (see figure 7–2) in which the name and birthdate are different than the chart in chapter 6. The use of a different name and birthdate is done to demonstrate the uniqueness of the number combinations and patterns that result from the calculation of each person's characteristics and development areas. It's virtually impossible for two charts to ever be alike unless the names and birthdates of two individuals were exactly the same and the chances of that happening are extremely unlikely.

The following characteristics and development areas define a sequence of events for us, that taken in combination as a whole, describe the nature of our life experiences in the form of a design and blueprint, a total picture of who we really are as an individual.

Characteristics and Development Areas of the Basic Chart
Destiny
Soul/Heart's Desire
Personality
Purpose
Life Goal
Birthdate Cycles

Challenges
Pinnacles
Soul Qualities

This design and blueprint, an owner's operating manual so to speak, which makes up your story, unfolds from the language of your numbers and their distinctive vibrational patterns. These patterns provide you with the blueprint for experiencing an exciting and fulfilling life. The vibrational patterns are then translated into written form through the interpretation of the language of numbers. The interpretation of the meaning of the numerical values was taught to the ancient priest-scientists, not by written texts, but through an intuitive process of learning, understanding, and knowing. This language of numbers provides a description of each "Number's" unique vibrational patterns and the influences the patterns have on your life and the world around you. The interpretation of these vibrational patterns was made possible with the unlocking of ancient secret codes by Chaldean priest-scientists that revealed the language of the numbers. The interpretative descriptions, like the calculation formulas, are correct and accurate to the most exact degree possible. This has been fully demonstrated by the uncanny accuracy of the results since the beginnings of Chaldean Numerology.

Knowing about the patterns of our characteristics allows you to have a better understanding of how you are designed. Some are born lovers, healers, leaders, diplomats, teachers, humanitarians, entertainers, builders, and more. By knowing what your blueprint reveals, you have a better understanding of your relationships, behaviors, compatibilities, and strengths and weaknesses, so you can make better choices in life.

For starters, the formulas for calculating the numbers of your name are based on a very straightforward application of the numerical values assigned to the sound-syllables "letters" of the Chaldean Alphabet (see table 7–1). The Chaldean number system has a very specific and unique formula that uses the Numbers 1 through 8 in its calculations, based on "sound vibrations" and "phonics" (association of letters with their sound values). The Chaldean Alphabet *does not have letters, per se*, as we know them in the West, but rather "sound-syllables." We use the word "letter" as interchangeable with sound-syllable *only* for the purpose of acknowledging that in today's world alphabets are commonly seen as containing "letters." Each letter or sound-syllable of the Chaldean Alphabet gives off vibrational energy which has an assigned "numerical value" (describing a specific set of vibrational patterns).

The Chaldean number system is the only accurate form of Numerology because it uses the original numerical value assignments and interpretive language for determining the vibrational patterns of your full name while other numerological systems do not.

However, before we discuss how to calculate each of the characteristics of your chart, it is important to display the original Chaldean formula and explain how to use it, noting that we first start off by applying the primary formula (see table 7–1) of turning letters into numbers. However, thereafter, each characteristic has its own unique calculation formula.

The Chaldean Alphabet formula is used throughout this chapter, as needed, and is shown in another form in table 7–2, where we first list the letters (sound-syllables) of the Chaldean Alphabet and then list the assigned numbers. This provides you two forms of matching letters to numbers, so that when you calculate each of the characteristics, you can more readily extract the number combinations from your name.

Chaldean Alphabet/Formula
Assigned Numbers with Letters Identified

1	2	3	4	5	6	7	8
A	B	C	D	E	U	O	F
I	K	G	M	H	V	Z	P
J	R	L	T	N	W		
Q		S		X			
Y							

Table 7–1

Chaldean Alphabet/Formula
Letters with Assigned Numbers Identified

A, I, J, Q, Y	1
B, K, R	2
C, G, L, S	3
D, M, T	4
E, H, N, X	5
U, V, W	6
O, Z	7
F, P	8

Table 7–2

Example of Turning a Name (Letters) into Numbers

W	I	L	L	I	A	M		M	I	C	H	A	E	L	S
6	1	3	3	1	1	4		4	1	3	5	1	5	3	3

Figure 7–1

There is a unique formula for calculating the numbers of the name distinct from the formula used for calculating the numbers of the birthdate. The numbers of the Name reveal the Soul/Heart's Desire, Personality, Purpose, and Soul Qualities, while the birthdate reveals the Destiny, Birthdate Cycles, Challenges, and Pinnacles. The calculation of the Life Goal number is the exception in that it is a combination of the Name and Birthdate. We touched on how to use the primary formula, and will describe the calculation of each characteristic in detail in the sections following.

The birthdate formulas will be explained a little later in this chapter when it's more appropriate to introduce yet another set of formulas used to determine the birthdate characteristics. Before we explain how to calculate each of the characteristics, you will need to know the meaning of what is termed the "root" number or a single-digit number of a "compound" number so that you will know when to reduce a number to its root single-digit number, or not to reduce the number, so that it remains a double-digit compound number (e.g., 14/5 versus 5). Table 7–3 shows all of the possible number combinations for the characteristics that either calculate out to be a single-digit or a special double-digit compound number based on what your numbers add up to be. If your numbers add up to be a single-digit number or a compound number, then that is the number you would use in your formula as the final numerical value. Table 7–3 shows the single-digit/double-digit compound number combinations assigned for each character trait (e.g., Soul/Heart's Desire, Personality, Purpose, and Soul Qualities), and development areas (e.g., Destiny, Birthdate Cycles, Challenges, and Pinnacles) and a combination of both, the Life Goal—and the number range across all characteristics and development areas as to what the numbers may calculate to be.

Single-Digit/Double-Digit Compound Number Combinations Assigned for Character Traits and Development Areas

Destiny	Soul Desire	Personality	Purpose	Life Goal	Cycles	Challenges	Pinnacles	Qualities
1	1	1	1	1	1	0	1	1
19/1	19/1	19/1	19/1	19/1	19/1	1	19/1	2
2	2	2	2	2	2	2	2	3
11/2	11/2	11/2	11/2	11/2	11/2	4	11/2	4
3	3	3	3	3	3	5	3	5
4	4	4	4	4	4	6	4	6
13/4	13/4	13/4	13/4	13/4	13/4	7	13/4	7
22/4	22/4	22/4	22/4	22/4	22/4	8	22/4	8
5	5	5	5	5	5		5	
14/5	14/5	14/5	14/5	14/5	14/5		14/5	
23/5	23/5	23/5	23/5	23/5	23/5		23/5	
6	6	6	6	6	6		6	
7	7	7	7	7	7		7	
16/7	16/7	16/7	16/7	16/7	16/7		16/7	
8	8	8	8	8	8		8	
9	9	9	9	9	9		9	
18/9	18/9	18/9	18/9	18/9	18/9		18/9	

Table 7–3

Calculation of the Nine Characteristics and Development Areas

Prior to discussing the calculations of each basic characteristic, we have laid out another Basic Numerology Master Chart (see figure 7–2) to show the calculation results for each characteristic and development area. Figure 7–2 shows the resulting numerical values of all of the nine major traits of the name and birthdate that define the design and blueprint of your life. If you compare figure 7–2 with figure 6–1, you will see that the overall make up of each chart is markedly different.

See Figure 7-2 on the Following Page.

Example of the Basic Numerology Master Chart

Name: William Michaels

Birthdate: 9/21/1938

The Nine Major Characteristics of the Basic Chart:

Destiny = 6
Soul Desire = 1
Personality = 7
Purpose = 8
Life Goal = 14/5
Personal Year (2006) = 3 (See chapter 13)

Birthdate Cycles & Challenges
Strengthen Weaknesses/Talents
Lessons in Life

(1–30) (30–57) (57 +)
9 3 3 (BD 9/21/1938)

(1–30)
1st Sub-Challenge
#6

(30–57)
2nd Sub-Challenge
#0

(Birth to Death)
Main Challenge
#6

(57 +)
3rd (Last) Sub-Challenge
#6

Pinnacles
Periods in Time–Like 4 Seasons
Apex of Life

(48 +)
4th Pinnacle
#3

(39–48)
3rd Pinnacle
#9

(1–30)
1st Pinnacle
#3

(30–39)
2nd Pinnacle
#6

Soul Qualities
(Soul Qualities 1–8, +More, –Less, 0 None)

SQ#1 = 5+ SQ#2 = 0- SQ#3 = 5+ SQ#4 = 2+ SQ#5 = 2- SQ#6 = 1 SQ#7 = 0- SQ#8 = 0-

Figure 7–2

Following are the step-by-step instructions on how to calculate the nine major characteristics and development areas, presented in the same order as shown in figure 7–2.

7.A Destiny (The Numbers from the Birthdate)

The Destiny number is gleaned from the Birthdate and is a combination of the Month, Day, and Year numbers. The Destiny is also known as the Life Path. We will first describe the step-by-step process for calculating the numbers of the Destiny. This will be followed by an actual real-time example (see figure 7–3) in illustration 7a that will walk you through the two-step calculation process. Once you have written the birthdate on a sheet of paper as shown in illustration 7a, you can follow the calculation process. (Note: Whenever we state "sheet of paper," we are referring to a prepared layout, which of course can also be a computer document, worksheet, form, or a design of your own.)

The definition and explanation of the Destiny are included in chapter 6, section 6.A. The description and meaning of the Destiny numbers are included in chapter 8, section 8.A.

Destiny Number
Two-Step Process on How to Calculate the Number
Step 1

First you will convert the Month, Day, and Year into numbers (e.g., September 21, 1938 becomes 9-21-1938). If the number of the month, day, or year is more than a single-digit number (called a compound number), such as 21, then you would add the digits of the compound number together and reduce it down to get a single-digit number, which is known as the root number. For instance, the 21 becomes 2 + 1 = <u>3</u> and the 1938 becomes 1 + 9 + 3 + 8 = <u>21</u>, further reduced down to 2 + 1 = <u>3</u>. In this case, the day and year are the same single-digit or root number. In Step 2, you will be shown the final additions necessary to arrive at the Destiny "numerical value" (vibrational patterns). [Note: If the Birth Day number is a Master Number (e.g., 11 or 22), then you would <u>not</u> reduce that compound number down before adding the numbers together which is the exception to the rule. If the Month, Day, and Year were September 11, 1938, then the calculation would be 9-11-1938 or 9 + 11 + 3 (1 + 9 + 3 + 8 or <u>21</u> or reduced to 2 + 1 = <u>3</u>) or a total of 23 or a <u>23/5</u> Destiny number that does <u>not</u> reduce down.]

Step 2

To finally arrive at the Destiny number, you will need to add the three birthdate numbers (Month, Day, and Year) together. The final calculation number can add up to either be a single-digit root number or a double-digit compound number such as shown in table 7–4. If the final calculation number adds up to be one of the special compound numbers as shown in table 7–4, then you would not reduce that compound number down to a single-digit number. However, if the calculated compound number is not listed in table 7–4, you would reduce that number down to a single-digit root number. These particular compound numbers provide significant additional information about that characteristic and that is why it is important to get a more in-depth interpretation of the actual meaning of the characteristic's patterns. (Note: Table 7–4 is an extraction of table 7–3.)

Double-Digit Compound Number Conversion Table

When the Final Number Adds Up To	The Number Converts To	Final Number Becomes
19	19/1	19/1
11	11/2	11/2
13	13/4	13/4
22	22/4	22/4
14	14/5	14/5
23	23/5	23/5
16	16/7	16/7
18	18/9	18/9

Table 7–4

Destiny Number

Illustration 7a: Calculating the Numbers of the Birthdate

Prior to showing the calculations in figure 7–3, we have included the Universal (calendar) Month numerical values (see table 7–5). (Note: A full discussion of the Universal Month is included in chapter 16.)

Example of Numerical Values Assigned to Universal Months

January	1	July	7
February	2	August	8
March	3	September	9
April	4	October	10 reduced to 1
May	5	November	11 reduced to 2
June	6	December	12 reduced to 3

Table 7–5

Example of Calculating the Destiny Number

	September	**21**	**1938**
Convert to	9	21*	1 + 9 + 3 + 8 = 21
Reduce to	9	21 = 2 + 1 + 3	21 = 2 + 1 = 3
Add	9+	3+	3+ = 15

15** (Compound Number)

Reduce to	1 + 5 = 6
Destiny Number	**= 6***** (Root Number)

Figure 7–3

* See chapter 16 for Universal Day numbers.

** See chapter 9 for Compound Number meanings.

***See chapter 8, section 8.A for the definition and explanation of the Destiny numbers.

7.B Soul/Heart's Desire (The Numbers from the Vowels of the Full Name)

The Soul/Heart's Desire number is found by calculating *only* the "Vowels" in the full name and is a two-step process. Vowels are A, E, I, O, U, and "Y." The "Y" is always a Vowel (see appendix B). The Soul/Heart's Desire also gives you your emotional perspective of life, the way you feel about the people and world around you. Again, as with the calculation of the Destiny number, we will describe the step-by-step process for calculating the numerical value of the Vowels—the Soul/Heart's Desire. This will be followed by an actual real-time example in illustration 7b that will walk you through the two-step calculation process.

The definition and explanation of the Soul/Heart's Desire are included in chapter 6, section 6.B. The description and meaning of the Soul/Heart's Desire numbers are included in chapter 8, section 8.B.

Soul/Heart's Desire Number
Two-Step Process on How to Calculate the Number
Step 1

> To find the number of the Vowels of the Name, lay out the Name on a sheet of paper with room to place numbers below the letters (see figure 7–4 in illustration 7b, noting that there is no middle name in this example, so the name appearing is the full name). Using the values shown in table 7–6, assign the correct number to the letters of the Vowels.

Step 2

To arrive at the Soul/Heart's Desire number, you will need to add only the Vowel numbers together as indicated in illustration 7b. The final calculation number can add up to either be a single-digit root number or a double-digit compound number such as shown in table 7–3. If the final calculation number adds up to be one of the special compound numbers as shown in table 7–4, then you would not reduce that compound number down to a single-digit number. However, if the calculated compound number is not listed in table 7–4, then you would reduce that number down to a single-digit root number. These particular compound numbers provide significant additional information about that characteristic and that is why it is important to get a more in-depth interpretation of the actual meaning of the characteristic's patterns. (Note: Table 7–4 is an extraction of table 7–3.)

Double-Digit Compound Number Conversion Table

When the Final Number Adds Up To	The Number Converts To	Final Number Becomes
19	19/1	19/1
11	11/2	11/2
13	13/4	13/4
22	22/4	22/4
14	14/5	14/5
23	23/5	23/5
16	16/7	16/7
18	18/9	18/9

Table 7–4

Chaldean Alphabet/Formula
Assigned Numbers with Letters Identified
Vowels Only

1	2	3	4	5	6	7	8
A				E	U	O	
I							
Y							

Table 7–6

Soul/Heart's Desire
Illustration 7b: Calculating the Numbers of the Vowels of the Full Name

Example of Calculating the Soul/Heart's Desire Number

W	I	L	L	I	A	M		M	I	C	H	A	E	L	S
	1			1	1				1			1	5		

1+ 1+ 1+ 1+ 1+ 5

Addition = 10* (Compound Number)

Reduced to 1 + 0 = 1

Soul/Heart's Desire Number = 1** (Root Number)

Figure 7–4

* See chapter 9 for Compound Number meanings.
** See chapter 8, section 8.B for the definition and explanation of the Soul/Heart's Desire numbers.

7.C Personality (Numbers from the Consonants of the Full Name)

Finding the Personality number is done by calculating only the Consonants in the full name and is a two-step process. Consonants are all the letters of the alphabet except for A, E, I, O, U, and "Y" which are the Vowels. This includes the "W" which is always a Consonant (see appendix A). Again, as with the Soul/Heart's Desire (Vowels) number calculation, we will first describe the step-by-step process for calculating the numbers of your Consonants. This will be followed by an actual real-time example in illustration 7c that will walk you through the two-step calculation process.

The definition and explanation of the Personality are included in chapter 6, section 6.C. The description and meaning of the Personality numbers are included in chapter 8, section 8.C.

Personality Number
Two-Step Process on How to Calculate the Number
Step 1

> To calculate the Consonant numbers of the Name, lay out the Name on a sheet of paper with room to place numbers below the letters (see figure 7–5 in illustration 7c, noting that there is no middle name in this example, so the name appearing is the full name). Now, using the numerical values shown in table 7–7, assign the correct number value to the letters of the Consonants.

Step 2

> To arrive at the Personality number, you will need to add all of the Consonant numbers together as indicated in illustration 7c. The final calculation number can add up to either be a single-digit root number or a double-digit compound number such as shown in table 7–3. If the final calculation number adds up to be one of the special compound numbers as shown in table 7–4, then you would not reduce that compound number down to a single-digit number. However, if the calculated compound number is not listed in table 7–4, you would reduce that number down to a single-digit root number. These particular compound numbers provide significant additional information about that characteristic and that is why it is important to get a more in-depth interpretation of the actual meaning of the characteristic's patterns. (Note: Table 7–4 is an extraction of table 7–3.)

Chaldean Alphabet/Formula
Assigned Numbers with Letters Identified

Consonants Only

1	2	3	4	5	6	7	8
	B	C	D				F
	K	G	M	H	V	Z	P
J	R	L	T	N	W		
Q		S					

Table 7–7

Double-Digit Compound Number Conversion Table

When the Final Number Adds Up To	The Number Converts To	Final Number Becomes
19	19/1	19/1
11	11/2	11/2
13	13/4	13/4
22	22/4	22/4
14	14/5	14/5
23	23/5	23/5
16	16/7	16/7
18	18/9	18/9

Table 7–4

Personality Number

Illustration 7c: Calculating the Numbers of the Consonants of the Full Name

Example of Calculating the Personality Number

W	I	L	L	I	A	M		M	I	C	H	A	E	L	S
6		3	3			4		4		3	5			3	3
6+		3+	3+			4+		4+		3+	5+			3+	3

Addition = 34* (Compound Number)

Reduce to 3 + 4 = 7

Personality Number = 7** (Root Number)

Figure 7–5

* See chapter 9 for Compound Number meanings.

** See chapter 8, section 8.C for the definition and explanation of Personality numbers.

7.D Purpose (The Numbers from the Full Name)

The Purpose number reveals what your mission in life will be. Finding your Purpose number is done by adding up all the numbers of the letters in your full name which is a three-step process. As with the Soul/Heart's Desire (Vowels) and the Personality (Consonants) numbers calculation, we will first describe the step-by-step process for calculating the numbers of your full name, or your Purpose. This will be followed by an actual real-time example in illustration 7d that will walk you through the three-step calculation process.

The definition and explanation of the Purpose are included in chapter 6, section 6.D. The description and meaning of the Purpose numbers are included in chapter 8, section 8.D.

Purpose Number
Three-Step Process on How to Calculate the Number
Step 1

To calculate the Purpose number, lay out the full Name on a sheet of paper with room to place numbers below the letters (see figure 7–6 in illustration 7d). Now, using the Chaldean Alphabet/Formula Assigned Numbers with Letters Identified (see table 7–1), assign the correct number value to each of the letters of the Name.

Step 2

To arrive at the Purpose number, you will need to add the numbers of the First, Middle, and Last Name together. Place the sum of the numbers of the letters of the first name underneath each corresponding letter of the first name as in figure 7–6. Where there is a middle name (or more than one), add the numbers of the letters of the middle name in the same manner as the first name. Finally, add the numbers of the last name in the same manner as the first name and middle name calculations.

Step 3

To arrive at the Purpose number, you will need to now add the number of the First Name to the number of the Middle Name to the number of the Last Name, as shown in illustration 7d. The final calculation number can add up to either be a single-digit root number or a double-digit compound number such as shown in table 7–3. If the final calculation number adds up to be one of the special compound numbers as shown in table 7–4, then you would not reduce that compound number down to a single-digit number. However, if the calculated compound number is not listed in table 7–4, then you would reduce that number down to a single-digit root number. These particular compound numbers provide significant additional information about that characteristic and that is why it is important to get a more in-depth interpretation of the actual meaning of the characteristic's patterns. (Note: Table 7–4 is an extraction of table 7–3.)

Chaldean Alphabet/Formula
Assigned Numbers with Letters Identified

1	2	3	4	5	6	7	8
A	B	C	D	E	U	O	F
I	K	G	M	H	V	Z	P
J	R	L	T	N	W		
Q		S		X			
Y							

Table 7–1

Double-Digit Compound Number Conversion Table

When the Final Number Adds Up To	The Number Converts To	Final Number Becomes
19	19/1	19/1
11	11/2	11/2
13	13/4	13/4
22	22/4	22/4
14	14/5	14/5
23	23/5	23/5
16	16/7	16/7
18	18/9	18/9

Table 7–4

Purpose Number
Illustration 7d: Calculating the Numbers of the Full Name

Example of Calculating the Purpose Number

W	I	L	L	I	A	M		M	I	C	H	A	E	L	S
6	1	3	3	1	1	4		4	1	3	5	1	5	3	3

6+ 1+ 3+ 3+ 1+ 1+ 4+ 4+ 1+ 3+ 5+ 1+ 5+ 3+ 3

Addition = 44*

Reduce to 4 + 4 = 8

Purpose Number **= 8**** (Root Number)

Figure 7–6

* See chapter 9 for Compound Number meanings.
** See chapter 8, section 8.D for the definition and explanation of Purpose numbers.

7.E Life Goal (The Numbers from the Birthdate and Name)

The Life Goal is the sum of the Destiny (birthdate) number plus your Purpose (full name) number, and represents the integration of your intuition (inner guidance, hunch, what is known as a "gut" feel) and your intellect (how you think about people, things, and the world around you). The numbers of your name, in conjunction with your birthdate, establish the framework for successful and rewarding experiences during the last half of your life. For, as you learn to get in tune to the unfolding patterns of your life experiences, all of your creative channels open up: Intellectual, Intuitive, Emotional, and Physical.

As with the previous characteristic number calculations, we will first describe the step-by-step process for calculating the numbers of your Life Goal. This will be followed by an actual real-time example in illustration 7e that will walk you through the two-step calculation process. Once you have calculated your Full Name (Purpose) number and your Birthdate (Destiny) number, this two-step process will give you your Life Goal number. Refer to section 7.A to calculate your Destiny number, and 7.D for your Purpose number.

The definition and explanation of the Life Goal are included in chapter 6, section 6.E. The description and meaning of the Life Goal numbers are included in chapter 8, section 8.E.

Life Goal
Two-Step Process on How to Calculate the Number
Step 1

To calculate the Life Goal number, you will first need to determine what the Destiny and Purpose Numbers are (see 7.A in illustration 7a to calculate the Destiny number and 7.D in illustration 7d to calculate the Purpose number. The sum total of these two numbers together equals the Life Goal "value."

Step 2

To arrive at the Life Goal number, you will need to now add the number of the Birthdate to the number of the Full Name as shown in illustration 7e. The final calculation number can add up to either be a single-digit root number or a double-digit compound number such as shown in table 7–3. If the final calculation number adds up to be one of the special compound numbers as shown in table 7–4, then you would not reduce that compound number down to a single-digit number. However, if the calculated compound number is not listed in table 7–4, then you would reduce that number down to a single-digit root number. These particular compound numbers provide significant additional information about that characteristic and that is why it is important to get a more in-depth interpretation of the actual meaning of the characteristic's patterns. (Note: Table 7–4 is an extraction of table 7–3.

Double-Digit Compound Number Conversion Table

When the Final Number Adds Up To	The Number Converts To	Final Number Becomes
19	19/1	19/1
11	11/2	11/2
13	13/4	13/4
22	22/4	22/4
14	14/5	14/5
23	23/5	23/5
16	16/7	16/7
18	18/9	18/9

Table 7–4

Life Goal Number
Illustration 7e: Calculating the Number

Example of Calculating the Life Goal Number

Birthdate (Destiny)	September 21, 1938	= 6
Full Name (Purpose)	William Michaels	= 8
Birthdate + Full Name	Total Sum	8 + 6 = 14* = 14/5
Life Goal Number		**= 14/5****

Figure 7–7

** See chapter 9 for Compound Number meanings.

7.F Birthdate Cycles (The Numbers from the Birth Month, Day, and Year)

The numerical values of each Birthdate Cycle are determined from the final, reduced-down digit of the Birth Month, Day, and Year numbers divided throughout your life into three major age spans as outlined in your Master chart under Birthdate Cycles (see figure 7–2). The vibrational patterns of each cycle will last for the duration of the particular age span you are in, which is unique to your birthdate. As shown in figure 7–8, the Birthdate Cycle numerical values are not "calculated" per se, they are simply derived from the "numbers" of the month, day, and year. However, the numbers (which are not vibrational numerical values) of the age span/duration of the Birthdate Cycles are, in fact, calculated.

The definition and explanation of the Birthdate Cycles are included in chapter 6, section 6.F. The description and meaning of the Birthdate Cycle numbers are included in chapter 8, section 8.F.

Using September 21, 1938, the numerical values of the three Birthdate Cycles are first shown in figure 7–8—the Birth Month number becomes the First Birthdate Cycle numerical value; the Birth Day number becomes the Second Birthdate Cycle numerical value; and the Birth Year number becomes the Third and last Birthdate Cycle numerical value. The Birthdate Cycle values then become a part of the formula for calculating the age span (duration) of the Birthdate Cycle.

Example of Calculating the Birthdate Cycle Numbers

	September	**21**	**1938**
Reduce to	9	21	1 + 9 + 3 + 8 = 21
Birthdate Cycle	9	21 = 2 + 1 = 3*	21= 2 + 1 = 3
Numerical Values	**= 9** (1st Cycle)	**3** (2nd Cycle)	**3** (3rd Cycle)

Figure 7–8

* The vibrational patterns of the Birthdate Cycles are determined by and keyed to the Cycle's base root number. This is the <u>only</u> instance where the Universal Day number is converted to the single-digit root number <u>except</u> when the numbers are the Master Numbers 11 or 22 in which case, those numbers don't get reduced down (e.g., 11 = 11/2 and 22 = 22/4 but for purposes of calculation, use eleven or twenty-two not 2 or 4).

Calculating the Birthdate Cycle age spans is a three-step process. In each of the steps we calculate the age span number for each of the Birthdate Cycles (Step 1–the First Birthdate Cycle, Step 2–the Second Birthdate Cycle, etc.). After all of the age span numbers have been calculated, the results will be displayed in figure 7–9, along with the numerical values of each Birthdate Cycle.

Birthdate Cycles
Three-Step Process on How to Calculate the Numbers of the Three Age Spans (Duration)

Step 1

The formula for the age span (duration) of your <u>First</u> Birthdate Cycle includes the number that results from subtracting the Birth Day from the Birth Month numerical value, <u>and</u> the maximum <u>base cycle span of years</u> (36). The calculation is as follows. Using the numerical values shown in figure 7–8, subtract the Birth Day (3) from the Birth Month (9). This number = 6 (9 - 3). The 6 is then subtracted from the Birthdate Cycle's maximum span of years (36). That is, 36 - 6 = <u>30</u>. The length of the first Birthdate Cycle span is 30 years, from age 1 to age 30, or from 1938 to 1968. (Note: The base number "36" is a mathematical "given" in the original Chaldean formula and is the standard used in the calculation of the age span of the First Birthdate and Challenge Cycle.)

Step 2

The <u>Second</u> Birthdate Cycle age span (duration) is 27 years, from 30 to age 57, or from 1968 to 1995. (Note: The "27" year duration is a mathematical "given" in the original Chaldean formula and is the standard used in the calculation of the age span of the Second Birthdate and Challenge Cycle.)

Step 3

> The age span of the Third Birthdate Cycle starts when the Second Birthdate Cycle has ended. In this case, the Third Birthdate Cycle span would begin in 1995 or at the age of 57 and continues until death.

Example of Calculating the Birthdate Cycle Age Span

September 21, 1938

	1st Birthdate Cycle	2nd Birthdate Cycle	3rd Birthdate Cycle
Birthdate Cycle Numbers (Vibrational Patterns)	**9**	**3**	**3**
	(These values are shown in figure 7–8)		
Age Spans (Duration)	**From Age 1–30** (1938 to 1968)	**From Age 30–57** (1968 to 1995)	**From Age 57 to Death** (1995 to ?)
	(These results were taken from the calculations in Steps 1–3 above)		

Figure 7–9

7.G Challenges (The Numbers from the Challenges Calculated in Age Spans)

The Challenges show the strengths and weaknesses that you must deal with in order to become more integrated. There are two interim Sub-Challenges (Minor Challenges) and a Third and last Sub-Challenge, in addition to the "Main" Challenge. The duration (age span) of only the First Sub-Challenge coincides with the age span of the First Birthdate Cycle in 7.F. The span of the Main Challenge is from Birth to Death, and is the overall Challenge you came into this lifetime to overcome.

There is a four-step process required to calculate all of the Challenges. The Sub-Challenges are the same duration as the Birthdate Cycles shown in section 7.F. The actual calculations for the Challenges are shown in each of the four steps. In each of these steps we will calculate both the numerical value (representing the specific vibrational patterns) of each of the Challenges (Step 1–the First Sub-Challenge, Step 2–the Second Sub-Challenge, etc.). Following the calculation of each Challenge's "Numerical Value," we will calculate the "age span" (duration) of the Challenge. After all of the Challenge numbers have been calculated, i.e., the calculation of the numerical values of each Challenge and the calculation of the age span (duration) of each Challenge, the results will be displayed in figure 7–10.

The definition and explanation of the Challenges are included in chapter 6, section 6.G. The description and meaning of the Challenge numbers are included in chapter 8, section 8.G.

Four-Step Process on How to Calculate the Challenge Numbers

Before proceeding to the four-step process for calculating the Challenge numbers, there are a number of basic criteria/mathematical "givens," derived from the original Chaldean formulas, to be aware of.

These criteria/givens are:

(1) For the First Sub-Challenge/Minor Challenge, the 36–year base span is a mathematical given from the original Chaldean formula.

(2) The duration of the First Sub-Challenge/Minor Challenge is always equal to 36 years minus the number that results from subtracting your Birth Day from your Birth Month numerical value, which starts the process.

(3) The Duration of the Second Sub-Challenge/Minor Challenge is always equal to 27 years (a mathematical given from the original Chaldean formula).

(4) The Main Challenge rules for your entire life and is from birth to death.

(5) The Third and Last Sub-Challenge/Minor Challenge rules for the remainder of your life.

(6) 11 and 22 are Master Numbers that never reduce down and are the exception to the rule when calculating a formula; these numbers would be added as shown, e.g., eleven, not 2 and twenty-two, not 4.

(7) In Numerology, when we are using the Chaldean formulas, we always calculate using base numbers, mathematically known as "absolute" numbers, uninfluenced and unaffected by the arithmetic sign. (Note: A negative number is converted to a base number. For instance, a -6 (minus 6) is bracketed by parallel lines (| |), as follows, |-6|. In mathematics, this is known as an absolute number and is equal to 6, a base number. If there is a minus sign (e.g., -6) in the answer, it is ignored (deleted) and resets to the appropriate base number 6.) This is because the vibrational patterns of the characteristics flow from the *Numerical Value* revealed by the calculations, not by its arithmetic sign, plus or minus (+ or −). The arithmetic sign (+ or −) is not relevant to the interpretation of numerological values.

First Sub-Challenge/Minor Challenge
Four Step Process on How to Calculating the Number
Step 1

Numerical Value (Vibrational Patterns)

The number of the First Minor Challenge, (Sub-Challenge), is calculated by subtracting the number of your Birth Month (September = 9) from the number of your Birth Day (21 = 2 + 1 = 3). That is, 3 – 9 = -6 = |-6| = 6 [see criteria/givens (7)]. The numerical value of the First Sub-Challenge = 6.

Age Span (Duration)

The age span duration of the First Sub-Challenge is calculated by subtracting the 6 from the base span of years, 36 [see criteria/givens (1)], to get the age span. That is, 36 - 6 = 30. The length of the First Sub-Challenge is 30 years, from age 1 to age 30, or from 1938 to 1968.

Second Sub-Challenge/Minor Challenge
Calculating the Number
Step 2

Numerical Value (Vibrational Patterns)

The number of the Second Minor Challenge, (Sub-Challenge), is calculated by subtracting the number of your Birth Year (1938 = 1 + 9 + 3 + 8 = 21 = 3) from the number of your Birth Day (21 = 3). That is, 3 - 3 = 0. That is, the numerical value (vibration) of the Second Sub-Challenge is zero (0).

Age Span (Duration)

The age span duration of the Second Sub-Challenge is not calculated, since its duration is a mathematical given in the original Chaldean formula for the Second Sub-Challenge [see criteria/givens (3)]. The age span (duration) of the Second Sub-Challenge is always 27 years long, from age 30 to age 57, or from 1968 to 1995.

Main Challenge
Calculating the Number
Step 3

Numerical Value (Vibrational Patterns) The number of the Main Challenge is calculated by subtracting the number of the Second Sub-Challenge zero (0) from the number of the First Sub-Challenge (6). That is, 6 - 0 = 6. The Main Challenge = 6.
Age Span (Duration) The age span (duration) of the Main Challenge is with you your entire life, from birth to death, [see criteria/givens (4)].

Third (Last) Sub-Challenge/Minor Challenge
Calculating the Number
Step 4

Numerical Value (Vibrational Patterns) The number of the Third (and final/last) Sub-Challenge is calculated by subtracting the number of your Birth Year (1938 = 1 + 9 + 3 + 8 = 21 = 2 + 1= 3) from the number of your Birth Month (September = 9). That is, 9 - 3 = 6. The numerical value of the Third Sub-Challenge = 6.
Age Span (Duration) The age span duration of the Third Sub-Challenge starts from the ending of the Second Sub-Challenge from age 57 until death.

Examples of Calculating the Challenge Numbers

	September 21, 1938	
Age Span (Duration)	(1–30) **1st Sub-Challenge**	(30–57) **2nd Sub-Challenge**
Numerical Value (Vibrational Patterns)	**#6**	**#0**
Age Span (Duration)	Birth to Death **Main Challenge**	(57 +) **(Last)** **3rd Sub-Challenge**
Numerical Value (Vibrational Patterns)	**#6**	**#6**

Figure 7–10

7.H Pinnacles (The Numbers from the Pinnacles Calculated in Age Spans)

Pinnacles are periods of development or personal growth that allow you to prepare for positive experiences that will present themselves to you. Where Challenges (see section 7.G) help you to open doors of opportunity that are closed, Pinnacles allow you to walk through doors of opportunity that are already open and waiting. The experiences of each Pinnacle are unique to each individual and are predetermined at birth. The numerical value (and therefore the corresponding vibrational patterns) of each Pinnacle is derived from the birthdate. In calculating the numbers of the Pinnacles, the formulas will use "addition" (adding the numbers of the Birth Month, Day, and Year), whereas the formulas for calculating the Challenge numbers used "subtraction."

Pinnacles are divided up into four age cycles spanning your entire life, and are defined by specific vibrational patterns tailored to each Pinnacle in the form of a numerical value assignment that represents a specific experience that will be attracted to you. They can also be explained as periods of time, like the changing of our four seasons. Whatever number is calculated for each Pinnacle will determine the type of experiences that will be generated by the vibrational patterns of the number. However, as always, your free will and choice will determine which of the experiences you will accept and acknowledge throughout your life, and of course, which you will pass by.

For example, if the First Pinnacle is a 6, then your experiences will be around domestic relations and adjustments, e.g., marriage, children, romance, etc. If the Pinnacle numerical value were a 14/5, then the type of experiences you would attract would be surrounded by change (changing jobs, moving, traveling, etc.), risk-taking, and possibly unexpected disruptions.

There is a four-step calculation process for the Pinnacles. In each of the steps we will calculate both the numerical value (representing the specific vibrational patterns) and the age span (duration) of each Pinnacle (Step 1–the First Pinnacle, Step 2–the Second Pinnacle, etc.). After all of the Pinnacle numbers have been calculated, i.e., the calculation of the numerical values of each Pinnacle and the calculation of the age span (duration) of each Pinnacle, the results will be displayed in figure 7–11.

The definition and explanation of the Pinnacles are included in chapter 6, section 6.H. The description and meaning of the Pinnacle numbers are included in chapter 8, section 8.H.

Four-Step Process on How to Calculate the Pinnacle Numbers

Before proceeding to the four-step process for calculating the Pinnacles, there are a number of basic criteria/mathematical "givens," derived from the original Chaldean formulas, to be aware of.

These criteria/givens are:

(1) The duration of the First Pinnacle is always equal to 36 years minus your Destiny (Birthdate) number, which starts the process. (Note: If your Destiny calculates to be a compound number versus a root or single-digit number such as 14/5, then the number must be reduced to the root number in order to subtract a single-digit number from 36 years. In this case, the 14/5 would be reduced down to a 5. The root number is always the end number of a compound number.)

(2) The Second and Third Pinnacles are 9 years in duration.

(3) The Fourth Pinnacle, which is the last/final Pinnacle, rules for the remainder of a person's life.

(4) 11 and 22 are Master Numbers that never reduce down and are the exception to the rule when calculating a formula; these numbers would be added as shown, e.g., eleven, not 2 and twenty-two, not 4.

(5) In Numerology, when we are using the Chaldean formulas, we always calculate using what is mathematically known as an "absolute" number, uninfluenced and unaffected by the arithmetic sign. We will call this a "base number" for matters of calculation. A negative number is always converted to a base number. For instance, a -6 (minus 6) is bracketed by parallel lines (| |), as follows, |-6|. In mathematics, this is the symbol/designation for an absolute number. The |-6| becomes a 6, the base number. That is, if there is a minus sign (–) in the formula's answer, it is equal to its base number (e.g., -6 = 6, -4 = 4, etc.). (Note: A characteristic's vibrational patterns flow from the base number [absolute numerical value] revealed by the calculations. The arithmetic sign [+ or –] is not relevant to the interpretation of the vibration of a number).

The Birthdate September 21, 1938 will be used for the four-step calculation process discussed. As stated, each of the steps will calculate both the numerical value (representing the specific vibrational patterns) of each Pinnacle and the age span (duration) of the specific Pinnacle.

First Pinnacle
Calculating the Number
Step 1

Numerical Value (Vibrational Patterns) The number of the First Pinnacle is calculated by adding the number of your Birth Day (21 = 2 + 1 = 3) to the number of your Birth Month (September = 9). That is, 9 + 3 = 12 = 1 + 2 = 3. The numerical value of the First Pinnacle = 3.
Age Span (Duration) The age span duration of the First Pinnacle is calculated by subtracting your Birthdate number (Destiny) = 6 (see calculations in section 7.A) from the base span of years, 36 [refer to the criteria/givens (1)], to get the age span (duration) of the First Pinnacle. That is, 36 - 6 = 30. The length of the First Pinnacle is 30 years, from age 1 to age 30, or from 1938 to 1968.

Second Pinnacle
Calculating the Number
Step 2

Numerical Value (Vibrational Patterns) The number of the Second Pinnacle is calculated by adding the number of your Birth Day (21 = 2 + 1 = 3) to the number of your Birth Year (1938 = 1 + 9 + 3 + 8 = 21 = 2 + 1 = 3). That is, 3 + 3 = 6. The numerical value of the Second Pinnacle = 6
Age Span (Duration) The age span duration of the Second Pinnacle lasts a period of nine years [refer to criteria/givens (2)]. The age span of the Second Pinnacle, which follows the First Pinnacle, is from age 30 to 39, or 1968 to 1977.

Third Pinnacle
Calculating the Number
Step 3

Numerical Value (Vibrational Patterns)

The number of the Third Pinnacle is calculated by adding the number of First Pinnacle (3) to the number of the Second Pinnacle (6). That is, 3 + 6 = 9. The numerical value of the Third Pinnacle = 9.

Age Span (Duration)

The age span duration of the Third Pinnacle, like the Second Pinnacle, lasts a period of 9 years [refer to criteria/givens (2)]. The age span of the Third Pinnacle, which follows the Second Pinnacle, is from age 39 to 48, or 1977 to 1986.

Fourth Pinnacle
Calculating the Number
Step 4

Numerical Value (Vibrational Patterns)

The number of the Fourth Pinnacle is calculated by adding the number of your Birth Month (September = 9) to the number of your Birth Year (1938 = 1 + 9 + 3 + 8 = 21 = 2 + 1 = 3). That is, 9 + 3 = 12 = 1 + 2 = 3. The numerical value of the Fourth Pinnacle = 3.

Age Span (Duration)

The age span duration of the Fourth Pinnacle is not calculated because the Fourth Pinnacle starts at the ending age of the third Pinnacle and continues until the end of your life. Therefore, the age span is from the age of 48, 1986, until death.

Example of Calculating the Pinnacle Numbers

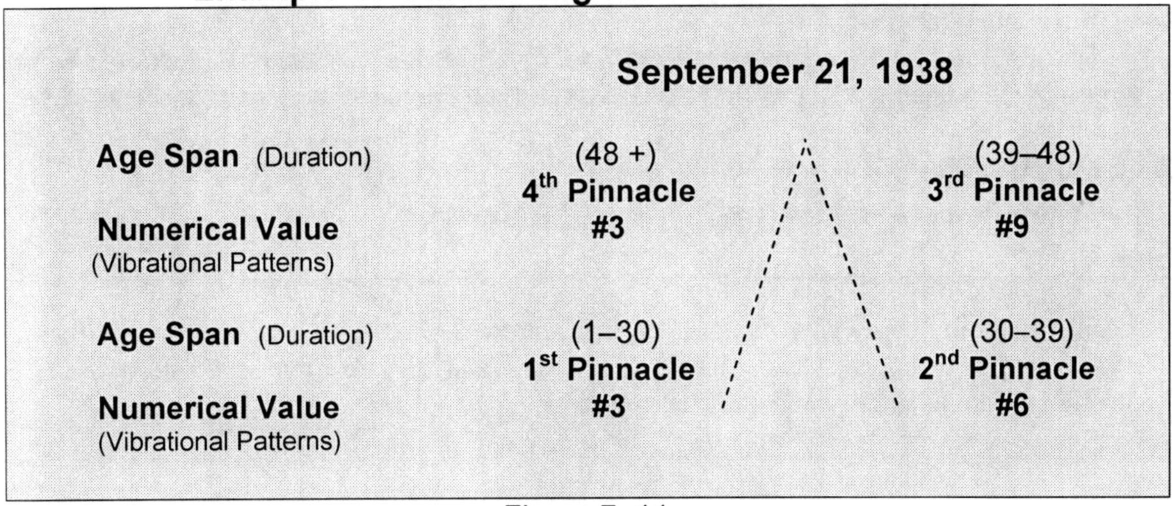

Figure 7–11

7.I Soul Qualities (The Numbers of the Letters of the Full Name)

There are eight Soul Qualities in the Basic chart, and each is assigned a numerical value (1 through 8) and a rating system based on the following formula which is used to calculate the Soul Qualities. These numbers indicate if the particular Soul Quality lesson has (1) already been developed and to what degree, or (2) if it is an area that must be developed in order to achieve your highest potential, or (3) if the lesson is Karmic.

To find your Soul Quality numbers, convert the letters in your name to numbers as indicated in the Example of the Soul Quality Conversion Values (Turning Letters into Numbers) (see table 7–8) using the Chaldean Alphabet/Formula (see table7–1) and count how many 1s, 2s, 3s, 4s, 5s, 6s, 7s, and 8s exist from the total number of letters in your full Name. The rating system was designed to interpret the development level of the individual for each of their Soul Qualities by using what is considered to be the normal standard for that value so you can compare the standard to what's in your chart.

Soul Quality Numbers 1 (SQ#1), 3 (SQ#3), and 5 (SQ#5), will have a normal value of a 3 while Soul Quality Numbers 2 (SQ#2), 4 (SQ#4), 6 (SQ#6), 7 (SQ#7), and 8 (SQ#8) have a normal standard of 1. You might find that when you convert the letters of your full name into numbers that your name does not have all of the eight Soul Quality values. Any missing Soul Quality values from your name represent a zero (0) or a Karmic lesson for you to resolve in this lifetime. The zero (0) indicates that in the past an area was avoided or not developed for whatever reason. When your Soul Quality values are less than the standard value, you have what are known as "must do" requirements to meet, if you wish to fulfill your life and reach a level of completion within.

The definition and explanation of the Soul Qualities are in chapter 6, section 6.I. The description and meaning of the Soul Quality Numbers are included in chapter 8, section 8.I.

Soul Quality Number

Three-Step Process on How to Calculate the Number

Step 1

Make a table to show how many of each of the Soul Quality values you have in the full Name by writing the Name on a sheet of paper (see table 7–8). Table 7–8 will be used to convert the letters of the Name into numbers.

Step 2

By using the following example in table 7–8, convert the letters in the full Name to numbers using the numbers assigned to letters in table 7–1.

Step 3

Count how many 1s, 2s, 3s, 4s, 5s, 6s, 7s, and 8s there are in the Name and indicate on your sheet of paper the total number for each Soul Quality.

Chaldean Alphabet/Formula
Assigned Numbers with Letters Identified

1	2	3	4	5	6	7	8
A	B	C	D	E	U	O	F
I	K	G	M	H	V	Z	P
J	R	L	T	N	W		
Q		S		X			
Y							

Table 7–1

Example of the Soul Quality Conversion Values (Turning Letters into Numbers)

Full Name	W	I	L	L	I	A	M		M	I	C	H	A	E	L	S
Conversion Numbers	6	1	3	3	1	1	4		4	1	3	5	1	5	3	3

Table 7–8

Example of Soul Quality Numerical Value Count

Soul Quality #s	1	2	3	4	5	6	7	8
Value Count	5+	0-	5+	2+	2-	1	0-	0-

Table 7–9

The plus sign (+) means that the count is greater than the standard number, and indicates where the "lesson" has been learned or talent perfected. The minus sign (−) means that the count is less than the standard, and indicates where the lesson needs to be developed. The standard for Soul Qualities 1, 3, and 5 is 3. Therefore, if your total adds up to be more than 3, then there will be a plus sign (+) next to the number it totals. Less than 3 will show a minus sign (−) next to the number. The standard for 2, 4, 6, and 8 is 1. Therefore, if the number totals more than 1 of those values, the sign shown will be a plus sign (+) next to the number since it is more than the standard number 1. Less than 1 will show a minus sign (−) next to the number. The zero (0) indicates where the lesson was avoided or that talent has not yet been developed.

Table 7–10 takes you through the process of interpreting the meaning and impact of the Soul Quality numerical values count shown in table 7–9. This will allow you to see the nature and importance of the information given to you through determining the effect of the Soul Qualities that you have already experienced and those Soul Qualities that you still have to develop.

Example of Soul Quality Numbers Counted and Explained for the Name William Michaels

Represents Soul Qualities 1–8	Converting Letters into Numbers Total Number of 1s, 2s, 3s, 4s, 5s, 6s, 7s, and 8s in the Name	Standard Rating System Number	What The Standard Rating System Means to You
1 Leader Pioneer Independent	5+ The plus sign (+) indicates that you have more than learned the lessons of leadership, pioneering, creative originality, and independence.	5+ Exceeds the Standard 3	The 5 count indicates you are highly developed as a leader/pioneer and have the potential to be just that, a leader/ pioneer wherever you are.
2 Diplomat Peacemaker Cooperative Spirit	0- There are no 2s in your Name so this is a zero (0-) or Karmic lesson to be learned in this lifetime.	0- Is less than the Standard 1	The 0- indicates that the traits of the SQ#2 have not yet been developed. You must overcome over-sensitivity and learn to be cooperative.
3 Self-Expression Sociability Entertainer	5+ You have more than developed the ability to express yourself in literature, arts, music, and you have a natural public presence.	5+ Exceeds the Standard 3	The 5 count indicates you are well-developed as an entertainer, have superb communications skills, and you excel socially.
4 Structure Foundation Loyalty	2+ You have more than developed the traits of a builder/carpenter who likes discipline, structure, and foundation.	2+ Exceeds the Standard 1	The 2 count indicates you have learned to put your affairs in order, are loyal, and know how to build a strong foundation.
5 Freedom Change Action	2- You are underdeveloped in this area with difficulty in balancing escape and dealing with reality.	2- Is less than the Standard 3	The 2 count indicates that more balance is needed, along with less scattering of your abilities, and a true understanding of freedom.
6 Cosmic Parent Counselor	1 You have developed the traits of being a cosmic parent, counselor, and community caretaker.	1 Is equal to the Standard 1	The 1 count indicates that you have learned to care for others in a domestic environment lovingly.

7 Intellect Educator Loner	0- There are no 7s in this name therefore it's a zero (0-) or Karmic lesson to be learned in this lifetime.	0- Is less than the Standard 1	The 0- indicates that the traits of the SQ#7 have not yet been developed. Learn how not to withdraw from participating in your life because you require solitude.
8 Ambition and Materialistic	0- There are no 8s in this name therefore it's a zero (0-) or Karmic lesson to be learned in this lifetime.	0- Is less than the Standard 1	The 0- indicates that you will need to learn how to make and manage money and to balance the spiritual and materialistic sides for harmony.

Table 7–10

As long as you have Soul Qualities that still need to be developed and understood, you will go through your life attracting people, places, things, conditions, and situations over and over and over again. Have you gone around and around and around in circles, seemingly facing the same identical situations to those that you thought you were done with? So, if you don't take care of these lessons and requirements (or most of them) by the end of your lifetime—well, you may just find yourself in a "future" lifetime continuing to go around those circles, attracting the same kind of environment, people, places, things, and conditions over and over again until you finally complete the lesson plan. When you do complete those remaining lessons and fully develop your talents, as shown by your Soul Qualities, you will then be capable of completing yourself (become wholly integrated), and be free to live a life unhindered by unfinished business.

###

Numbers–The Powerful Bridge Beyond

Chaldean Numerology for the New Millennium

Chapter 8:
The Language of Root Numbers and Special Compound Numbers

Introduction

Where chapter 6 gave you the definitions and explanations of each of the major characteristics of a Basic Numerology Master Chart, and chapter 7 provided you with the detailed instructions and calculations for the numbers of each characteristic, chapter 8 will give you an in-depth meaning and description of both the "root" numbers and special (high importance) compound numbers of each characteristic. Chapter 8 is, in essence, providing you with the "interpretive language" of numbers.

Now, understanding this interpretive language will give you an opportunity to become more informed about your life than you ever thought possible. You will find information about (1) the major events taking place (or about to take place) in your life, (2) the options that can be available to you, (3) making correct choices and decisions, (4) taking right action, (5) opening new doors and finding open doors to walk through, (6) your personal and business relationships, and more.

The language of numbers is the basis for interpreting and understanding the vibrational patterns of your numbers, and will provide you with "advice" from an exceptionally reliable source—your personal design and blueprint—so that you will not have to depend on the words or opinions of others for guidance and counseling. It doesn't mean you can't listen to "outside" input, but who knows what's best for you more than you? This understanding will allow you to bring out the best within you, to give equal recognition and acceptance to all that you are, and to express all of your talent and ability, in a manner and at a time of your choosing, not someone else's.

The Meaning and Description of the Language of Your Numbers

8.A Destiny (The Language of the Numbers of the Birthdate)

The definition and explanation of the Destiny are included in chapter 6, section 6.A. The calculation of the number of the Destiny is included in chapter 7, section 7.A.

Number 1 Destiny

If you have a Number 1 Destiny, you were born to be a *leader* of mankind, gained through your own initiative, independence, and originality of thought—a *pioneer* who paves the way for others to follow. You were meant to be in the driver's seat, not a passenger. Creativity and ambition are an inherent part of your thinking patterns. The force behind this ambition, the great sense of humor, and the innate executive ability all combine to make a great leader. The Number 1 likes to be in charge and leave the minor details to others. You also have no fear of exploring new territories, or of letting anyone or anything stand in the way once a commitment has been made. However, for your greatest success, it is important to be reasonable in all relationships with others and not become too domineering, strong-willed, conceited, or driven by greed. Ideally, owning your own business or functioning as an executive fulfills your desire to have the finer things in life that success brings. This vibration is well-suited for a partnership in marriage.

Number 19/1 Destiny

With a Number 19/1 Destiny you have what can be called the most fortunate of all numbers because the Number 19 includes all of the traits of the Number 1 Destiny combined with the traits of the Number 9, the number of the humanitarian and healer. In addition, the 9 includes the vibrations of all the other single-digit Root Numbers (1–8), which make it a powerful force. The two Numbers of the 19 rest upon the Root Number 1, which reinforces individuality, determination, originality, creativity, and ambition, as well as an added sense of humor needed for true success. The Number 1 functions best as a leader.

Number 2 Destiny

The Number 2 Destiny will move you toward being known as a *diplomat,* or *peacemaker* for mankind. Intuitively you know what people feel and need in addition to being a master at dissolving misunderstandings. The nature of the 2 includes cooperation, receptivity, tact, courtesy, agreeability, and the ability to maintain peace—giving you the potential ability to see both sides of the issues, to settle disputes, and to mediate for a peaceful resolution. Goodwill toward others is your magic power for success. Your talent for detail combined with the desire to work with others to complete their plans is inborn in you and accomplished through a cooperative spirit. This is the partnership number that prefers to follow rather than being aggressive. The vibration also represents a "two-of-a-kind," and is the perfect partner and companion, ensuring continual balance. Possible career paths are in the areas of coaching, counseling, teaching, and medical-related endeavors. Be careful not to become so emotional or sensitive that you repress your talents and hold back from confrontation for the sake of maintaining the peace, and as a result cause internal anger and resentment.

Number 11/2 Destiny

If the Master Number 11/2 is your Destiny, you belong to the public in the capacity of a *super diplomat* or *peacemaker*. It is electrical in nature and intensified to a much higher level of emotional and nervous energy, idealism, and the aspiration to be in the limelight. It wants you to "shine your light across the land." However, you must inspire by your own example, by living your own ideals. Be careful not to become so emotional or sensitive that you repress your talents because of fear of confrontation, causing internal anger and resentment. The Root Number 2 brings graciousness, cooperative spirit, tact, and the ability to see both sides of the issues. Direct the nervous and emotional energy of the 2 into positive channels or activities. The power and strength of the double 1 includes creativity, originality, inventiveness, and the desire for leadership of the Number 1. If you develop your talents, you could excel in the TV, motion picture, radio, or literary fields. Learn to depend on your intuition and inner guidance system. Even young children with the 11/2 Destiny show early signs of wanting to be seen.

Number 3 Destiny

The Number 3 Destiny directs you to help people realize the magic power of cheerfulness and inspiration through your creative imagination and talents as an *entertainer*. You have the gift of words and a quick sense of humor. You are intuitive, versatile, have the ability to gain knowledge quickly, and have no difficulty making friends. Romance, beauty, the arts, and love are important elements of this vibration, in addition to being well-suited for a partnership in marriage. Talents include being a writer, speaker, musician, singer, and other lines of creative endeavors. The ability for self-expression and humor combined, draw financial and social success. There is the tendency to scatter energies, talent, emotions, and money, so try to maintain a balance in your life. Be careful how you handle your money and responsibilities because you have a tendency not to pay attention to your affairs or to be organized. Guard against being too critical of others, impatient, and intolerant.

Number 4 Destiny

The Number 4 Destiny is the sign of the *carpenter, mason, or builder*. The purpose is to build a solid foundation and bring forth new ideas for the benefit of mankind. The builder feels a deep satisfaction and accomplishment in physical work and considers work to be play versus work, as others perceive it to be. The Number 4 can best be described as being honest, ethical, hardworking, loyal, dependable, workaholic, detail-oriented, disciplined, controlled, orderly, and very conservative. Success comes by utilizing great talent for establishing system and order in any field of management. Careers are more likely to be in the areas of management, organization, carpentry, construction, accounting, or legal. This vibration is well-suited for a partnership in marriage as structure and foundation are very necessary for true happiness. Be careful not to become too stubborn, rigid, rude, controlling, and stuck in your ways, as it will be detrimental to your success.

Number 13/4 Destiny

The vibration of the Number 13/4 Destiny is a more powerful form of the Number 4. And, it has all the traits of the 4—the gift of detail, discipline, loyalty, hard work, and the desire for a solid foundation in life. The extra power of the 13/4 comes from the combination of the 1 and 3. The creative power of the Number 1 and the ambition and desire for self-expression of the Number 3 may result in feeling overwhelmed by the combined high-energy vibrations of these numbers. However, the 13 has its roots in the 4, which balances and stabilizes the energy of the 13 vibration with discipline, foundation, and practicality. Since those with this vibration will need to work harder to accomplish any task, they must remained focused, and not scatter their energies.

Number 22/4 Destiny

Since the Number 22/4 Destiny represents a Master Number, it has a much higher level of energy than the Number 4, and operates on a universal plane of endeavor. The 22/4 Destiny represents the *master carpenter, mason, or builder.* The double 2s increase the power of the intuitive ability, imagination, emotional and nervous energy, and cooperative spirit of the Number 2. The 22 rests on the Root Number 4, which represents foundation, framework, discipline, loyalty, detail, and the ability to work hard. Success can be yours in diplomatic arenas, in politics, in real estate, as a financier, as a promoter, or as a super-athlete or explorer. This charged vibration represents increased creativity and intuition. Therefore, there is a need to strive for a balance between the emotional traits of the 2, and the influence of the practical and disciplined 4. There will be more of an interest in service and humanity than ever before during this vibration.

Number 5 Destiny

The Number 5 Destiny represents freedom as the keynote and password throughout life. The 5 Destiny represents the vital force of freedom and progress and is highlighted by change, variety, travel, and unexpected adventure. You are a progressive individual and will desire to learn the right use of freedom, constantly seeking the new and untried, and gaining insight through the understanding of all classes and conditions of people. You are a natural in the use of "words in action" (writing, reporting, selling, promoting, and investigating). You are meant to be out in the public arena displaying the sparkle of your imagination and your gift for communications to keep progress on a forward and upward path. Your magnetic energy brings action and excitement to your environment and attracts the opposite sex.

Number 14/5 Destiny

The Number 14/5 Destiny has its roots in the Number 5 which symbolizes freedom, progress, communication, variety, and change. The 1, which is masculine, represents creativity, original ideas, and leadership ability, while the 4, which is feminine, sits between these two numbers, and represents structure, order, discipline, and restriction. The differing vibrational patterns in this combination 14 can create a conflict in the way progress and decisions are made, making it a potentially disruptive vibration. Commitment is the key, for setting goals, maintaining order wherever possible for emotional stability, avoiding overindulgences, and maintaining faith. In the world of business, the vibration of the 14/5 may add the possibility of risk, as it is the number of speculation in business ventures. And, for marriage or investing, the 14/5 may be a contentious vibration.

Number 23/5 Destiny

The Number 23/5 Destiny is considered to be the second most fortunate of numbers after the 19/1, as it is the best of all of the 5 number combinations. The Number 2 (feminine) brings a vibration of peace, diplomacy, and receptivity to the self-expression and creativity of the social Number 3 (masculine). The 2 and 3 together have their root in the Number 5 which brings action, variety, change, freedom, communication, and travel. Together these numbers represent a very creative, lively, and pleasant vibration.

Number 6 Destiny

The Number 6 Destiny is often called the *cosmic parent, teacher, or counselor,* and emphasizes service and devotion to family and community as the core of this existence. The essence of the Number 6 is to learn the meaning of responsibility, and how to balance opposites. Seek to keep the scales of justice in balance. This is the domestic number with a great desire to love and be loved. Those with this Destiny generally have a tendency to be very sensual and charismatic in nature. The 6 is also a humanitarian and may pursue a mission in life to comfort and uplift others toward a higher, finer life as a cosmic parent whose focus is primarily on family, friends, and community. Family and marriage are the key elements to happiness and contentment, so this is an excellent vibration for marriage. Love, truth, beauty, and harmony are cornerstones of your world. You have an innate ability for artistic expression and appreciation of fine arts.

Number 7 Destiny

The Number 7 Destiny represents self-preservation, the drive to seek out the wisdom and the knowledge of the Universe, and teach it to others. These are the keynotes of the 7 Destiny vibration patterns. You have the attributes of a healer, educator, scientist, and minister. Seek and discover the reality behind the appearance, for your destiny is to discover the truth and answers to the world's problems from "within." You are destined to be one of the educators of the world, to discover and understand the mysteries that lay hidden. Resist the tendency to withdraw from the demands of the ordinary life in order to delve into deeper levels of the spirituality and mysticism. Inner magnetism will attract others to you even though there is the appearance of reservedness, aloofness, and aloneness on the surface. Do not insist on partnerships. You also can be inventive and scientific, since the Number 7 is very analytical, comprehensive, and contemplative. You need the finer things in life to experience the joy of living. Truth, beauty, and harmony are critical desires of the soul.

Number 16/7 Destiny

A Number 16/7 Destiny represents a Karmic lesson. Whenever the 16/7 shows up on your chart, it has the potentiality to disrupt things and may cause circumstances to fall apart causing you loss and some humiliation. With the Number 16/7 Destiny, there can be conflict between the aggressive individuality of the Number 1 (masculine) versus the need of the Number 6 (feminine) to serve family and community. However, the wisdom, intelligence, and comprehension of the Number 7 soon bring about a recovery. The lesson revolves around the ego (what is sometimes called the "little" Self), the giving up of micro-managing, so to speak, and getting in touch with the larger picture of your life. The 16/7 is about the destruction and dissolution of the old and birth of the new. The lesson of the 16/7 brings with it inner housecleaning and balance, bringing you into a higher consciousness and closer union with the source of life. It results in a spiritual rebirth that opens up your heart and mind to an entirely new awareness in your life. This would be viewed as a path of progress and great spiritual growth, once you have a better understanding of why you choose this lesson and how you benefit by keeping a balance between "I," (the Number 1) and "We," (the Number 6).

Number 8 Destiny

The Number 8 Destiny is known as the number of the *organizer*. The 8 is ambitious and materialistic, is endowed with the executive ability to organize and supervise the affairs of others, is generally in a high-level position in the business or commercial sector, or in the financial world, and is the number of sound judgment—the qualities that bring position, authority, money, and recognition. The Number 8 Destiny gives you natural executive ability, and a talent for decision making, as you are intuitive, efficient, dynamic, and capable. However, it is important to strive for balance between the material and spiritual world in order to gain the wisdom necessary for your success. In your quest for power and wealth, you can best serve all by ensuring that you do the right thing so everyone will enjoy freedom of action. Beware of greed, materialism, and losing sight of improving the plight for mankind by your personal accomplishments and riches. A lasting reward will come through your own efforts—strength of character, mastery over self, and helping to improve the plight of mankind. Choosing a partner with a similar and equal ambition ensures a better chance for a successful marriage. The Number 8 Destiny is to understand the laws that govern money, and to pass on that understanding to others.

Number 9 Destiny

The Number 9 Destiny is that of the *humanitarian* or spiritual dreamer who inspires others through dedication and service to the benefit of mankind, not for personal gain. The Number 9 must be objective and have a universal outlook on life. It is an energetic, impersonal, and emotional vibration in nature that works for the upliftment of mankind. Service in or with humanitarian organizations is emphasized—whether it is political, social, spiritual, psychological, or medical. Stay focused, as the greatest success will come from a public environment, versus smaller crowds. Teaching, healing, writing, music, and art are all natural areas of expression for the 9 individual. Other characteristics that add to success and happiness include tolerance, compassion, love, understanding, and generosity, in addition to having learned forgiveness. Remember, "soul" satisfaction is more important than materialistic rewards.

Number 18/9 Destiny

The Number 18/9 Destiny is a very powerful vibration, a vibration of high emotional and intellectual energy and the vibration of great leaders. This vibration requires a person to seek positive paths to express this highly, electrical drive. The 1 symbolizes independence, leadership, and drive along with the executive ability, sound judgment, and efficiency of the 8. The root number is the Number 9, a vibration of compassion, force, energy, healing, and the universal interest in all of humanity. The combined traits of the 18/9 are qualities of powerful leaders dedicated to social, political, medical, and religious changes in the world.

8.B Soul/Heart's Desire (The Language of the Numbers of the Vowels)

The definition and explanation of the Soul/Heart's Desire are included in chapter 6, section 6.B. The calculation of the number of the Soul/Heart's Desire is included in chapter 7, section 7.B.

Number 1 Soul/Heart's Desire

The Number 1 Soul/Heart's Desire is to be a true leader, independent, self-reliant, and living life according to what you believe. It brings with it the desire to be at the front of life's parade. This creative and original mind, and pioneer spirit that likes to be in charge, will naturally assume the lead and direct others rather than being a subordinate. However, there is a need here to cultivate tact, diplomacy, and patience, and to avoid the appearance of being arrogant, dominating, and overdoing things. Number 1s are driven to operate from the strength of their convictions, to endure and overcome difficult challenges, and to succeed through remarkable willpower. Be careful not to become ruthless in your decision making and behavior. If you become impatient and intolerant, you may become too dominant and unpopular, causing unpleasant reactions— express yourself with courtesy, graciousness, and sincerity, in order to be recognized as a respected leader. The Soul/Heart's Desire is to love deeply. Romance will remain faithful and enduring when the love is fully returned, and the loved ones live up to the standards of charm, cleverness, and individuality. Don't allow pride, dignity, and reserve to keep you from acting or being romantic. Be aware of your strong self-restraint, which gives you the appearance of being cold and distant, although the desire to love deeply and be the head of the household is so important.

Number 19/1 Soul/Heart's Desire

The Number 19/1 Soul/Heart's Desire is a most powerful vibration on the soul level. It is emphatically the desire to be Number 1, and leave all details to others. The 1 also represents leadership with creative and original ideas, while the vibration of the Number 9 adds the emotions and vibrations of all the numbers. This is a high-energy force at the center of one's being that must be expressed in a positive way for the best results.

Number 2 Soul/Heart's Desire

The Number 2 Soul/Heart's Desire is all about partnerships, seeking companionship not leadership, and devoting their entire life to a partnership as they fall in love easily. The keynotes of the Number 2 are peace, harmony, cooperation, kindness, and thoughtfulness. Friendliness is your byword. You are very sensitive and emotional, and you seek the comfort of companionship, partnerships, and camaraderie. Generally, you give in instead of confronting the situation, doing things when you should not, for the sake of peace. Your gentleness and tendency to act in a nonresistant manner often make it difficult for you to stand up against a dominant person. Being sensitive and emotional in nature, you are not fond of display or aggressiveness, and may be too easygoing for your own good. The Number 2 needs encouragement and appreciation not only from their loved ones, but also from their peers. You can be easily hurt by criticism and become angry, sometimes showing a temper and speaking bluntly when hurt or upset. Diplomacy and tactfulness are natural to you, giving you the innate skills for arbitration and peacemaking. Develop confidence to fight uncertainty and doubt. Also, your success can be enhanced, if you develop discipline and a definite purpose. Sympathy and feelings for others make you appealing and attractive to the opposite sex.

Number 11/2 Soul/Heart's Desire

The Number 11/2 Soul/Heart's Desire is a Master Number because it contains the Master Number 11, and represents the Number 2 raised to a much higher level of energy and imagination. The 11/2 is both intuitional and inspirational, with the continual desire to reveal the vision of beauty available to everyone. It is a "magnetic" vibration, and indicates an "electrical" individual with originality, a natural ability to lead, and intuition. The double 1 brings leadership, creativity, and originality, combined with the detail, diplomacy, sensitivity, cooperative spirit, and emotional energy of the Number 2 to produce a very high vibrational force. You have the innate abilities to become a Super Diplomat or Peacemaker, but you must cultivate human understanding through the inherent cooperation, kindness, and thoughtfulness of the Root Number 2. You will always have the desire to be in the public limelight passing on truth. Even children with the 11/2 Soul/Heart's Desire want to be recognized.

Number 3 Soul/Heart's Desire

The Number 3 Soul/Heart's Desire represents self-expression and creativity, which form the keynotes of this joyful and social vibration. As a Number 3, you desire beauty and laughter in your environment. You can find great pleasure by learning to express your thoughts and imagination in a lighter vein. The Number 3 has the innate talent to express creativity in the verbal arts such as acting, writing, speaking, singing, or in the field of art. You are a natural entertainer in any environment. You seek knowledge, ambition, and independence, while cultivating tolerance, patience, and concentration. Love rules the life of the Number 3 Soul/Heart's Desire, a romantic by nature who loves deeply. You are a charming companion because of being well-balanced from a mental and emotional standpoint, but may turn away when admiration and affection become commonplace. The self-confidence of the 3 is built upon the approval of the opposite sex and admiring friends. You may have the tendency to keep feelings on a surface level, hiding any difficulty in expressing inner feelings and personal thoughts. It is best to plan goals early and enjoy "the now," as you tend to scatter your energy. You are great at coming up with ideas but have difficulty following through to completion. A dreamer at heart, you would much rather be happy than practical. Inspiration and imagination are your finest characteristics. Use these characteristics intelligently to attain the best that life has to offer. You like to do things grandly and on a large scale. And you like nice environments, protection, the comforts of life, and the elegance of living. The key to success is maintaining a balance between your creative side and self-discipline. Don't become so self-absorbed in yourself on the surface level that you pass up your life entertaining others as a smoke screen rather than being a participant in life.

Number 4 Soul/Heart's Desire

The Number 4 Soul/Heart's Desire is the sign of the carpenter or builder who thrives on hard work and detail. Work is essential to your life. However, you may have a tendency to become a workaholic. Things practical, analytical, methodical, orderly and reliable appeal to the Number 4. And loyalty, stability, respectability, and dependability are important to you. Your inner desire is to build a solid foundation in life based on law, order, self-discipline, and loyalty. You are practical, hardworking, and orderly, in your home and need a complete plan on which to build a solid foundation in life. In business, home, and love affairs, you are rather conservative in thought and action. However, the key to success for harmony and balance in your life is flexibility. You may dislike things that are unfinished or incorrect, and react unfavorably to change and innovation. You may have an affinity to carpentry, pottery, metalworking, or mechanics. The Number 4 Soul/Heart's Desire is the serious lover who is loyal and dependable. Honesty and sincerity are at the heart of your motives along with a strong determination to succeed. The home environment and family provide the sense of security that the 4 desires. You may not have a flare for romance in lovemaking, and are easily embarrassed by too much sentiment, but you take care of your own.

Number 13/4 Soul/Heart's Desire

The Number 1 and Number 3 of the 13/4 Soul/Heart's Desire form a combination of masculine energy that radiates leadership, creativity, and aggressive self-expression. However, this power and drive is somewhat restricted by limitations of the Root Number 4—detail, hard work, and discipline. The 13/4 vibration brings a strong desire for foundation, discipline, and success. The Number 1 represents strong leadership while the 3 brings the creative self-expression and energy.

Number 22/4 Soul/Heart's Desire

The Number 22/4 Soul/Heart's Desire is a Master Number bringing higher aspirations than that of the Number 4 and a much greater energy and force that represents hard work, discipline, and the desire for foundation in life. The 22 vibration stands for the "ideal realized." The 22/4 Soul/Heart's Desire motivates you to become a "Master Builder," with the potential of creating the foundation for a great humanitarian work. The challenge of the 22/4 vibration is to maintain a balance between the sensitive and emotional Number 2, and the disciplined 4. You have the ability to make useful and practical things both magnificent and uplifting. You continually strive for perfection. You need to continuously cultivate a steadfast adherence to your ideals in the midst of materiality and conflict.

Number 5 Soul/Heart's Desire

The Number 5 Soul/Heart's Desire vibration represents personal freedom, change, progress, movement, variety, and action. The 5 is highly enthusiastic, resourceful, and creative, and thrives on being a part of the excitement of the world. You have fast mental and physical reflexes, as well as a very strong power of intuition from within that aids you in clear thinking in the time of a crises. You are naturally clever, witty, and curious. With change, action, movement, versatility, and freedom as your bywords, you are spurred on by the dislike of routine, detail, and conformity. The unexpected and exciting are more stimulating than ordinary day-to-day existence. Extremely flexible, you can stop on a dime, change directions or plans on a moment's notice without thinking twice, and without becoming disappointed. Success can come to you through "words in action" in writing, speaking, investigative reporting, and other endeavors in the field of communications. Lack of freedom and variety may lead to a feeling of dullness, discontent, unrest, and dissatisfaction, causing you to act hastily and impulsively, and to do things, which may lead to sorrow or regret later. You are ambitious, with the tendency to have too many irons in the fire, scattering your forces and finances, and undertaking more than you can successfully carry out. Be careful not to play the role of a hero out to save the world. This causes commitments to be made that may not be able to be kept later, even though your intentions were honorable. Because your desire is to please everyone, the tendency is to take care of others first, often feeling resentment after the fact that you placed yourself last.

Number 14/5 Soul/Heart's Desire

The Number 14/5 Soul/Heart's Desire vibration has all the traits of the Number 5, such as the desire for complete freedom, progress, variety, and change needed to be happy. The Number 1 desires to express freedom and leadership with its creative and original ideas. However, the 1 and the 5, both of which are active, aggressive, and masculine, have the restriction of the feminine, receptive Number 4 between them, which adheres to discipline, attention to detail, and hard work. This can bring about the feeling of being held back, a feeling of frustration which may create a sense of rebellion.

Number 23/5 Soul/Heart's Desire

The Number 23/5 Soul/Heart's Desire is the best vibration of all the 5 Number combinations. The Number 2, which emphasizes peace, diplomacy, cooperation, and receptivity, leads the creative, joyful, self-expressive, and ambitious 3. The 2 and 3 have their root in the 5, which needs complete freedom, variety, travel, and change to be happy. Combined together, these numbers create a pleasant, enjoyable, and lively vibration.

Number 6 Soul/Heart's Desire

The Number 6 Soul/Heart's Desire is about love, truth, beauty, harmony, and justice. You will desire to give service to others in your home and community—as teacher, counselor, parent, friend, and humanitarian. The 6 is typically categorized as an idealist and an inspirational cosmic parent. You want to feel and know love on a personal as well as on a universal level of awareness. Love, marriage, and the need of a home and family environment are essential to the Number 6. Great success can be yours when you learn to balance your feelings and thinking, your emotions and intellect. This Soul/Heart's Desire is the most loving of all the numbers and is very protective. You will shower loved ones with attention, gifts, and expressions of love, but may demand the expression of love and approval in return. You must balance two extremes. One, be careful not to sacrifice yourself for love, family, or service. And two, be very aware <u>not</u> to be possessive and "smothering," or you will cause those you love to feel trapped, which will force them to flee.

Number 7 Soul/Heart's Desire

The Number 7 Soul/Heart's Desire is introspective, intellectual, philosophical, and spiritual. The Number 7 is considered "the" mystical number of completion. The greatest asset of the 7 is intuition and inner voice. Your intuition is finely tuned, and it can be said that you have an illumined intellect. The Number 7 is a visionary at heart, seeking the odd, the mysterious and the unusual. Self-preservation and the need to spend time alone are important to the Number 7, thus presenting some potential difficulty in forming successful partnerships. Avoid isolation and indifference, and do not become cynical toward others because of your need for privacy or spending time alone. Although the Number 7 Soul/Heart's Desire is very selective in friendship and romance, it also has somewhat of an "indifferent" nature as it can live with or without love. Never marry out of convenience or for social reasons. Although you are deeply emotional (but afraid to show it), learn to overcome the tendency to be reserved, conservative, and withdrawn. A natural-born teacher and advisor, the Number 7 has a wealth of knowledge to share with others. Have faith in life itself and in people, and do not permit your quiet, reserved nature to suppress you. Your challenges, as an intellectual, are to understand the meaning of "faith," and experience your emotional side, which ultimately will result in growth and satisfaction.

Number 16/7 Soul/Heart's Desire

The Number 16/7 Soul/Heart's Desire is a vibration seeking truth, knowledge, and wisdom. The Number 1 stands for the need to express the creative and original ideas of leadership. The Number 6 devotes its energies to the service of the family and community. And, the Number 7 is the loner aspect that demands time alone. Since self-preservation is essential to the 7, the reverberation of the vibrations between these numbers creates a challenge of its own and may cause friction.

Number 8 Soul/Heart's Desire

The Number 8 Soul/Heart's Desire is to gain power and success in life on all levels, for this is a materialistic vibration. The perception is that money is necessary in order to get the most out of life. You have all the stamina, courage, judgment, drive, and talents needed to be a successful business executive, leader, or manager. The Number 8 Soul/Heart's Desire requires a balance between the material and spiritual planes of life for the best results. You respect power and success. You see power, acclaim, money, and authority as a means to get quality from all levels of life. The 8 Soul/Heart's Desire represents involvement in large operations, and belongs to the world of important endeavors, especially in the financial/commercial world. You dislike laziness, weakness, lack of strength of character, and anything second best. The Number 8 Soul/Heart's Desire seeks a strong and capable mate and wants its loved one to be equal to its ambition and drive. You have a warm love-nature, but must be alert not to defer your love-nature and place it low on your list of priorities, often being too busy to be romantic for long periods of time. Be very careful not to treat your romantic involvements in the same manner as you would direct and execute business and other affairs, making things of the heart seem impersonal and unimportant. And, be careful not to take the lead too positively in your love affairs for you can unconsciously drive others away by being too aggressive, causing others to experience disillusionment.

Number 9 Soul/Heart's Desire

The Number 9 Soul/Heart's Desire desires to be a humanitarian and of service to the world on some level as a *universal sister/brother,* advancing the cause of humanity. The Number 9 has a compassionate heart. You give freely of yourself without thoughts of your own discomfort, and you have boundless faith in your own unending source of supply and energy. Since the 9 has the combined vibrations of all the other numbers, it gives you a very sensitive, emotional, and romantic nature. However, your deep sense of commitment and drive toward perfection may detract from who you really are and tend to make you appear impersonal and aloof, which is far from the truth. Be aware of feeling superior, for you may express an arrogant attitude. Forgiveness, patience, and sympathy should always be foremost in your heart. You have a deep desire and need for personal love, but you belong to the Universe. As such, you need to be deeply aware of and attentive to your emotions so that you do not suffer through them. You can have personal enjoyment in your life, but taking things, people, or events too personally may bring you pain or grief. However, be careful not to neglect your personal loved one, by waiting until you are about to lose them. When you find your true love and nurture it, it will be a partnership for life.

Number 18/9 Soul/Heart's Desire

The Number 18/9 Soul/Heart's Desire is the number of great world leaders. They desire to always protect and serve. They can be political leaders, military leaders, or leaders in the field of medicine. Highly emotional and intellectual in nature, the Number 18/9 has all of the leadership abilities, as well as the creative and original ideas of the Number 1. The Number 8 brings with it a sound, intuitive judgment and efficiency, while the Number 9 brings the vibration of service to humanity with it, having the energy of all the numbers combined to create something great in the world. The 18/9 is a very focused and powerful number that desires to be recognized.

8.C Personality (The Language of the Numbers of the Consonants)

The definition and explanation of the Personality are included in chapter 6, section 6.C. The calculation of the number of the Personality is included in chapter 7, section 7.C.

Number 1 Personality

The Number 1 Personality will make an impression on others as a leader with a very pleasant, persuasive, and confident manner. However, the Number 1 can be seen as either courageous and daring, or self-indulgent, domineering, and selfish. Which "person" do you want to be seen as? Which one do you want to express? Be careful not to appear forceful or aggressive as this appearance can intimidate others. At times you may wish such a reaction, but you may find those that you care about backing away. Many people will react to you as a pioneer or a promoter of new and creative enterprises. A Number 1 Personality is well-groomed, dignified, and generally wears fashionable business suits/dresses in his or her own unique bright and cheerful style. Being overweight would contradict the image of the 1 Personality. Your taste in clothes should be in straight lines, loose, but well-fitted, accentuating your physique.

Number 19/1 Personality

The Number 19/1 Personality on any level is a very fortunate number. It is the Number 1 in all its best aspects. The double 1s emphasize the qualities of good leadership, which are added to the magnetic force of the Number 9. You radiate self-confidence, and creative and inventive abilities to those around you.

Number 2 Personality

The Number 2 Personality appears neat, clean, and radiates peace, tact, and diplomacy to others. This vibration has a pleasant personality, gentle manner, cooperative spirit, and a willingness to help others. People see you as harmonious, unobtrusive, and as someone who listens to both sides of the issues. A knack of selecting clothes should be cultivated, for loud or showy apparel would not be appropriate for your unobtrusive, gentle, and pleasant personality. Instead, wear styles and adapt them to your own personality choosing soft, flowing, easy-to-wear clothing, which would add more sparkle to your passive life.

Number 11/2 Personality

The Number 11/2 Personality is a Master Number that uplifts the vibration of the Number 2. While the 2 is peaceful, sensitive, and plays the role of a partner who avoids confrontation or being in charge, the 11/2 having a much higher vibrational force than the 2 resonates strong leadership, courage, originality, and creativity (from the double 1), and is highly emotional and electrical in nature, due to increased sensitivity, willingness to help others, and the radiating of peace and harmony (from the Number 2). The 11/2 Personality is seen as a gifted counselor with an extraordinary understanding of the human psyche. Channel the nervous energy for best results.

Number 3 Personality

The Number 3 Personality is seen as the life of the party, friendly, sociable, and popular, with the easy ability to express completely in an uplifting and charming manner. These traits and a relaxed air help you to appear successful and ambitious to others. You give off an aura of strong willpower and a sense of determination, and authority. Many will see you as having no worries or concerns. You may tend to draw enemies who are jealous of you just because they think you are successful, whether or not you are. The Number 3 Personality enjoys dressing up, wearing fine clothing and jewelry, and is both attractive to the opposite sex and attracted to the opposite sex. Being of an artistic nature may lead you to wearing extreme glamour styles, but regardless, remember to dress in good taste.

Number 4 Personality

The Number 4 Personality gives the impression of being conservative, orderly, and self-reliant. You want to be judged on the basis of your work performance rather than on appearance. So, you appear to others as disciplined, practical, and stable, one who thrives on hard work, and one who always has their nose to the grindstone. Even as a child, you demonstrated these same characteristics. You are seen as a tower of strength, and even may have square shoulders. You tend to wear earth colors and conventional clothing. Choose clothes that harmonize with your personality—wearing neat, tailored styles with more of a flair. Wear brighter colors and looser fitting clothing with less severe lines. Be careful not to overdress.

Number 13/4 Personality

The Number 13/4 Personality is a powerful masculine combination of the ambitious leadership ability of the Number 1 and the power of self-expression of the Number 3. All of this power is somewhat restricted by the limitations of the Root Number 4 which emphasizes detail, hard work, discipline, and a desire for foundation in life. The 13/4 Personality has these same attributes of the 4, but with an intense desire to be successful.

Number 22/4 Personality

The Number 22/4 Personality is seen as a *Master Builder*. The Number 22/4 is a Master Number that raises the Root Number 4 to a much higher, more intense energy level. The double 2 brings heightened emotional energy, tact, and diplomacy to the vibration. You appear as someone who listens to and sees the truths of both sides of the issues. The Root Number 4 brings discipline, structure, and foundation to the vibration. You make a distinct impression on others, with the ability to influence, having considerable strength and self-confidence. Be careful not to become too overbearing, as others will see you only as a "know-it-all" and avoid you. Become more aware of the feelings that may motivate another person, and respect those feelings. The combination of the 2s and the 4 make you appear to be as solid as a rock with an appearance of financial stability.

Number 5 Personality

The Number 5 Personality is seen as curious, free-spirited, adventurous, versatile, and carefree—as one who is always ready for a change. You charm people with your great sense of humor, sunny disposition, and vivid imagination while giving off magnetic and interesting vibrations which permeate around you. You build for present happiness. The desire to enjoy the now and face life fearlessly is very refreshing to those around you. You are inclined to be up-to-date on your clothing selection at all times—stylish, and versatile in selection. Be careful not to go to extremes. Don't select flashy clothes for the sake of being flashy or your image will be diminished in the eyes of others. Enhance your image by selecting styles appropriate for the occasion.

Number 14/5 Personality

The Number 14/5 Personality has all the traits of the Number 5, such as the desire for complete freedom, progress, change, variety, and to be happy. The Number 1 wants to express freedom, as well as leadership with its creative and original ideas. The Number 1 and the 5 have between them the restrictions of the Number 4 that adheres to discipline, detail, and hard work. This may very well give one the feeling of being held back, and can create a sense of rebellion and disruption.

Number 23/5 Personality

A Number 23/5 Personality vibration is the best of all of the Number 5 combinations. It reflects the desire for the peace and harmony of the Number 2, mingled with the social, creative ability, and joy of the Number 3. The Root Number is 5, which desires freedom, change, travel, and variety. Together these numbers create a pleasant, creative, and lively vibration.

Number 6 Personality

The Number 6 Personality is seen by others as sympathetic, harmonious, neat, balanced, and as having it all together. You reflect a quiet nature that appeals to all those who are seeking advice and comfort in their lives. You enjoy the "quiet" of meditation and contemplation. You are seen as loving many forms of art and music, flowers, and gardening. You are a natural-born interior designer and have excellent taste in color and style when you choose to be fashionable. However, you are more concerned with your personality than your appearance. You may be less conscious of the style of clothing you wear and prefer more comfortable clothes over the statement the clothes will make. Regardless of the clothes you choose, you should always be well-dressed, and give thought to the way you look and appear to others.

Number 7 Personality

The Number 7 Personality appears to be mysterious and different, serious, subtle, aloof, exclusive, reserved, highly independent, and self-sufficient—requiring solitude and peace. You must guard against becoming arrogant and often appearing withdrawn. It is common for people to see your focus turn inside of you in the middle of a conversation. Some may look at you as if you were a "loner." You are seen as having intelligence, wisdom, and as being highly educated. You are hard to get to know, but once the barrier is broken, your aloof and quiet personality becomes friendly toward others. You gain much esteem by being well-dressed, well-groomed, and by looking intelligent and wise to others. Good style for you involves straight lines, with touches of sparkle and dash. Expensive clothing brings you the confidence you need for show and tell.

Number 16/7 Personality

The Number 16/7 Personality is aloof, selective, and gives much attention to self-preservation. The Number 7 is known for intellectual pursuits and the desire for wisdom. The 16/7 sometimes appears as an enigma that baffles understanding, and is seen as both a participant in world affairs and as someone avoiding them like the plague. The Number 1 is the expression of creative and original ideas for leadership, while the Number 6 reflects the desire to give time and energy to service, family, and the community. The Number 7 appears to withdraw into solitude out of the world, which creates a possible conflict of interest with the 1 and 6 influences. The challenge is the competition between the 1, free individual, the 6, service provider, and the reserved, loner aspect of the 7.

Number 8 Personality

The Number 8 Personality gives off the impression of power, authority, strength, and ambition, with an exceptional ability to influence others. Your appearance of natural authority, competence, and enthusiasm attract people with resources. People are drawn to you because they sense your sureness and effectiveness. You know how to deal with the material and business problems you face. Your personality is seen as well-balanced and efficient, which may tend to make people see you as friendly, persuasive, and dominant. For the Number 8 Personality, it is always important to be well-groomed, and to present the picture of success to others. Your clothing may be a bit flashy, but in good taste, since quality is a top priority in selecting clothes. You always like the best and will present a picture of success, knowing you dislike cheap things or being second best. You prefer plaids, tweeds, and heavier types of clothing (sports clothes). There is a touch of showmanship in clothes selection, whether for social or business events.

Number 9 Personality

The Number 9 Personality is sincere, well-balanced, truthful and noble, and dedicated to the service of others, as a "big brother" or a "big sister." You are generous, sympathetic, and a guardian of mankind. You may appear to be romantic and an idealist. You are very much in control of the image you send out to others, as you are elegant, graceful, and charismatic. You are a magnetic personality, but sometimes lack the force of following through in developing friendships. Try to improve your style in clothes by adding more color, which better suits your magnetic personality. You may feel that wearing black is fashionable; however, you should not wear black as you often do, unless it fits the occasion. However, you would go further with the use of color to better suit your magnetic personality.

Number 18/9 Personality

The Number 18/9 Personality is a very powerful reflection of the Number 9 qualities, combining with the leadership of the Number 1 and the sound judgment and efficiency of the Number 8. The 1 and 8 have their root in the Number 9, which combines the vibrational force and energy of all the numbers, as well as humanitarian spirit.

8.D Purpose (The Language of the Numbers of the Total Name)

The description and explanation of the Purpose (Total Name) are included in chapter 6, section 6.D. The calculation of the number of the Purpose is included in chapter 7, section 7.D.

Number 1 Purpose

The Number 1 Purpose is to be a leader, as you have a pioneering spirit and a creative and original mind. You are self-reliant, independent, and have a strong will to accomplish your goals in life. Your success will come by "being your own person" through your talents, abilities, interests, and individuality, that is, through your own efforts. You must develop your powers of concentration and visualization to the utmost to achieve your goals, but be very aware to "not" become set and fixed in your ways. You are a natural born leader, pioneer, promoter, or executive management type. You will be given opportunities to help others discover their own individuality. Be cognizant of a tendency toward selfishness and seeming indifference to organization, group, team, or partner goals.

Number 19/1 Purpose

A Number 19/1 Purpose has the most fortunate of numbers. The Number 1 is positioned both at the beginning and ending of the number, indicating an enhanced leadership through originality and creative ideas. It is also known as the Alpha (1) and the Omega (9), encompassing all things. The Number 9 has the magnetic energy of all the numbers incorporated within its vibration. Your Purpose is to lead and to demonstrate respect for the rights of others.

Number 2 Purpose

The Number 2 Purpose in life is to play the role of peacemaker or diplomat. You have the ability to establish peace, balance, and harmony, for you can see both sides of the issues and have patience in handling details. The key to success with the Number 2 Purpose is working in association with others, not by competing. You possess great powers of cooperation, diplomacy, and subtle persuasion. It is important to develop these assets to perfection if you want the best from life. For the 2 Purpose, sharing and partnership are the best approach in experiencing your environment. You have great insight into the feelings of others. The arts, music, museums, and libraries give you much pleasure and opportunity.

Number 11/2 Purpose

The Number 11/2 Purpose is a Master Number, and lifts the Number 2 to limelight activities. The 11/2 is the number of the inspirational visionary, who is generally called to action for some great cause. You can be a super diplomat, super mediator, or super peacemaker. This vibration is "magnetic," and indicates an "electrical" individual with originality and intuition. The double 1 brings leadership, creativity, and originality. When combined with the detail, diplomacy, cooperative spirit, and emotional energy of the Number 2, the 11/2 produces a very high vibrational force. You can become a moving force in any endeavor, since people are "naturally" attracted to you and may tend to "follow" your lead as a result. You can find success as an evangelist, minister, reformer, or as a psychologist or psychoanalyst. However, because of the power, energy, and "electricity" of the 11/2 (and great responsibility), not all choose to respond, being quite satisfied with fulfillment within the lower vibration of the Root Number 2.

Number 3 Purpose

The Number 3 Purpose carries with it the natural ability for self-expression and the talent for a vivid and creative imagination. This is an optimistic vibration, and your success is tied directly to your gift of words that will let you achieve through writing, acting, speaking, or any medium that involves the creative word of self-expression. You are to arouse spirit and imagination so that others may learn how to experience the lighter, more joyful, lighter side of life. To scatter your energy and forces, and use your talents in self-indulgence at this time of life is to waste the opportunity for a wonderful use of the power of imagination you were given and diminish your success. The 3 Purpose can find success in literature, theater, opera, publishing, movies, or as a society leader or organizer. Concentrate on not scattering your talents by completing one activity at a time before moving on to avoid not accomplishing your original goals.

Number 4 Purpose

The Number 4 Purpose is to give form to new ideas that are permanent and lasting for the benefit of mankind. The Number 4 is the symbol of foundation, framework, and the "square." As a builder, your fulfillment comes from hard work and determination. The ideals of honesty, straightforwardness, and equality are of second nature to you—and you can help others by passing on your understanding to them. Your ability to establish system, order, and organization will bring you success in any field of management. You are hardworking, dependable, efficient, and loyal which helps to instill confidence to those around you. You can succeed as a carpenter, mason, contractor, or instructor.

Number 13/4 Purpose

The Number 13/4 Purpose is a very powerful expression of the Root Number 4. It combines the aggressive and masculine energy of the Number 1, the leader, and the Number 3, self-expression and ambition. At the base of the 13/4 is their Root Number 4 (feminine energy), which adds the talent for detail, hard work, discipline, structure, and foundation. The proper use of this combined power can form foundations for the benefit of others. However, do not let the "opposite" energies of the 13 (aggressive) and the 4 (structure) become potentially disruptive. Be sure to moderate and guide the power of these combined energy influences.

Number 22/4 Purpose

The Number 22/4 Purpose is a Master Number and contains the vibrational patterns of the Master Builder or Mason. The double 2 makes the tact, diplomacy, cooperative spirit, emotional and nervous energy of the number 2 a very powerful vibratory force in dealings between people, organizations, and nations. It is the combination of the emotional and nervous energy of the 2 with the discipline and structure of the Root Number 4 that raises the 22/4 to a much higher level. It is the number of international fame and activity. With the 22/4 Purpose, you can achieve the position of super statesman or become the head of an international organization or foundation. You have the potential to pave new roads on which others will follow from advancements that you have discovered. Where the 4 lays the foundations for home and community, the 22 does it for the world. The vibration brings the energy and ability to form foundations for the benefit of others.

Number 5 Purpose

The Number 5 Purpose in life is to promote freedom and liberty for all. This involves bringing forth new ideas for the purpose of expansion and progress and to pass these concepts on to others. The Number 5 Purpose inspires words in action. You can find success in writing, speaking, communications, journalism, investigative reporting, public relations, and public administration. Since the 5 Purpose empowers a life of action, change, and movement, you should find success working in the public arena or supporting civic improvement. Learn that change means progress, growth, and expansion, not confusion, uncertainty, or unpredictability. The Number 5 Purpose is versatile, clever, and courageous. However, be aware that too many irons in the fire and scattered forces can indeed lead to uncertainty.

Number 14/5 Purpose

The Number 14/5 Purpose also represents the Root Number 5 which is the number of change, variety, travel, and communication. The 14/5 Purpose can sometimes reflect disruption and confusion. The Number 1 represents creativity, originality, and leadership, and desires freedom as an individual. The vibrational pattern which stands between the 1 and the 5 energies (masculine, aggressive) is the Number 4, which requires hard work, foundation, discipline, structure, and detail. It is the mixing of the 1, 4, and 5 energies in this manner that can create a disruptive vibration which produces restrictions, pulling you between the aggressive 1 and 5, and the passive 4. This interaction sometimes leads to a sense of rebellion with a need to challenge the status quo unreasonably. Understand these energies and the play of these combined patterns, and use them to their greatest effect for your success. The 14/5 Purpose is known as the number of speculation, e.g., real estate, gambling, speculative stock market endeavors, etc.

Number 23/5 Purpose

The Number 23/5 Purpose is the best of all the 5 Number combinations. It combines the peace, diplomacy, and cooperative spirit of the Number 2 (which leads the 23) with the self-expression, creativity, and lightheartedness of the Number 3. The 2 and 3 have their root in the 5, which is change, variety, travel, and communication, making this a pleasant vibration.

Number 6 Purpose

The Number 6 Purpose is keynoted by the phrase "Doing unto others as you would have them do unto you," to give comfort and service to others whether it is done in the home or out in the community. You are the "cosmic" parent or teacher in service to home and community, and your success depends on how much you can do for others. You will be successful if you work from a position of great responsibility and trust, and inspire the people you serve. Your rewards will come through your service, love, and protection. Since harmony, rhythm, love, and beauty are paramount in your life, many types of music will appeal to you, as well as the finer arts. You will be a strong influence in establishing harmony and beauty in every environment where you abide, whether in your home or in your community.

Number 7 Purpose

The Number 7 Purpose is to be the educator of the world and to understand all the mysteries (physical and/or metaphysical) of this Universe, and to share specialized knowledge gained in life with others who seek to understand these mysteries. Your philosophical mind enables you and drives you to seek out the ultimate in truth. The 7 Purpose is a deep thinker and needs to spend time alone and in silence. Opportunities lie in the fields of education, science, or study. And time may be given to writing, invention, and to the unusual, even odd, lines of endeavor. Partnerships may not be successful for you unless you really work at it, even though the 7 Purpose has an innate sympathy for others, a sensitive nature, and inner power and substance. Learn to see the reality behind the appearance through understanding, wisdom, and discrimination. Learn the difference between what is real and what is illusion. You may desire to withdraw from the "world" and become absorbed in more introvert activities.

Number 16/7 Purpose

The Number 16/7 Purpose is the number of completion, reflection, and intellectual pursuit that is always governed by the need for self-preservation. The individuality and leadership aspects of the Number 1 versus the Number 6, which is the devotion to family and community, tend to compete with the desire of the 7 to be alone. Again, like the 13/4 Purpose, this Purpose number can be disruptive and unsettling because of the interaction of one, the "outward" looking aspects of the 1 and 6 with the "inward" looking desire of the 7, and two, the mixture of masculine (aggressive) energies of the 1 and 7 with the feminine (passive) energies of the 6. Remember that the true nature of this number is to seek information, absorb it, understand it, and then teach it to others. The Number 16/7 Purpose is also known as a Karmic number with lessons to be learned during this disruptive vibration.

Number 8 Purpose

The Number 8 Purpose is to attain financial recognition and success and then share this success and knowledge with others. You are to learn about the relationship between material and spiritual power and to pass that learning on. The 8 Purpose represents an innate intuitive judgment, and requires the right use of sound judgment if you want the best results. Your sharp sense of judgment can bring you success in a court of law or in business and finance. With these qualities, opportunity to supervise, regulate, and direct the affairs of others will be easily obtained. Positions such as in research, investigation, advisory boards, counseling, and executive management give you personal satisfaction. Power, organization, and executive ability are natural to you, but demand good character, self-discipline, and courage. Do not let any failures discourage or anger you (they're only temporary), and do not desert your purpose or ideals, for doing so will bring unhappiness into your life.

Number 9 Purpose

The Number 9 Purpose is to give humanitarian service, of the highest standard, to the world. Bywords of the 9 Purpose are compassion, tolerance, understanding, as well as service. You must live above the jealousies, fears, and the greed of mankind to experience a successful life. You can achieve that success as a spiritual leader, teacher, healer, or as a philanthropist. Learn to give freely of emotions through inspiration, kindness, and understanding. Love and companionship will come through work done for all people—regardless of race, creed, culture, or politics. It is important to include the arts, philanthropy, and romance in your life to help you maintain a personal view of what you are undertaking. Stay impartial; for taking things too personally or too seriously can bring you unnecessary pain. You can have all the success that you want by living up to your ideals. If you find that you must make unwanted sacrifices, face them, and resolve them.

Number 18/9 Purpose

The Number 18/9 Purpose is the number of great spiritual and humanitarian leadership. It is the most powerful expression of the Root Number 9. The Number 1 represents creative and original ideas of leadership and combines with the efficiency and sound judgment of the Number 8. Along with this, the 9 includes the vibrations of all the numbers to produce a high vibratory force.

8.E Life Goal (The Language of the Numbers of the Sum of the Name and Birthdate)

The description and meaning of the Life Goal number given here is a predominant influence over the last half of your life. The definition and explanation of the Life Goal (the sum of your Destiny number and your Purpose number) are included in chapter 6, section 6.E. The calculation of the number of the Life Goal is included in chapter 7, section 7.E.

Number 1 Life Goal

The Number 1 Life Goal gives you an even greater opportunity to express all of the ambition and drive of the leadership role of the 1. You will have the opportunity to fill a "leadership" role, or to be a "pioneer" of new ideas. If you are prepared, your creative originality will be enhanced, and action and independence can be yours. Be aware not to be stubborn and opinionated, over-dominant, or "too" set in your views. If so, success could be dampened.

Number 19/1 Life Goal

The Number 19/1 Life Goal is a powerfully positive vibration of energy and represents leadership filled with original, creative, and inventive ideas. The Number 9, which stands between the two 1s, represents the vibrational energy of all the numbers. The two 1s emphasize and reinforce the qualities of leadership, making the 19/1 Life Goal one of the most fortunate of numbers. The 19/1 sets up the latter period in life for success, if you are ready.

Number 2 Life Goal

The Number 2 Life Goal emphasizes the field of diplomacy. You could enjoy great success as an advisor, counselor, mediator, or peacemaker. You may even work for the public using your talent for detail and gathering of data while creating a climate of peace and harmony around you. Your bywords are cooperation and association. Be careful not to bend over backwards too much in working with others, or you could become a doormat. Involve yourself in the finer arts, such as in music, dancing, or art.

Number 11/2 Life Goal

The Number 11/2 Life Goal is a Master Number, with the double 1 enhancing the originality and creativity of the leadership qualities of the 1, making it a very dynamic number. This combined with the detail, diplomacy, cooperative spirit, and emotional energy of the 2 produces a very high vibrational force. It suggests that this is a time to do something inspirational in the latter part of your life. Limelight, leadership, and distinction are signified. Many spiritual and religious leaders fall under the 11/2 vibration. Since the Number 11/2 is electrical in nature, communications fields are open to you. Opportunities will also avail themselves to you in high "energy" fields such as power generation, aviation, aerospace, electronics, and inventions.

Number 3 Life Goal

The Number 3 Life Goal is an opportunity for you to express yourself now more than any other time in your life. Your natural flair for communication along with a great sense of humor and vivid imagination, combine to make this vibration very exciting. Self-expression is the keynote of this vibration—in speaking, writing, or acting. Speaker, entertainer, publisher, author, and movie director are position opportunities for success and fulfillment. Avoid any tendency to scatter your energies, and concentrate on a few "select" goals.

Number 4 Life Goal

The Number 4 Life Goal is the time to give form to many of your own ideas for the benefit of others. You can lay the foundations upon which others can build their dreams. Your talent for organization based on system and order will be very important factors in your success. And, there is much for you to accomplish in your latter years—promoting goodwill through orderliness, honesty, and straightforwardness. Success and rewarding outcomes will come through discipline, attention to detail, and respecting everyone as being equal.

Number 13/4 Life Goal

The Number 13/4 Life Goal is a more powerful expression of the aggressive and masculine energy of the Number 13, which combines the leadership of the 1 and the ambition and self-expression of the Number 3. The root of the 13/4 is the Number 4, the builder, which adds the talent of detail, discipline, hard work, and the desire for foundation in life. This is the time to help build various foundations for the benefit of all.

Number 22/4 Life Goal

The Number 22/4 Life Goal is a Master Number and will energize and enhance the attributes of the Number 4, which include discipline, foundation, structure, hard work, and attention to detail. Intuition, emotional and nervous energy, cooperative spirit, partnership, and diplomacy of the double 2 are enhanced and combined to raise the 4 to a new level called the Master Builder. The 22/4 is the Number of worldwide fame and for forming foundations for the benefit of others. You can be the "builder" in the practical or physical (mundane) world as well as in the world of ideals and metaphysics.

Number 5 Life Goal

The Number 5 Life Goal promises a great amount of activity in the latter part of your life. The accent will be on travel, variety, and freedom of thought and action—letting go of the old and experiencing the untried. You could shine as a writer, an investigative reporter, or find success in the communications arena in such way as to benefit mankind. However, avoid being too diversified or reaching out in so many directions, that you lose track of your real goals.

Number 14/5 Life Goal

The Number 14/5 Life Goal is the number of change, variety, communication, and travel, but you must be aware to keep focused and disciplined. The Root Number 4 (structure, passive), which requires attention to detail, discipline, hard work, and foundation, stands between the aggressive Number 1, which represents active individualism and leadership, and the Number 5, which represents freedom and travel. This combination of vibrational energy may produce some restrictions, and in any kind of business venture, could represent risk and speculation. The 14/5 Life Goal is sometimes known as the number of speculation, which means that you can be a salesman or a speculator (whether it is real estate, stocks, or gambling).

Number 23/5 Life Goal

The Number 23/5 Life Goal is also a number of change, variety, communication, and travel. However, instead of being overshadowed by risk and speculation, the sensitivity, tact, cooperative spirit, and diplomacy of the Number 2 combines with the creative ability and self-expression of the Number 3, to form very lively and pleasant vibrational patterns within the attributes of the Root Number 5. The 23/5 Life Goal is the best of all the Number 5 combinations, and presents a good time in life to experience it all.

Number 6 Life Goal

The Number 6 Life Goal reflects a time in the latter part of your life when you will have the opportunity to be the "cosmic teacher and parent," devoted to family and community services as a humanitarian. Your responsibilities, duties, and success lie in helping and guiding others and working for the betterment of mankind. You should also find satisfaction in your home life and financial security in your career.

Number 7 Life Goal

The Number 7 Life Goal vibrational patterns present an ideal opportunity to share all the wisdom and knowledge that this number attracts, when you could become known as an educator of great wisdom and understanding. Your greatest success will come through teaching and passing on intellectual and spiritual truths. This time of your life can provide great insights which come to you through meditation and contemplation. Be aware to avoid the desire to become an introvert and withdraw, for this will limit your experiencing.

Number 16/7 Life Goal

In the Number 16/7 Life Goal, the Root Number 7 is a number of intellectual pursuits, self-preservation, and completion. The individuality and leadership of the Number 1 and the devotion to family and community of the Number 6, will tend to compete with the desire of the 7 to be a loner. This may give rise to some discontent, and may even be a hindrance to prompt action when required.

Number 8 Life Goal

The Number 8 Life Goal in the latter days of your life gives the promise of recognition, authority, and power to those who are determined to succeed in life. Opportunities in positions of authority, power, and judgment will offer themselves to you. If you have exercised discipline and determination, and your executive and directive abilities are well-established, you may be drawn into commercial business or financial ventures, such as real estate or banking. If your interest is in the field is law, your goal can be realized as a judge.

Number 9 Life Goal

The Number 9 Life Goal reward in the latter years comes through serving the world in humanitarian and universal pursuits. Opportunities for fulfillment will come to you more through a "larger" view of things than through a "personal" view. You can achieve goals of success in the medical, political, or philosophical arenas as a doctor, nurse, psychiatrist, metaphysician, or political office holder. You can shine as a writer and lecturer on subjects that deal with service to humanity.

Number 18/9 Life Goal

The Number 18/9 Life Goal is the vibration of famous world leaders. The 18/9 is a more powerful expression of the Root Number 9. It represents all the qualities of leadership of the Number 1 and the efficiency, sound judgment, recognition, and authority of the Number 8. The 9 is the Number of completion that combines the energy and vibrations of all the numbers, producing a very powerful universal force. This is the time to take a holistic view of life and to serve society on a humanitarian or universal level.

8.F. Birthdate Cycles (The Language of the Numbers of the Birth Month, Day, and Year)

The definition and explanation of the Birthdate Cycles are included in chapter 6, section 6.F. The calculation of the numbers of the Birthdate Cycles is included in chapter 7, section 7.F.

Number 1 Birthdate Cycle

The Number 1 Birthdate Cycle requires that you develop your individuality to the utmost. It is important to be independent and rely on your own resources for a lot is expected of you, especially if it is your first cycle. Likewise, it is important to develop your creative talent and your original and inventive ideas.

Number 19/1 Birthdate Cycle

The Number 19/1 Birthdate Cycle gives you the opportunity for success as a humanitarian leader in the public arena. The 19/1 begins with a Number 1 (the Alpha of numbers), which represents leadership, creative originality, action, and independence. It stands before the Number 9 (the Omega of numbers), which has within it the vibrational energies of all of the other root numbers, and is the number of the humanitarian. The 9 is followed again by the 1 (encircling the 9), which completes a circle of power, and makes the 19/1 the most fortunate of numbers. As a leader, it is important for your success that you assume the right attitude toward others for the best result.

Number 2 Birthdate Cycle

The Number 2 Birthdate Cycle is the period to be receptive and cooperative with others, and is a partnership number that requires you to become more tolerant and patient. In this cycle, it is important for you to avoid the tendency to be very emotional and sensitive. If the 2 Birthdate Cycle appears as a first cycle, the young person may require counseling.

Number 11/2 Birthdate Cycle

The Number 11/2 Birthdate Cycle is a Master Number and is a period of time for illumination and a chance to be in the limelight. The double 1 indicates leadership with original and creative ideas, as well as the desire for freedom of action. The Root Number 2 shows diplomacy, partnership, detail, and emotional energy. The ideals and inspirational nature of these numbers could lead to success in the public arena as a peacemaker.

Number 3 Birthdate Cycle

The Number 3 Birthdate Cycle is the time to be joyful, live life to the fullest, and develop any talent and creative abilities you may have. It is the number of romance, joy, ambition, and success.

Number 4 Birthdate Cycle

The Number 4 Birthdate Cycle is about building better foundations in life, noting that this is not the time for pleasure or play. It also requires that you be practical and economical, and organize your plans to bring forth new ideas for the benefit of others. You may feel some limitations financially or in expressing yourself.

Number 13/4 Birthdate Cycle

The Number 13/4 Birthdate Cycle is a powerful masculine vibration, with the Number 1 representing leadership and individuality with the need for freedom to function, and the Number 3 vibration representing self-expression and ambition. They sit upon the Root Number 4, which requires structure, hard work, discipline, detail, and the need for foundation. Therefore, it is necessary to be patient and work through any difficulties during this vibration to get the best results, as the Numbers 1, 3, and 4 in combination may cause some conflicts. Because of the powerful energy of this number, it is wise to maintain good health habits and not overwork.

Number 22/4 Birthdate Cycle

The Number 22/4 Birthdate Cycle is a Master Number and is considered to be the time of the Master builder. The cooperative spirit, emotional energy, and intuition of the double 2 raises the Number 4 to a much higher level. The 4 is known for attention to detail, discipline, structure, hard work, and the talent for bringing form to new ideas to benefit mankind. It is important to use all this talent to help others in order to enjoy success.

Number 5 Birthdate Cycle

In the Number 5 Birthdate Cycle, the desire for freedom, expansion, and change prevails. You are best suited working in the public arena. This is the time for freedom without neglecting your responsibilities, so that the proper use of your freedom can add to your success. An increased interest in sex or other indulgences can lead to impulsive behavior. Travel, change, and having variety in life make this an exciting time. Try to improve your charm and appearance and keep on the move.

Number 14/5 Birthdate Cycle

The Number 14/5 Birthdate Cycle brings with it a period of change—the potentially conflicting vibrational energies involved make it unusually dissimilar to the Root Number 5 vibration. This is due to the aggressive, masculine influences of the Numbers 1 and 5, in contrast to the solid, disciplined Number 4. The 1 brings with it leadership, creative originality, and individuality. The 5 wants change, variety, travel, freedom, and action. However, the Number 4 stands between these aggressive energies as a restrictive or restraining force. The 4 wants attention to detail, structure, hard work, and foundation. Thus, it is not a "true" freedom number in the manner of the 5, and therefore, you must stay aware of a potential disruptive nature in the 14/5 vibration. Progress can be made, but patience and balance is required. Some people use this time to bring about change in the established rules of conduct, politics, government, etc.

Number 23/5 Birthdate Cycle

The Number 23/5 Birthdate Cycle is the best combination of all the 5 Number combinations. The tact, diplomacy, detail, and partnership need of the Number 2 join with the self-expressive joy and creative ability of the Number 3. Their Root Number 5 wants change, variety, travel, and the joy of freedom. It can be a lively, pleasant, and exciting period of time. Although, it is important to enjoy this period, always remember what the proper use of freedom really is—bringing forth new ideas for the purpose of progress, growth, and freedom from restriction, which you pass on for the benefit of humanity.

Number 6 Birthdate Cycle

The Number 6 Birthdate Cycle centers on responsibility and adjustment in the affairs of home, family, and community. If the 6 were the last Birthdate Cycle, it would indicate the need to bring and maintain balance and harmony in your domestic life, and be committed to community service.

Number 7 Birthdate Cycle

The Number 7 Birthdate Cycle is dominated by spiritual growth and understanding wisdom. It will call for greater examination of your own thoughts, desires and conduct, increased mental activity, studying, and the setting aside of time for meditation to achieve peace. Strive to bring the beauty of the intangible nature of spirituality and your physical existence into balance, in order to bring the poise that you desire. Though you may prefer to work alone, try not to let aloofness and/or negativity control your life.

Number 16/7 Birthdate Cycle

The Number 16/7 Birthdate Cycle is a completion period with the accent on spiritual growth, introspection, and intellectual and educational pursuits dominating. You may experience having less physical energy than normal, with a tendency to withdraw somewhat, therefore, appearing aloof. The Number 16/7 may produce a conflict of priorities. This may happen for two reasons. The first reason is the potential effect of the masculine, aggressive aspects of the Number 1 coming into close proximity of the feminine, receptive aspects of the Number 6. The Number 1 is the desire for leadership, individuality, and creative originality versus the 6 which is a team/family-oriented vibration dedicated to family, home, and community service. The other potential conflict comes from the desire of the Root Number 7 to withdraw and be alone, which is not the desire of the 1 and 6. The 16/7 is also considered a Karmic number which indicates there are lessons to be learned. Since it can be a potentially disruptive vibration, it is best to stay aware and focused, be patient, and keep yourself occupied and involved in the world around you during this cycle.

Number 8 Birthdate Cycle

The Number 8 Birthdate Cycle is a powerful vibration concerned with activities in finance, business/commercial, and legal endeavors. More than ever, you must rely on your own efforts instead of trusting to luck. As a first cycle, it may mean too much financial and social freedom, which could give rise to problems and adjustments later on. As a last cycle, it may be the opportune time to increase your financial and social independence, since you have had the chance to incorporate the lessons of experience.

Number 9 Birthdate Cycle

The Number 9 Birthdate Cycle suggests an interest in humanitarian service and is devoted to serving mankind as opposed to pursuing personal interests. It does not mean that you must give up having a personal life; it only means that your personal life will have second priority. This cycle can be a very emotional time of life, particularly if it appears as a first cycle, since you will not have had a chance to form a mature and informed perspective of life. As an adult, you need to cultivate tolerance and more compassion. The 9 belongs to the world, making this Birthdate Cycle not the best time for marriage.

Number 18/9 Birthdate Cycle

The Number 18/9 Birthdate Cycle is a most powerful vibration. The 18/9 is the Number of great leaders associated with either social, political, military, religious, and medical arenas. It forms a magnetic force to do good works benefiting mankind. The Number 1 is leadership with creative and original ideas along with the desire for independence. The Number 8 brings power, sound and intuitive judgment, and efficiency to the equation. Along with these elements, their Root Number is 9, which has all the vibrational energy of all the numbers, and represents completion, force, energy, healing, universality, compassion, and objectivity.

8.G Challenges (The Language of the Numbers of the Challenges)

The definition and explanation of the numbers of the Challenges are included in chapter 6, section 6.G. The calculation of the numbers of your Challenges is included in chapter 7, section 7.G.

Number 0 Challenge

The Number zero (0) Challenge is known as the challenge of *choice.* You have reached a point in your development where it is your right and your responsibility to choose which path to accomplishment, if any, you are willing to take. If you rely on others to make your choices in life, you are still responsible for the outcomes, good or bad. The circle represents the Universe; it has no beginning and it has no ending. The zero (0) Challenge means that you have fulfilled the lessons of the Soul/Heart's Desire, reached a place of completion, and can now contribute to helping others fulfill their Soul's lesson plan, or not. It provides you with the opportunity to apply "all" or "none" of the lessons learned. You have the knowledge and talents of all the numbers. Develop and apply creative ideas. You can use your talents, abilities, knowledge, and determination to succeed in life to the benefit of humanity, or you can ignore success, compassion, and empathy—drifting through life doing whatever you please without caring about anyone or anything around you, vacillating to please others, and accomplishing nothing.

Number 1 Challenge

The Number 1 Challenge requires that you develop self-reliance, will power, courage, and the desire to succeed. Any feelings of revenge, belligerence, and resentment which may have resulted early in your life must be overcome, if you wish to move forward with success. You may have been criticized, put down, or held back by relatives, friends, or teachers. Being overly aggressive can bring you experiences of humility. Instead, develop and apply creative ideas, and command the respect of others.

Number 2 Challenge

The Number 2 Challenge represents sensitivity in your life. You must now learn how to develop self-confidence by using your own creative ideas, developing and using your own talents, and cultivating a broad viewpoint. All of your physic powers are inborn so try to develop them to the utmost. Learn to trust the intuition and psychic powers that are inherent within you. Avoid the tendency to become a doormat—be self-confident, be yourself. Keep from vacillating to please others and accomplishing nothing. You are very sensitive and may find it very hard to forgive and forget.

Number 3 Challenge

The Number 3 Challenge indicates that before you can become successful, you will need to develop the ability to create expressively through the arts, as in writing, acting, music, or speaking. The Number 3 Challenge also requires that you learn how to express yourself verbally, develop yourself socially, and enjoy the company of people. Get involved in public affairs, but avoid scattering your energies, efforts, and talents.

Number 4 Challenge

The Number 4 Challenge requires that you establish system and order in your life now. But, avoid over controlling things or being controlled. Let things flow naturally. You are meant to give form to your own ideas for the benefit of others. Be careful not to be stubborn and opinionated, for it could hold you back from success and moving forward in life. You may dislike routine jobs, tend to put off things, or worry needlessly, all of which are traps which will also hold you back.

Number 5 Challenge

The Number 5 Challenge calls for the proper use of freedom in your life, both for yourself and for others. You may want freedom at any price, but do not seek freedom in order to avoid responsibilities. If you allow restlessness to control your life, real success may never be fully achieved. Though you resist all confinement, you still need to build and maintain a solid foundation. Be aware of an increased interest in sex and other indulgences which can lead to impulsive behavior. Learn the lesson to discard, what to let go and when to let go, to make room for the new. The desire for travel, change, and variety can make this an exciting time. The right use of your desire for freedom can make you successful at promotion, advertising, travel, or public relations.

Number 6 Challenge
The Number 6 Challenge is a domestic number concerned primarily with assuming the responsibility for affairs of the home and the community. Deep within the nature of the Number 6 Challenge is the desire to be the head of the household, while at the same time, there is the temptation to become possessive and domineering. Since you are overly idealistic about what is wrong and right, avoid becoming self-opinionated and self-righteous. Don't expect or try to make everyone adjust or conform to "your" rules or way of thinking or you will be resented. For true love and companionship, you must learn to respect, not just tolerate, the views of others. Everyone is entitled to their own point of view.

Number 7 Challenge
The Number 7 Challenge shows that you need to conquer any feelings you may have of resentment toward prevailing conditions or limitations in your life. If you feel rebellious against these conditions and limitations, you must change the circumstances. You may appear aloof and reserved, hiding your true feelings. Eliminate this conflict by developing faith in your own self- worth and your soul. It is important to develop your mind and keep faith in yourself.

Number 8 Challenge
The Number 8 Challenge requires that if you work hard and have good values, that is, if your motives are straightforward and above board, you will have an excellent chance for recognition, success, and financial reward. If you are afraid of loss and limitation, you may very well experience lack and limitation. The 8 Challenge is known as the "Balance of Power" challenge. This means that you must see both the material and spiritual side of power and money, and bring them into balance. You believe that personal freedom is based on material possessions.

8.H Pinnacles (The Language of the Numbers of the Pinnacles)
The definition and explanation of the Pinnacles are included in chapter 6, section 6.H. The calculation of the numbers of the Pinnacles is included in chapter 7, section 7.H.

Number 1 Pinnacle
The Number 1 Pinnacle marks the beginning of a new 9–year cycle in which you will now have a real chance to develop leadership, creativity, and your own originality of thought. This is a cycle that will bring new beginnings, new projects, change, and action. As a first Pinnacle, this could be a very difficult period, for a lot of responsibility may be placed on you. This responsibility may be more than you want to handle, causing you to feel rebellious. However, this responsibility gives you a chance to express your individuality, independence,

and abilities, and to stand on your own two feet—your path to success. If the Number 1 is found on any other Pinnacle, it provides you with the opportunity to develop your own ideas, but demands determination and courage.

Number 19/1 Pinnacle

The Number 19/1 Pinnacle opens the door for the opportunities of a new 9–year cycle and sets up the most fortunate time for success. It is a powerful vibration because the Number 1, which stands for the leadership of creative and original ideas, leads the 19/1. The Number 9, which brings the energetic vibration of all numbers combined, stands at the center of the 19/1. And the end 1, which follows and encircles the 9, completes a circle of power, making the 19/1 one of the most fortunate of number combinations. As a leader, it is important that you assume the right attitude toward others for the best result. This Pinnacle may also bring some new lessons to be learned.

Number 2 Pinnacle

The Number 2 Pinnacle is an opportunity for success through patience, detail, cooperative endeavors (including relationships), and sharing. Although the 2 is a number of emotional energy, it is not an aggressive vibration. As such, you will need to cultivate diplomacy, tact, harmony, and a cooperative spirit. This is a time for partnerships and associations rather than for individual endeavors. If this is a first Pinnacle, a young person could be very emotional, requiring understanding and counseling.

Number 11/2 Pinnacle

The Number 11/2 Pinnacle is the time to open up the consciousness for spiritual growth. It is a time of spiritual expansion, illumination, and fame. The two 1s represent pillars of strength, which emphasize and enhance the aspects of the 1—leadership, independence, originality, creative ideas, and inventiveness. The double 1 vibration plus the emotional and nervous energy of the Number 2, make this an "electrical period." If you fully develop your talents, you will get the chance to be in the limelight.

Number 3 Pinnacle

The Number 3 Pinnacle gives you the grand opportunity to express your creative and artistic abilities more then ever before. Your imagination and feelings will be on top. You could have opportunities for writing, speaking, interior designing, stage, movies, and/or music. Put forth effort to develop your creative talent, for a new energy force is operating in your life to bring you happiness and success.

Number 4 Pinnacle

The Number 4 Pinnacle is the time to build a good foundation for your future and to put ideas into form that will benefit others. This time calls for work not play, and constant service and effort. Your inner responses should be to "discard" the old and make ready for expansion. As a first Pinnacle, a young person may go to work and enter the job market early. The 4 Pinnacle may also be your first chance in life to complete a great work. This may be a slow period, but it will be very sure one.

Number 13/4 Pinnacle

The Number 13/4 Pinnacle brings you an opportunity to build a new foundation for the future. The Number 13 brings together the masculine and aggressive energy of leadership and independence of the Number 1, and the ambition and self-expression of the Number 3. The feminine and receptive Root Number 4, requires work, discipline, detail, foundation, and structure. It is important to maintain good health habits during this energetic, hardworking year. Be careful not to become a workaholic.

Number 22/4 Pinnacle

The Number 22/4 Pinnacle is a Master Number. The double 2 brings a magnified sense of electrical, emotional, and nervous energy, and raises the Number 4 to a much higher level. For your greatest success, this is a time to think on a much larger scale in terms of commitment, energy, and hard work, for the Number 22/4 has the vibratory power to bring forth new ideas for the benefit of mankind. It is the number of international affairs and worldly activities.

Number 5 Pinnacle

The Number 5 Pinnacle brings the desire for more freedom, movement, and change than any other time. Although you may experience restlessness and uncertainty, make the most of this unsettled time and be a part of the world. The keynotes of the 5 Pinnacle are travel, new experiences, and new friends. Working in the public arena is the best place for you during this period such as in advertising, selling, and public relations.

Number 14/5 Pinnacle

The Number 14/5 Pinnacle brings much change, the chance for travel, and possibly a period of some disruption. The 14/5 puts the feminine, receptive, and discipline-oriented vibrations of the Number 4 between the masculine, aggressive, and action-oriented vibrations of the Number 1 and the Number 5. This brings a challenge to balance the different demands of these interacting vibrations. The Number 1 brings leadership with new and creative ideas, individuality, and independence. The Root Number 5 wants to express complete freedom, variety in life, and constant change. Since the 4 centers on hard work, structure, discipline, and foundation, a potential conflict and disruption could occur between the interacting energies of the 1, 5, and 4.

Number 23/5 Pinnacle

The Number 23/5 Pinnacle carries with it the most pleasant of all the 5 Number combinations. The Number 2 is known for cooperation, tact, diplomacy, emotions, and partnerships. The Number 3 stands for joy, self-expression, and creative energy. The Root Number 5 represents freedom, variety, travel, communication, and change. Care should be taken to act in a responsible way during this lively, pleasant, and exciting period. Be aware to curtail overindulgences in any area.

Number 6 Pinnacle

The Number 6 Pinnacle emphasizes duty and responsibility to the family, the home, and the community. This is a Pinnacle that favors marriage; if you do get married, it will be a good one. This can be a very productive, happy period of time, settling down, and putting your life in order and laying your foundation to build security. An early marriage or family responsibility may occur in the first Pinnacle.

Number 7 Pinnacle

The Number 7 Pinnacle should be centered on spiritual growth, the search for more knowledge, and understanding of all the deeper forces of the Universe. Interest should be in spiritual progress, not material accumulation. Your inner response to this time should be one of poise, self- examination, and waiting. This is not the best time for marriage unless the lessons of life have been learned. You must be honest, patient, and understanding in personal relationships and partnerships, or difficulty may result. If the 7 Pinnacle appears as a first Pinnacle, the young person will need good nutrition, education, and lots of understanding and patience from the parents.

Number 16/7 Pinnacle

The Number 16/7 Pinnacle is the time for introspection, spiritual growth, and intellectual pursuits. During this period there tends to be less physical energy to offset the high mental activity. The Number 1 brings with it the desire for leadership, individuality, and creative originality versus the 6 which is a team/family-oriented vibration dedicated to family, home, and community service. Added to these vibrations is the affect of the Root Number 7, an intellectual and introspective vibration that desires to withdraw and be alone, which are not the desires of the 1 and 6. So it's important to be patient, and to understand that this is a time to be focused on mental housecleaning and spiritual growth.

Number 8 Pinnacle
The Number 8 Pinnacle is an excellent period for the success and the financial gain that you want. However, this requires stamina, courage, ambition, and constant effort. If you rely on your ability to make sound judgments, and not luck, you can obtain a position of authority and fame. Careful management of the finances is important since success brings financial rewards, and money can be lost as easily as it's earned.

Number 9 Pinnacle
The Number 9 Pinnacle is the number of completion, and brings with it the desire to give up old thought patterns and habits that no longer nurture your life, and are no longer of value to your life and style of living. This could be a highly charged and emotional period that may be difficult for you. Some relationships may even end in order to stimulate new growth. The 9 Pinnacle carries with it a talent for art, beauty, and a universal mentality. There is a lot of opportunity for business success that will allow you to live the full life that you desire, once your lessons have been learned. As a first Pinnacle, the 9 can be a very emotional time for you as a young person, due to facing and resolving many new challenges.

Number 18/9 Pinnacle
The Number 18/9 Pinnacle has very high energy, and it is electrical in nature. The 18/9 Pinnacle is the number of great leaders associated with social, political, military, religious, and medical arenas. The 18/9 forms a magnetic force to do good works benefiting mankind. The Number 1 is leadership with creative and original ideas along with the desire for independence. The Number 8 brings power, sound judgment, and efficiency to the equation. Along with these elements is the Root Number 9, which has the vibrational energy of all the numbers, and represents completion, force, energy, healing, universality, compassion, and objectivity. This is the time to be impersonal and think of service on a universal level for the best results.

8.I Soul Qualities (The Language of the Numbers of the Soul Qualities)
The definition and explanation of the Soul Qualities are included in chapter 6, section 6.I. The calculation of the numbers of the Soul Qualities is included in chapter 7, section 7.I.

Number 1 Soul Quality
Leadership/Pioneer/Originality

The Number 1 Soul Quality is the self-reliant pioneer who has creative and original ideas, a good sense of humor, and likes to be the boss. If you do not have any of the following letters in your full name (A, I, J, Q, or Y), as assigned to the Number 1 in the Chaldean

Alphabet/Formula (see table 7–1), then you would have a "count value" of zero (0-) for the Number 1 Soul Quality. A zero (0-) value represents a Karmic lesson in this lifetime, indicting the need to develop yourself through your own efforts, abilities, and drive in order for you to succeed as a leader paving the roads for others to follow. A Soul Quality assigned a number with a plus sign (+) means that the person has been developing this quality and exceeds the normal value indicated. A number value followed by a minus sign (–) means the person has not yet reached the particular level of understanding for that Soul Quality and has more work to do in that area in order to achieve balance and full potential. (The meaning of a "normal" value is more fully addressed in chapter 6, section 6.I.)

Number 2 Soul Quality

Partner/Sensitivity/Mediation

The Number 2 Soul Quality is a cooperative, sensitive, and non-aggressive vibration which thrives in a partnership. The essential Number 2 qualities include skills utilizing detail, data collection, cooperation in the spirit of partnership, development and use of physic ability, and sensitivity to the needs of others. If you do not have any of the following letters in your full name (B, K, or R), as assigned to the Number 2 in the Chaldean Alphabet/Formula (see table 7–1), then you would have a "count value" of zero (0-) for the Number 2 Soul Quality. A zero (0-) value represents a Karmic lesson in this lifetime, indicating you must learn to be more sensitive to the needs of others, be cooperative, and develop your skills for detail. A Soul Quality assigned a number with a plus sign (+) means that the person has been developing this quality and exceeds the normal value indicated. A number value followed by a minus sign (–) means the person has not yet reached the particular level of understanding for that Soul Quality and has more work to do in that area in order to achieve balance and full potential. (The meaning of a "normal" value is more fully addressed in chapter 6, section 6.I.)

Number 3 Soul Quality

Creativity/Sociability/Self-Expression

The Number 3 Soul Quality gives you the inborn desire to express yourself through creative and artistic channels. You are romantic, social, and ambitious with the tendency to "scatter" your energies. If you do not have any of the following letters in your full name (C, G, L, or S), as assigned to the Number 3 in the Chaldean Alphabet/Formula (see table 7–1), then you would have a "count value" of zero (0-) for the Number 3 Soul Quality. A zero (0-) value represents a Karmic lesson in this lifetime, indicating that you have the need to continue to develop yourself socially and verbally, as well as in a creative, self-expressive manner, for these traits are either still lacking or need to be improved. A Soul Quality assigned a number with a plus sign (+) means that the person has been developing this quality and exceeds the normal value indicated. A number value followed by a minus sign (–) means the person has not yet reached the particular level of understanding for that Soul Quality and has more work to do in that area in order to achieve balance and full potential. (The meaning of a "normal" value is more fully addressed in chapter 6, section 6.I.)

Number 4 Soul Quality
Structure/Foundation/Discipline

The Number 4 Soul Quality signifies the "builder," whose purpose is to form new ideas for the benefit of others. The "builder" is loyal, hardworking, detail-oriented, disciplined, and good in management. A zero (0-) value for the 4 Soul Quality is seldom to be found, as it is the basis of all human desire and effort. If you do not have any of the following letters in your full name (D, M, or T), as assigned to the Number 4 in the Chaldean Alphabet/Formula (see table 7–1), then you would have a "count value" of zero (0-) for the Number 4 Soul Quality. A zero (0-) value represents a Karmic lesson in this lifetime, indicating you must begin to develop these abilities and build a solid foundation in your life through hard work, discipline, and determination. A Soul Quality assigned a number with a plus sign (+) means that the person has been developing this quality and exceeds the normal value indicated. A number value followed by a minus sign (–) means the person has not yet reached the particular level of understanding for that Soul Quality and has more work to do in that area in order to achieve balance and full potential. (The meaning of a "normal" value is more fully addressed in chapter 6, section 6.I.)

Number 5 Soul Quality
Freedom/Change/Adaptability

The Number 5 Soul Quality represents movement, change, travel, progress, communication, and curiosity to make this "the" sparkling vibration. This is similar to the 4 Soul Quality, in that a zero (0-) value for the 5 Soul Quality is also seldom found, for the people of the world have a very natural desire to express freedom and the other abilities and talents of the 5. If you do not have any of the following letters in your full name (E, H, N, or X), as assigned to the Number 5 in the Chaldean Alphabet/Formula (see table 7–1), then you would have a "count value" of zero (0-) for the Number 5 Soul Quality. A zero (0-) value represents a Karmic lesson in this lifetime, indicating you must begin to develop these abilities, and learn to respond, adapt, and work to be a part of the world while maintaining balance in your life—balancing your "freedom" with your "responsibilities." A Soul Quality assigned a number with a plus sign (+) means that the person has been developing this quality and exceeds the normal value indicated. A number value followed by a minus sign (–) means the person has not yet reached the particular level of understanding for that Soul Quality and has more work to do in that area in order to achieve balance and full potential. (The meaning of a "normal" value is more fully addressed in chapter 6, section 6.I.)

Number 6 Soul Quality

Cosmic Parent/Counselor/Relationships

The Number 6 Soul Quality is a domestic vibration, devoted to partnerships, family, home, and service to the community, which are the "core" life of the Number 6. These qualities, including artistic talent, make this a very magnetic vibration. If you do not have any of the following letters in your full name (U, V, or W), as assigned to the Number 6 in the Chaldean Alphabet/Formula (see table 7–1), then you would have a "count value" of zero (0-) for the Number 6 Soul Quality. A zero (0-) value represents a Karmic lesson in this lifetime, indicating you must strive for a good balance between your emotions and intellect, learn about service to others, and adapt and respond to domestic challenges and experiences that are designed to show you the way. A Soul Quality assigned a number with a plus sign (+) means that the person has been developing this quality and exceeds the normal value indicated. A number value followed by a minus sign (–) means the person has not yet reached the particular level of understanding for that Soul Quality and has more work to do in that area in order to achieve balance and full potential. (The meaning of a "normal" value is more fully addressed in chapter 6, section 6.I.)

Number 7 Soul Quality

Educator/Intellect/Faith

The Number 7 Soul Quality is an intellectual vibration which is reserved, selective, aloof, and analytical, but also magnetic. If you do not have any of the following letters in your full name (O, or Z), as assigned to the Number 7 in the Chaldean Alphabet/Formula (see table 7–1), then you would have a "count value" of zero (0-) for the Number 7 Soul Quality. A zero (0-) value represents a Karmic lesson in this lifetime, indicating you must develop your technical and intellectual skills, while at the same time, seek a deeper meaning in your life to know what real "Faith" is all about. A Soul Quality assigned a number with a plus sign (+) means that the person has been developing this quality and exceeds the normal value indicated. A number value followed by a minus sign (–) means the person has not yet reached the particular level of understanding for that Soul Quality and has more work to do in that area in order to achieve balance and full potential. (The meaning of a "normal" value is more fully addressed in chapter 6, section 6.I.)

Number 8 Soul Quality

Ambition/Balance/Judgment

The Number 8 Soul Quality is about compassion, sound judgment, ambition, and a desire for fame and success, making this an energetic vibration. If you do not have any of the following letters in your full name (F, or P), as assigned to the Number 8 in the Chaldean Alphabet/Formula (see table 7–1), then you would have a "count value" of zero (0-) for the Number 8 Soul Quality. A zero (0-) value represents a Karmic lesson in this lifetime, indicating you must assume all responsibility for your life, and learn all there is about money and material possessions, i.e., how to make money, how to manage money, and how to "spend" it. In addition, it shows that you need to understand the meaning of "balance" between the "spiritual" and "material" planes in order to bring about harmony in your life. A Soul Quality assigned a number with a plus sign (+) means that the person has been developing this quality and exceeds the normal value indicated. A number value followed by a minus sign (–) means the person has not yet reached the particular level of understanding for that Soul Quality and has more work to do in that area in order to achieve balance and full potential. (The meaning of a "normal" value is more fully addressed in chapter 6, section 6.I.)

###

Chapter 9:
General Description of Compound Numbers

Introduction

One of the most exciting and interesting aspects of Numerology is the interpretation of compound numbers. In the study of the language of numbers (Numerolinguistics), compound numbers permit one to read between the lines, because they give you additional information that refines and expands on the basic (single-digit) root number meaning.

A root number or single-digit number like the Number 6, say for example, can have a double-digit Compound Number of 15, 24, 33, 42, or 51, etc., each of which gives a different emphasis or "twist" to the 6 root meaning. That is, a 15/6 will reveal certain specifics of the Root Number 6, keyed around the patterns of the Numbers 1 and 5. A 24/6 will reveal slightly different specifics keyed around the patterns of the Numbers 2 and 4, while other Root Number 6 compound numbers will reveal their own special flavor within the overall 6 vibration. Although the vibrational patterns of these different compound numbers still fall within the overall environment of Root Number 6, they define a uniqueness that the particular compound number brings to the 6 environment. This is similarly true for all of the root numbers; the Root Number 1 has Compound Numbers of 10, 19, 28, 37, or 46, etc.; the 2 has 11, 20, 29, 38, or 47, etc.; and so on through the 9, which has the Compound Numbers of 18, 27, 36, or 45, etc. This uniqueness of the compound numbers is another reason why your Numerology chart, your story, your "owner's" manual, as we say, is, for all intent and purpose, completely and totally yours. That is, there is no one else whose numbers and story are the same as yours.

The full range of compound numbers that we will cover starts with the Number 10 and ends with the Number 54. Beyond that range, the interpretation process gets redundant in the sense that the numbers can be understood by the relationship of the compound number's single-digits, that is, by looking at the vibrational patterns of the single-digit number that "leads" and the single-digit number that "follows," having a secondary and supporting role. For example, the Number 6 is the primary influence of the Number 63 and, when combined with the meaning of the Number 3, provides a unique interaction of patterns (different than, say, the 54) within the Root Number 9 environment. When interpreting the language of anyone's numbers, you get a more complete meaning and effect of compound numbers by looking at the influence of the root numbers within the Compound Number (e.g., 54 = [9], 37 and 10 = [1], 48 and 12 = [3]) to understand how they interact with each other.

However, when you see the Number 63, you know that it will be similar to the Number 36, but with variations in the 36 due to the dominance of the 3, being first, instead of the 6. However, both the 63 and the 36 have the same Root Number 9 that determines the tone of the unfolding patterns. As stated before, a repetitive pattern of interpretation develops which allows you to quickly and easily determine the influence of a particular compound number in relationship to current events. The Number 64 is similar to (but not the same as) the 46 which reduces down to the 10, and has the Root Number 1. The Number 74 is similar to the 47, which reduces down to the 11, and has the Root Number 2, etc.

This process permits you to see why some of the compound numbers may create confusing or disruptive environments, or appear as if they do—where opposite energies or conflicting vibrational patterns touch each other's vibrations. This may cause you to have an uncomfortable or "negative" reaction to an event, situation, circumstance, person, or place. However, without knowing the "real" cause of your conflicting emotions or negative responses, you may misunderstand or misinterpret the true nature of the environment that feels so negative or repelling, and as a result, incorrectly respond or react to the events around. You could very well end up blaming and humiliating someone inappropriately (not even counting your own embarrassment or humiliation), becoming emotionally upset for the wrong reasons (and maybe never be able to make right an unintentional wrong), or making choices or decisions which you wished you could change, etc.

In addition, and prior to, the descriptions from the section on "The Generic Language of Compound Numbers," for each double-digit compound number through the Number 54, we will provide a generic look under the "Discussion of the Interpretive Process," at the how, why, to what extent, etc., of the relationships between the single-digit numbers of compound numbers. Not all compound numbers will be discussed, but enough will, so that an understanding of the nature of the interpretive process can be demonstrated. We hope that you will at least have some appreciation of the language of compound numbers, after the discussion of the interaction of the single-digit numbers that make up the compound number.

To reiterate, the first single-digit number of the compound number is the primary or dominant influence, while the second number plays a supporting role, or creates an underlying pattern (in the form of, perhaps, a stage) upon which the first number operates and functions. Not only are the interactions of the single-digit numbers shown, but also the manner in which each compound number operates within the vibrational patterns of its root number, the final reduced sum (single-digit) of the numbers that make up the compound number. The vibrational patterns of this root number set the <u>tone</u> for the compound number's impact and influence on its environment.

In addition, certain compound numbers have compound numbers within them, as well as the root number. Examples of these numbers are the Number 29 = 11 = 2 (e.g., 11 is a Compound Number within the Compound Number 29 and the Number 2 is the Root Number), the Number 37 = 10 = 1 (e.g., 10 is a Compound Number within the Compound Number 37 and the Number 1 is the Root Number), and the Number 59 = 14 = 5 (e.g., 14 is a Compound Number within the Compound Number 59 and the Number 5 is the Root Number). The vibrational patterns of the compound numbers within the compound number also have an influence on the unfolding environment of the original number.

Numbers–The Powerful Bridge Beyond

Chaldean Numerology for the New Millennium

Most numerologists doom certain compound numbers to some tragic and dreaded future. They say that these Compound Numbers (e.g., 13, 14, and 16) are negative, too powerful for us, jinxed, or worse. As a result, many who come in contact with those numbers may feel unlucky, doomed, or despairing because a picture of negativity seems to have invaded their harmony. And yes, if these numbers are misinterpreted, the energy of the vibrations of a number can set up what feels like a pattern of potential negativity. However, in reality, it is not the number per se that causes a negative reaction, nor can a number, in and of itself, bring misfortune with it. Negativity and misfortune are the results of misinterpretation, miscalculation, misunderstanding, and sometimes the result of a "knee-jerk" reaction to something to which we emotionally overreact. However, always remember, numbers are neutral. Numbers, per se, are not good or evil, right or wrong, positive or negative. Whatever you are involved in will move toward success as long as you flow with and are in tune to the vibrational patterns of the environment which is unfolding.

Another interesting aspect of compound numbers is the zero (0), which plays a very significant and important role in the interpretation of compound numbers. For instance, the Number zero (0), by itself, means either "potential" or "choice." In relation to one's Challenges (closed doors to be opened), it is known as the Challenge of Choice. In combination with another number, it is a number of potential. When the zero (0) (whether a single zero or more than one) is connected to the root number, it gives that number or makes that number have "open-ended" potential. The zero (0) provides an added dimension to the patterns of the single-digit root vibration. In other words, it increases its vibrational potential. The more zeros attached to a number, the greater the potential in the patterns of that number. When the zero (0) is attached to a compound number, your chances for success will be increased. For instance, in the case of the Number 10 (or the Number 100), the zero increases the potential of the Number 1 which is the number of individuality, leadership, originality, and creative ideas, thereby enhancing the success of such events operating in the environment of the 10 vibrational patterns. The zero magnifies the abilities and enhances the honor and prestige of the root number, while providing a success-oriented influence. The analysis and evaluation of compound numbers which follows has never been undertaken in the detail and scope presented here. We have done it this way to allow for a greater understanding and usage of compound numbers. In most existing published information on compound numbers, the reader is told what a certain number means, but never told "why" the compound number means what it does.

Discussion of the Interpretive Process

Before we provide you with an extended listing of Compound Numbers (10 through 54) with their meanings at the end this chapter, we will first discuss what is involved in the process of evaluating and understanding "why" the compound number means what it does.

You can accept the meaning and description of the various compound numbers or you can begin the process of understanding the interpretation of compound numbers. You will also begin to understand how to integrate the various single-digit number vibrational patterns within the compound numbers with the root numbers. In order to ensure as detailed a presentation as we can, we have selected several compound numbers for discussion as the best way to demonstrate and clarify the understanding of the process of interpreting the language of numbers. The treatment of the selected compound numbers will show you the diversity of the meaning of the individual numbers, and how they either blend or unite with each other or have potentially conflicting energies and patterns. You will also be able to examine how you can effectively work with this diversity for the most successful and positive outcomes, by understanding how to maximize the strengths and minimize the conflict and opposition. The Compound Numbers that we have selected for discussion are 10, 11, 12, 13, 16, 17, 18, 19, 21, 22, 23, 25, and 27.

First, in order, comes the Number 10/1, which is the first step in the cycle of compound numbers, and the vibrational pattern which leads into the process of interpreting the language of compound numbers. This is a high-vitality number, not only by virtue of the Number 1 vibrations, but also by virtue of the fact that the 10 starts the cycle of compound numbers. The 10 is the Number 1 raised up in potential by virtue of the zero (0). (You can refresh your memory of the importance of the zero (0) and its impact on the choices and potential that we are offered, in the previous discussion of the zero (0) earlier in this chapter.) The 10 is also the symbol of the return to "wholeness"—having gone through the full circle of Root Number (1 through 9) vibrational patterns returning to the beginning by way of the 10.

The next number is the Number 11/2 which we have spoken of before. It is a Master Number and has much symbolism around it. The Number 11 represents equilibrium between two extremes. If you have ever seen Greek temples, you become aware of the upright columns of marble which hold up the roof over the entrance that leads into the temple. It is a Number of idealism (2) combined with aspiration (1), making it a very charismatic vibration. The 11/2 is also the number of the psychic, the visionary, and the dreamer. Intense emotions, dramatic flair, and much nervous energy are keyed around the Number 11/2. Your intuition will operate at a very high level. The Number 2 is the Root Number of the 11, which magnifies the vibratory force of the 2. The 11 enhances the Number 2 attributes, whereby sensitivity is increased, creative imagination is magnified, and the ability of diplomacy (being able to see both sides) is enhanced. The two 1s (double emphasis) enhance creative originality of the 1. And, it is a limelight number because of a presence of the charismatic energy, intensified imagination, and creative originality, along with the leadership emphasis of the Root Number 1. These things make the 11/2 a very favorable influence in connection with public events.

The Number 12/3 has as its Root Number the 3, which is the number of self-expression, intuition, and integration (the trinity: body, mind, and soul). The Number 3 is also a number of ambition, social contact, and public endeavor (as a speaker or entertainer). Since it is ambitious, in the sense of being goal-oriented (which, in our society, equals the pursuit of money), the 3 is also a number of money. The 12/3 has within its patterns, the Number 1, which being first in order, dominates, and brings with it the aspects of leadership, individuality, and unity. The 12 also has the Number 2 as secondary influence. The vibrational patterns of the 2 bring with them cooperation, partnership, sensitivity, tact, and creative imagination. These two numbers have qualities, which when brought together, interact very favorably. The number of individuality is combined with the number of cooperation.

It should be especially noted that compound numbers are important in the sense that they reveal additional (between the lines or behind the scenes) information about your environment, ensuing events, or developing situations which have been identified by the single-digit root vibrational pattern. A compound number also brings with it the identity of certain talents, within the root number, which are latent in its unfolding patterns.

For instance, if we take a look at the reverse placement of the digits of the 12, where the 1 was dominant and the 2 subordinate, we have the Number 21, it also has the Root Number 3, but creates a different pattern of influence, in that the 2 leads and the 1 has a supporting role. The 21/3 is the most favorable of the threes because the Number 2, cooperation, partnership, receptivity, sensitivity, and imagination, is the dominant influence instead of the Number 1. The dominance of sensitivity, cooperation, and imagination operating in an environment of the 1, individuality, innovation, and leadership, ensures a cooperative environment emphasizing the promotion and acceptance of new ideas, new beginnings, new associations, and anything which involves self-expression. The Number 21 governs public activities, social events, publishing, entertainment, and dramatic endeavors. Anyone who might be involved in theatre arts, singing, dancing, or speaking will find the 21 a very favorable pattern within which to perform.

The Number 13/4 has been considered as *the* most unlucky number in all of history. It is also the most abused of all the numbers. Again, as stated before, the truth of the matter is that a number, in and of itself, can not be lucky or unlucky, fortunate or unfortunate, balanced or disruptive. The 13/4 is not at all unlucky or unfavorable in connection with unfolding events surrounding a person. The misconception is based on the fact that the 13/4 is a very powerful number, having a very strong and aggressive vibratory force. It is the combination of two of the most masculine of Numbers, the 1 and the 3, both of which are directive, active, outward moving, and dynamic in nature. The Number 1 is the number of individuality, leadership, and the pioneering spirit of blazing new trails. The 3 is the number of ambition, creative self-expression, and public endeavors. You have two strong vibrational patterns working in combination with each other, which magnifies and emphasizes their natural attributes and forces. Whenever anyone walks into an environment which is dominated by the vibratory force of the 13/4, the vibratory influences are so strong that the environment sometimes becomes confusing, disruptive, and too uncomfortable for you to flow with. As a result, accidents may occur, mistakes may be made, or luck may go sour. And so naturally, the 13 has been blamed for causing bad things to happen. However, this does not have to be the case. It depends on the whether or not you are informed or superstitious. In fact, the 13/4 is a very good number to have on one's side, because it brings with it potential favorable vibrational patterns that can help one achieve success in active endeavors. In addition, the 13/4 has as its root the Number 4, which is the number of foundation, discipline, practicality, hard work, and dependability. The root vibration of the 4 gives stability to the 13 by virtue of the foundation, which becomes a base to operate from. One of the most negative reactions to the Number 13 is that the desires of the 1 and 3 may be somewhat hampered, restricted, or limited, because the 4 is a very structured number and places a framework or box around the creative potential of the 1 and the 3. Therefore a person may feel that their creativity, abilities, choices, or actions are restricted and limited when they operate within the environment of the 13/4 but, that does not have to be so.

The Number 16/7 is considered a very negative and disruptive number in most, if not all, reference materials—portending danger and hardship. With a vibrational pattern that the 16/7 has, you have three things occurring which cause people to misjudge or misunderstand the nature of the energy of the vibrations operating within the influence of the 16/7. People either fail to prepare for the dynamic of the 16/7 or do not have the presence or understanding to protect themselves from such energies. You have the Number 1 present, the Number 6, and the Number 7, which is the Root Number of the 16. The 1 is the individual, the leader, the pioneer. The 6 is the number of dedication to family and service to the community, as well as harmony and balance. This results in an initial seeming conflict, between the leadership, upfront, stage center, vibrations of the 1, and the service to family and community (where family and community, not the individual, are number one) of the 6. Now tie that in with the vibratory influence of the Root Number 7. The 7 includes the vibrational aspects of the loner, the meditative, introspective, and analytical approach to things. These are not desires of the 1 or the 6 vibrations.

You also have the law of preservation influencing the 16/7 patterns. In fact, the law of preservation rules the 16/7. The 7 seeks to preserve the truth. The 1 is the vibration which emphasizes the preservation of the ego, or the individuality. And the 6, the Number of the family, seeks to preserve the family unit. Since preservation and survival are part and parcel of the 16/7 vibration, this brings with it the need for and the use of caution and care in doing things (taking care to preserve). You get an interplay of action between the patterns of each single-digit number within the compound number. When something happens in the environment which seems to act like the 16, and at the same time the 16 is showing on an office door, the conclusion of the traditional numerologist is that the 16 is causing the problem. However, the real cause of the problem is the failure of those within the environment to understand the nature of the unfolding energies, patterns, and events. Traditionalists continue to say that you should look out for a number such as the 16, because it is negative in its influence. Or, they tell you to avoid any number whose vibrational patterns are difficult to interpret. What should be said, instead, is that when you walk into an environment where the vibrational patterns may cause you uncertainty or discomfort, allow yourself to be aware of the nature of the vibrations which surround you. In that way, you can prepare yourself for potential events or circumstances that are unfolding in the environment and be able to experience your surroundings as an informed person. Remember that numbers, in and of themselves, are neutral.

The Number 17/8 is the best of the Number 8 root vibrations. It is made up of the Number 1 which is creativity, originality, and individuality, and the Number 7 which has the intellectual, scientific, and mystical vibrational patterns. As a result, the 17/8 demands proof of the validity of things. The 17/8 person must be shown the proof of the pudding, which of course is in the taste, before they will buy anything. It has behind it the Root Number 8, which is the business, finance, and commercial number. It is particularly successful for endeavors in banking, executives in a corporation, or individuals heading their own businesses. It is a number of vitality through the courage of the 1 and the power of the 8. It is a comfortable vibrational pattern to work or play in because it brings together the intuition and sound judgment of the 8, the intellectual attributes of the Number 7, and the emotional and pioneering drive of the 1. Although the Root Number 8 brings with it power, ambition, and authority, the fact that it is feminine and receptive in nature brings a great deal of balance to the directness of the 1 and 7 which are masculine and active.

The Number 18/9 combines three numbers which are dynamic, active, and forceful. It is a very powerful vibrational influence which blends the independence and leadership of the number 1 with the power and judgment of the Number 8, and the completion, healing, energy, and humanitarian drive of the Root Number 9. The 18/9 is universal in nature. The 18/9 vibrations will be felt anytime there is change or upheaval. Things spiritual and medical come under the influence of the 18 from the Root Number 9, which is the number of healing and metaphysics, and from the 8, which represents intuitive judgment. The greatest significance of the power of the 18/9 comes from the mission of Jesus Christ. His Purpose (mission or "calling") was the Number 18/9. The name Jesus vibrates to the 9, and the name Christ vibrates to the 9, which when taken together equal 18. And, we all know that Jesus Christ was the forerunner of the greatest spiritual and religious upheaval in the history of man.

The Number 19/1 is considered the most favorable of all the numbers. The 19 is the individual (the Number 1) operating in an arena of universality (the Number 9). It is the most success-oriented vibratory force that exists. It unites the vibrational patterns of the 1 (leadership, originality, creative and innovative ideas, pioneering determination, and individuality) and the 9 (energy, emotion, healing, compassion, and service to humanity). In addition, the 9 includes the vibrational energy and attributes of all the root numbers. The 1 is known as the Alpha of numbers while the 9 is the Omega. Generally, very little can go wrong or awry under the influence of the 19/1, since the protective envelope of each number comes into play when an event or situation calls for it. However, if the person who is within the protective envelope of the 19/1 acts inappropriately and incorrectly with conscious intent, or fails to stay alert and aware of the negative signs and allows things to go wrong, the damage that they can do or the damage that could be done to them is mitigated by the influence of the 19/1. (see the description and meaning of the Compound Number 19 in chapter 9 in connection with what is called the test of character.)

The Number 22/4, like the 11/2, is a Master Number. The number of its root vibration is the 4. The 22/4 is the 4 vibratory force raised up in emphasis and intensity. Where the 4 represents foundation, framework, hard work, discipline, and detail, the 22/4 represents the Master Carpenter, Master Builder, or Cosmic Mason who is engaged in the laying of a foundation upon which the greater community of the world can build a much stronger society. The foundation can be physical, social/political, or spiritual. The Number 22 constructs the road upon which others tread. The double 2 in the compound number amplifies the intuitive, receptive, and imaginative faculties of the 2, while magnifying the potential to see all sides of the issues. And it enhances the talent of the 2 for detail, combined with the desire to work with others to complete their plans. The power of the 22 more than doubles the intensity of the single-digit. The 22/4 governs the things of the earth through the Root Number 4. People who operate within the vibrational influence of the 22/4 need to be aware of the necessity to maintain balance between the sensitivity of the 2 and the practicality of the 4. The Number 22/4 person can remain at the level of the single-digit patterns of the 4 and become a good bricklayer, building contractor, or carpenter—or fulfill the full potential of the 22 and become the leader of an international foundation, dedicated to providing the groundwork for others to build upon, particularly if the goal is cooperation between all people. The Number 22/4 vibration has a much greater potential for achievement than its Root Number 4, although there is no guarantee that the potential will be realized.

The Number 23/5 is the most fortunate of all the 5 root vibrations, and is the second most fortunate number in Numerology, after the Number 19. It brings together the Number 2 which is cooperation, partnership, sensitivity, diplomacy, agreeability, and receptivity, with the Number 3 which is ambition, self-expression, sociability, imagination, and lightheartedness. The Number 2 dominates the compound number, which allows the receptivity and cooperative spirit of the 2 to provide the channel for bringing success to the 23/5 vibrational patterns, while the ambitious 3 gives added strength to this very high potential vibratory force. The best influences of both the 2 and 3 come together with optimum results, with the Root Number 5 patterns setting the tone of the 23/5 vibration. Remember that the 5 is the Number of freedom, communications, action, change, and movement. All of the Numbers of the 23/5 emphasize some aspect of rapport and communications. The Number 2 represents cooperation, the 3 represents speaking and the public, while the 5 is the number of communications (words in action). Anyone involved with acting, singing, lecturing, selling, public relations, investigative reporting, advertising, or entertainment (where words and communications are involved) will prosper under the influence of the 23/5.

Next, the Number 25/7 is the most fortunate of the Number 7 root vibrations. It is considered a very spiritual vibrational pattern, and is known as the number of prophecy and intuitive experiencing. The 25/7 has a primary influence of the 2 with its sensitivity, receptivity, and cooperative spirit operating in the environment of the Number 5, which represents freedom, movement, seeking new and untried experiences, expanded horizons, and communication. This combination of the 2 and 5 functions within the vibrational patterns of the Root Number 7, which sets the tone for intellectual, introspective, and mystical endeavors. The Number 7 is the number of a highly tuned (illumined) intellect, meditative experiencing, introspection, scientific courage (physical or metaphysical), and seeking the truth of reality behind the appearance. The 25/7 influence enhances spiritual endeavors, is perfect for meditating on or about reality, and increases the anticipation of receiving inner understanding of outer relationships.

The Number 27/9 is the most spiritual, but not necessarily the most success-oriented (materially speaking that is) of all the numbers. It can be a fortunate number for certain material happenings and events related to humanitarian endeavors but it is not a material number per se. The Root of the 27/9 is the Number 9, which is the number of the metaphysician, healer, and humanitarian, and contains the vibratory energy of all root numbers. The 9 sets the tone for the unfolding vibrational patterns of the 27/9. Within the 27/9 is the Number 2, which is the primary or dominant influence of the compound number. The vibrational patterns of the 2 bring with them cooperative spirit, sensitivity, vivid imagination, receptivity, and the ability to see both sides of an issue, situation, or event clearly. The influence of the Number 7, being the secondary aspect of the Compound Number 27, is the tempering or supportive vibration, and represents the number of the mystic, the illumined intellect, and the seeker of the truth of reality. The blending of the vibratory energy of the 9 and 7 make the Number 27/9 very significantly spiritual in effect. All of the aspects of the Numbers 2, 7, and 9 taken together imbue the 27/9 with a vibratory force that governs the areas of healthcare and healing (whether of body, mind, or soul), including nurses, physicians and metaphysicians, healers, surgeons, hospitals, spiritual centers, and protective services such as police and firemen whose purpose is to help keep our society safe and unharmed from forces within, and the military, who are the nation's protective arm against harm or damage from outside forces.

With the study of the discussions and the information provided in the meanings and descriptions of the Compound Numbers in chapter 9, you should develop enough of a familiarity of the ways in which vibrational energies blend, combine, and interact. In addition, you will be able to understand why, under what conditions, and in what circumstances interacting vibrational patterns can influence a particular environment, and the manner in which you determine what those influences will be.

Numbers–The Powerful Bridge Beyond

Chaldean Numerology for the New Millennium

The Generic Language of Compound Numbers

Too many books on Numerology and too many numerologists will state what compound numbers mean, but do not even make an attempt to give you an understanding as to why the numbers mean what they do, and how the descriptions and interpretation are arrived at. We hope that the information and explanation about the meaning of compound numbers shown in the above discussion and listed below will at least give you some insight into understanding the language of compound numbers. It is the compound number which gives you an added dimension—additional information about one's self, others, and important events in one's life.

Number 10 Compound Number

The Compound Number 10 is a high-vitality vibration which starts the cycle of compound numbers. Spiritually, it is a return to wholeness. Zero (0) signifies an eternal source or a universal source. However, when the zero (0) is joined with the Number 1, it increases the potential of the 1. With the 10, the inherent ability of the Number 1 to lead is magnified. The 10 enhances originality, creative ideas, honor, and prestige, and is a success-oriented vibrational pattern (whether for seemingly good or evil purposes). The significance of the 10 is seen in the Ten Commandments as shown in the Old Testament of the Bible in the book of Exodus, chapter 20, verses 2–17. The Ten Commandments, which are also known as the Decalogue (Greek for "The Ten Words"), give recognition to the universality of the 10. The significance of the 10 can also be seen in the book of Genesis, chapter 18, verse 32 where Abraham spoke with God and said, "Please, let not my Lord grow angry if I speak up this last time. What if there are at least ten there?" "For the sake of those ten," he replied, "I will not destroy it."

Number 11 Compound Number

The Compound Number 11 or 11/2 is a Master Number which represents two upright columns that lead into the inner temple of our being. It contains two 1s, which amplifies the creative originality, inventiveness, and individuality of the Number 1, as well as elevating the leadership quality to a higher level of inspiration. The symbolism refers to equilibrium or balance between two extremes. The 11/2 is the Number of idealism (the Number 2) combined with the aspirations of the 1. It raises the vibratory force of the 2 up by magnifying the imagination, romanticism, inventiveness, sensitivity, and emotional energy of the 2. The 11/2 vibrational patterns are charismatic, magnetic, and electrical, and are keyed to limelight activities. The 11/2 Compound Number is the number of the psychic, visionary, and dreamer, and is intensely emotional, establishing patterns suited for the use of great nervous energy and dramatic flair. An 11/2 must be aware that the intellect may attempt to control the magnetism of the 11 and misdirect its energy.

Number 12 Compound Number

The Compound Number 12 has the Number 3 as its Root Number. The 3 denotes self-expression, ambition, and integration (3–in–1, mind, body, and spirit). The 12 vibrational pattern is made up of the Number 1 (which dominates since it is first in order), representing leadership, unity, individuality, creative ideas, and originality, as supported by the Number 2, which brings cooperation, receptivity, sensitivity, creative imagination, and diplomacy. It provides favorable environments for self-expression, writing, debating, and speaking engagements. Significance is found in the 12 Disciples of Christ; 12 Tribes of Israel; 12 Sons of Jacob; 12 Months of the Year; 12 Signs of the Zodiac; 12 Powers of Man; and 12 Hours AM/12 Hours PM.

Number 13 Compound Number

The Compound Number 13 is the most abused of all numbers. It is not unfortunate as has been supposed for all these ages, only that its power is misunderstood or misinterpreted. This occurs because of the combination of the Number 1 and 3, both of which are masculine, directive, aggressive, and forceful. It is a number of leadership, creative ideas, and individuality (the 1) reinforced by self-expression and ambition (the 3). As a result, one may feel overpowered by such a high concentration of aggressive energy, and become disconcerted, confused, and mistake-prone. However, the 13 still has as its roots the Number 4, which represents practicality, down-to-earthiness, detail, discipline, framework, and foundation. The 13 vibrational pattern is structured from its Root 4, and is driven into a rut (groove) by the one-way emphasis of the force of the 1 and the 3, resulting in creativity being potentially stifled. If used properly, the power of the 13 can be directed to build or form many different structures and foundations. The most significant and outstanding significance of the 13 comes from the fact that the United States of America was established upon the foundation (4) of 13 original colonies, with the 13 stars and stripes on the first flag. America also represents the individual (1) and self-expression (3). For America and its people, the 13 was indeed a very lucky number. The 13 can be seen in the lost tribe of Israel which was the 13th tribe. Additional recognition of the 13 includes the missing 13th floor of most office and apartment buildings, 13 cards per suit in a deck of 52 cards, and 13 loaves of bread in a "baker's" dozen.

Number 14 Compound Number

The Compound Number 14 has as its root the Number 5, which represents change, action, versatility, and communications (words in action). It is business-oriented in that the individuality and inventiveness of the Number 1, supported by a foundation provided by the Number 4, discipline and structure, can flourish in the environment of the Root Number 5. However, it is "business"-based on changing conditions, action, or quick turnaround. This makes the 14 Compound Number the number of speculation and includes sales, gambling, real estate, or stock market activities. Speculation implies risk and uncertainty due to the action and changeability vibrational pattern of the 5. However, it is not necessarily negative, if the risk has been measured, planned for, and managed. The 14 with its Root 5, properly directed, can bring excitement and variety into one's experiencing. The major significance of the 14 is seen in the book of Matthew of the New Testament of the Bible where it speaks of 14 generations (the "change" points in their travels) in the historical experience of the people of Israel. Spiritually speaking, it denotes a time of change or shifting in each individual's inner experiences.

Number 15 Compound Number

The Compound Number 15 is the individual (the Number 1) operating in the environmental patterns of communications, freedom, movement, and action (the Number 5), and has the Root Number 6. The 15 is considered a number of youthfulness, due to the Root 6 bringing balance, harmony, truth, love, service, and family, combining with the individual (the 1) operating upon a stage of freedom and action (the 5). The opportunity for success in developing original ideas (the 1) is enhanced and increased. The energy flow that comes from the individual in the center of the arena of action becomes a magnet for financial or material success, as well as a focal point toward which others are drawn in their need to find help, support, or counseling.

Number 16 Compound Number

The Compound Number 16 represents the individual (the Number 1) operating in an environment of people, community, service, and teaching (the Number 6). The Root Number of the 16 is the Number 7, which brings with it the desire to withdraw (the loner/privacy), introspection, faith, intellect, perfection, and aspects of mysticism. The law of preservation rules the 16 (preserving the individual, the family, and privacy), and brings with it the desire for continuity, and the use of caution and great care. As a result, the 16 may result in procrastination, delays, waiting, taking no action, etc. The seeming discontent and impatience that may arise from the 16 vibrational influence is most probably due to two things—the competition between the 1 which emphasizes individuality and leadership, and the 6 which emphasizes devotion to family and service to the community—and the loner aspect (the desire to withdraw) of the 7 versus the upfront/participatory desires of the 1, and the "service" to family and community of the 6. Favorable environments for the 16 are intellectual, mystical, and scientific, which makes it a good vibrational pattern for educators, editors, counselors, and healers.

Number 17 Compound Number

The Compound Number 17 blends the Number 1, creative, inventive, original, and individual, with the Number 7, mystical, scientific, and intellectual—and demands proof of the validity of things. The 17 brings with it the power, judgment, intuition, expansiveness, and efficiency of its Root Number 8, along with a financial, business, and commercial orientation. It is a number of vitality, courage, and ambition, which governs large things and affairs. The 17 carries with it a success-oriented vibrational pattern in banking, insurance, real estate, as an executive for a company, or as the head of your own business. With regard to financial success, the 17 is considered a number of fortune and happiness. This is so because of the outward flowing and goal-oriented aspects of the 1 tempered by the quiet inner understanding and strength of the 7, while enhanced by the good sense of judgment inherent in the 8.

Number 18 Compound Number

The Compound Number 18 combines the independence, leadership, and individuality of the Number 1 with the power, efficiency, and judgment of the Number 8, which brings with it the interaction of leadership vibrations with intuitive judgment. It is set upon a base of its Root Number 9, which represents completion, transformation, energy, healing, universality, compassion, and objectivity. The 18 Compound Number is highly emotional, energetic, and intuitive in nature, and governs law, politics, medicine, and spiritual (the 9) arenas. It is known as the number of great leaders, particularly those associated with social/political, military, medical, and spiritual change and upheaval. Great leaders function very well within an 18/9 vibrational pattern or where the 18/9 influence is evident. The greatest significance of the 18 lies in the fact that it was the Birthname (purpose, mission) vibration of Jesus Christ, who was the forerunner of the greatest spiritual and religious upheaval in the history of man—past, present, and future.

Number 19 Compound Number

The Compound Number 19 is considered the most blessed of all the vibrational patterns. This combination includes the vibrational patterns all of the root numbers. It is the beginning (the 1) and the ending (the 9)—the Alpha and Omega. Fortune seems to follow this number. With this vibrational pattern influence in someone's life experiences, they could work very hard to make a mess of it, and still be blessed with success, even if limited. The 19 Compound Number is the individual operating in the universal arena, a combination of creation and completion. It governs professions rather than businesses; that is, you can find success as a musician, politician, aviator, lawyer, salesman, electrician, or a specialist in most, if not all, areas in the medical field.

(Note: Be aware that the 19 vibration surrounds you or your environment with such a feeling of protection or immunity that you may take things for granted without pausing to ensure that nothing is hidden or ignored that could be detrimental to you or your family's well-being. You must always be alert to and aware of what is going on in your surroundings and for any desire on your part to act inappropriately or incorrectly with conscious intent. The Number 19 protective envelope can lessen consequences, but it cannot, in and of itself, "prevent" consequences. When operating within the influence of the 19, the mixture of the patterns within your environment can bring about what is called a test of character when too great a feeling of or dependence on safety causes you to take things for granted. Bottom line, if, under any circumstances, something doesn't feel right, even in the slightest degree, take the time to step back and be sure that you understand the meaning of just what doesn't feel right before acting. Again, although the 19 vibration can dampen a negative experience, it cannot prevent the experience from occurring. Only you can! Always maintain your responsibility to stay awake and aware and use discretion and right action, no matter what it may seem like around you.)

Number 20 Compound Number

The Compound Number 20 contains the zero (0), which gives an open-ended potential to the qualities of the Number 2—enriched imagination, magnified receptivity and diplomacy, heightened sensitivity, and a strong understanding of the nature of cooperation. The 20 Compound Number has a natural mediator or peacemaker vibration, and is considered the most fortunate of the 2s. Many will be attracted to the vibrational pattern of the 20 to receive spiritual, mental, and psychological support. The pattern of the experiences of the 20 develops from spiritual success and not particularly from material success.

Number 21 Compound Number

The Compound Number 21 has the Root Number 3, which represents a vibrational pattern of self-expression, public activities, social popularity, and writing. The 21 is the most favorable vibrations of the 3. Unlike the Number 12, the 21 Compound Number is dominated by the cooperative spirit, receptivity, agreeability, and imagination of the 2, which is first in place, and prevails over the aggressive, directed, individualistic, and independent aspects of the 1. Since the qualities of the Number 2, imagination, sensitivity, receptivity, and cooperation prevail, being first, the independence, originality, and leadership aspects of the Number 1 support the 2 vibrational impact, giving added strength and forcefulness to the patterns of the 21. As a result, the 21 Compound Number is a highly magnetic vibrational pattern. The 21 governs books, publishing, and editorial activities as well as being beneficial for dramatics, music, and public speaking.

Number 22 Compound Number

The Compound Number 22 or 22/4 is a Master Number with the attributes of the Root Number 4 raised up and magnified in vibratory force. Where the Root 4 represents foundation, framework, discipline, and detail, the 22 Compound Number represents the Master Builder. The double 2 amplifies the intuitive and imaginative faculties of the Number 2, as well as the ability to see all sides of an issue or concern. The Master Number 22 operates in a worldwide and international arena, and represents both the laying of a foundation upon which great humanitarian organizations are built and the paving of roads upon which others will walk and follow. The 22 governs things of the earth (the Number 4). With the 22, balance is needed between the sensitive and emotional 2, and the practical and disciplined 4.

Number 23 Compound Number

The Compound Number 23 is considered the most fortunate of numbers after the Number 19. It blends the aspects of the Number 2, cooperation, imagination, tact, partnership, and receptivity with those of the Number 3, self-expression, intuition, public activities, and social events. The 2, the 3, and the 23 Root Number 5, all emphasize communication, sociability and creative expression, writing, speaking, selling, lecturing, music, acting, and teaching. The action, change, freedom, movement, and travel aspects of the Root 5, in conjunction with the sensitivity and nervous energy of the 2 and the energy scattering effect of the 3, make this a mercurial vibrational pattern. Solid values and distinct purpose will reap the greatest harvest from the free-flowing vibration of the 23 Compound Number.

Number 24 Compound Number

The Compound Number 24 combines the Number 2, partnership, with the vibrational patterns of the Number 4, discipline and foundation, within an environment of the Root Number 6, love of home and family. The patterns of the Root 6 emphasize beauty, balance, harmony, and service. The patterns of receptivity, creative imagination, cooperation, and sensitivity of the 2 combined with the discipline, detail, framework, and dependability aspects of the 4. The blending of the 2, 4, and 6 indicates success in people-oriented areas of endeavor—for example, counseling (legal, psychological, and financial), beauty salons/barber shops, real estate, facilitation, etc. The harmony of the 6, plus the cooperative spirit of the 2, plus the dependability and loyalty of the 4, makes the 24 vibrational pattern very magnetic, and will attract attention and generate power by its unfolding possibilities.

Number 25 Compound Number

The Compound Number 25 is the most fortunate and the most spiritual of the Root Number 7. The 25 Compound Number is the number of prophecy and intuitive experiencing. The sensitivity, receptivity, creative imagination, and cooperative spirit of the Number 2 operates in an environment of freedom, change, movement, and words of the Number 5, and blends with the attributes of the Root 7, which represents intellect, meditative introspection, and the desire to find the reality behind the appearance. The environment of the 25 vibrational pattern enhances and illuminates the understanding of spiritual revelation and mystical experiences.

Number 26 Compound Number

The Compound Number 26 Root Number is 8, with attributes of power, energy, expansiveness, strong judgment, and executive ability, and sets the tone for the effect of the 26 vibrational patterns. Also, the 8 thrives in the arena of business, finance, and commerce. Within the 26 Compound Number is the ability for seeing both sides of the issues (the Number 2), which is active in an environment of teaching, counseling, service, family, and community (the Number 6). This combination of the 2 and 6 are enhanced by the vibrational patterns of the Root 8 and indicate success in politics, large humanitarian organizations, executive management, or running your own business. The combination of the 2 (partnership) and the 6 (love, family) indicates an early marriage and a long one. However, be aware of the potential for conflict which may be felt due to an interaction of the power, energy, ambition, and executive authority of the Root 8 with the sensitivity, cooperation, and receptivity vibrations of the 2.

Number 27 Compound Number

The Compound Number 27 is the most spiritually-oriented of all the numbers. It combines the creative imagination, cooperative spirit, and the ability to see both sides of an issue of the Number 2, and the intellectual perception and interest in the mysterious aspects of life of the Number 7. The "spirituality" of the 27 Compound Number is further accentuated by the vibrational pattern of its Root Number 9—energy, healing, universality, and objectivity. The 27 governs areas of health and medicine, physicians, metaphysicians, healers, surgeons, military and police. It is an excellent vibration for writing and lecturing on any of these subjects. The sensitivity along with the nervous energy of the 2 and the force and energy of the 9 make this an "emotion" driven vibration with a sometimes overly sensitive reaction to one's environment.

Number 28 Compound Number

The Compound Number 28 which reduces to a Root Number of 1, sets the tone (an overarching vibrational umbrella) for the Compound Number 28, which emphasizes creative imagination and sensitive understanding of the Number 2 operating in an environment of power, energy, expansiveness, and judgment of the Number 8. The 28 produces highly effective influences in areas of executive and leadership positions of large organizations, and with law, judges and courts. The 28 can work well with partnerships (since the 2 dominates), and can use the power and judgment of the 8 for making proper changes in course or direction. Care should be taken to make wise use of the judgment abilities of the 28 before taking any action.

Number 29 Compound Number

The Compound Number 29 combines a very personal vibrational pattern (the Number 2) with a very impersonal vibrational pattern (the Number 9). It has extreme vibrations within it as well as intense emotional potential. Both the 2 and the 9 have highly emotional vibrations as well as a great deal of nervous energy. In addition, within the 29 is another compound number, the Master Number 11, which brings a very "electrical" and dynamic vibration to the 29 party. As a result, the 29 has been interpreted as a number to be avoided. However, that is not true. Since the 2 is accented, being first, it is the dominant and major influence in the unfolding vibrational pattern of the 29. The 29 represents the 2, the number of the peacemaker, diplomat, cooperation, and partnership, operating in an environment of the 9, healing, force, energy, and universality. Add this to the fact that the root vibration is also a 2 and has the presence of the 11 pattern inherent in it—you will find that the 29 can be a very exciting and charismatic environment. It is both very spiritual and inspirational, due to the influences of the 9 and the 11 pattern potential.

Number 30 Compound Number

The Compound Number 30 has all of the possibilities and potential of the Root Number 3 vibrational pattern, self-expression, intuition, ambition, money, drive, and sociability, magnified with the addition of the zero (0). The arena of dramatic expression is emphasized (verbal arts), particularly acting, speaking, singing, etc. This is a favorable number for authors, playwrights, and publishers.

Number 31 Compound Number

The Compound Number 31 has the Root Number vibration of the 4, which represents discipline, detail, hard work, structure, routine, and loyalty. The predominant number is the 3, whose vibrational pattern includes self-expression, integration, ambition, public endeavors, and socialization. It is supported by and operates in an environment of the Number 1 whose vibrations are conducive to leadership, individualism, the opportunity to pioneer new fields, originality, and creative ideas. The structure, detail, and discipline of the 4 may tend to limit the potential of the 31, but cannot totally contain it. This vibratory influence is conducive to good business sense and practicality. The 31 Compound Number is not as powerful as the Number 13 due to the control and dominance of the 3, self-expression, sociability, and integration instead of the 1, independent, individualistic, and determined.

Number 32 Compound Number

The Compound Number 32 has, along with the Root Number 5, vibrations of freedom, action, and communications (words in action), the Number 3, self-expression, verbal arts (writing, public speaking, lecturing), ambition, and sociability, which dominates. And, although the overall vibrational pattern of the 32 Compound Number is very similar to the 23, the 32 is not as balanced and stable as the 23, which has its major influence derived from the dominant 2—the number of friendships, cooperation, agreeability, and partnerships. This vibratory influence is good for the quick study of different languages.

Number 33 Compound Number

The Compound Number 33 is the most favorable of all the Number 6 vibrational patterns. The 33 combines the overall vibrational pattern of the Root 6—harmony, balance, love, service, values, teaching, beauty, and truth which sets the tone of the environment, with a magnified and raised up vibration of the double 3. This double 3 combination enhances self-expression, is highly ambitious, stresses big business, is a strong money number, and is very public in nature. The focus of the power of the double 3 is toward maintaining balance and harmony of the Root 6. The high concentration of self-expression, of ambition, and of strength that flows out of the double 3s make it a good number for revolutionaries and anyone else who challenges concepts, attitudes, dogma, conditions that are out of balance, and rigid or obsolete values.

Number 34 Compound Number

The Compound Number 34 blends the vibratory force of the Number 3, which manifests self-expression, intuition, and integration, in an environment of discipline, foundation, detail, and framework of the Number 4. The Root Number of the 34 is the 7, which governs intellect, analytical abilities, desire for knowledge of the mysterious aspects of life, meditation, and introspection. It is finely tuned both spiritually and psychically due to the discipline of the 4, the intuition of the 3, and the highly tuned intellect of the 7. The influence of the patterns of the 4 along with the intellectual and analytical aspects of the 7 indicates that a scientific career and field of endeavor would be successful.

Number 35 Compound Number

The Compound Number 35, which has the Root Number 8 vibrations of power, material gain, judgment, and business, financial, and commercial success, blends the Number 3 vibrational pattern of writing, public speaking, lecturing, publishing and the Number 5 vibrational pattern of freedom, action, movement, communications (words in action), indicating a very great emphasis on things literary as well as on material rewards. Being first, the 3 dominates so that writing books, publishing, and public speaking show great promise and potential for success.

The forcefulness and ambition of the 3 in conjunction with the changeability of the 5 can create a scattering of energy and efforts. So, be constantly aware of this scattering effect, stay focused, and use the power of the 8 and its inherent vibration of good judgment in all decisions.

Number 36 Compound Number

The Compound Number 36 is the most success-oriented number in Numerology, after the Compound Numbers 19 and 23. It is the most favored of the Number 9 vibrations for material success, for it combines the attributes of the Number 3, self-expression, intuition, and ambition, with the attributes of the Number 6, harmony, balance, community, service, teaching, and counseling. The Root Number of the 36 is the 9, which represents energy, universality, humanitarianism, healing, and emotional expression. The 36, which emphasizes creative self-expression, healing, or personal counseling, would prove favorable for metaphysical teaching centers, or any center, organization, and business. It is also a good vibrational pattern for "teaching" hospitals, or medical referral and consultation businesses.

Number 37 Compound Number

The Compound Number 37 not only has the Root Number 1 vibration with its individuality, leadership, pioneering spirit, and creative originality, but the 37 also has a Compound Number within a Compound Number, the Number 10, which is high vitality with increased potential for success. The Number 3 brings the vibrational patterns of self-expression, ambition, intuition, verbal acuity, and public involvement into combination with the Number 7 vibrations of a highly tuned intellect, a meditative and introspective view of things, and the desire to seek the reality behind the appearance. The 3, which is the number of entertainment, friendship, and social popularity dominates the 37, and is further enhanced by the gregariousness of the Root 1, in its desire to be "Numero Uno," in all that it does.

Number 38 Compound Number

The Compound Number 38 has a compound number within it, the Number 11 (3 + 8). The Root Number of the 38 is the 2, which is also the Root Number of the 11. The 38 Compound Number is dominated by the Number 3, which is a very strong masculine number of self-expression (verbal arts), sociability, and intuition operating in an environment of the Number 8, a very strong feminine number of power, judgment, efficiency, and expansiveness. Added to this combination of single-digit numbers is the inherent qualities of the 11—charismatic leadership, magnified imagination, intense emotions, and idealism, and is keyed to limelight activities. The blending of these vibrational patterns makes for a very spiritually powerful vibrational pattern. The 38 Compound Number is endowed with an exceedingly powerful vibration, which has been misinterpreted and misunderstood. This misinterpretation has been caused by a seeming conflict between the 3 vibration, masculine, directive, and active in nature and the 8 vibration, feminine, receptive, passive in nature—a misconception arrived at by looking at the co-mingling of these vibrations as opposing one another, i.e. oppositional forces. However, in the case of the 38, the 3 and 8 are not opposites but rather complements—highly intuitive, highly charismatic, and highly psychic in nature.

Number 39 Compound Number

The Compound Number 39 contains within it the Compound Number 12 vibrational patterns as well as the Root Number 3 vibrational patterns. With the 3 first in sequence and dominant, the emphasis of the 39 is on self-expression, intuition, and integration inherent in the 3. The 3 then operates within the environment of the Number 9, which represents healing, spirituality, emotional energy, universality, objectivity, and the humanitarianism. The Number 12 brings with it the Root 3 traits as well as the blending of individualism (1) and cooperation (2). Although not the most favorable of the Root 3 vibrations, the 39 is the most powerful. The greatest strength of the 39 is in the inner and outer vibrations of self-expression, which governs writing, lecturing, dramatics, music, and publishing.

Number 40 Compound Number

The Compound Number 40 has all of the possibilities and potential of the Root Number 4 vibrational patterns—discipline, hard work, detail, methodology, foundation, and loyalty—magnified by the combination of the zero (0) with the 4. The influence of the zero, which represents potential and choice, enhances the pattern of achievement with the 40 functioning in the environment. The 40 Compound Number indicates completion of a major endeavor, such as the laying of a foundation or "establishing a framework," in both the physical and metaphysical sense. The 40 patterns are favorable for development of a well-defined and executed plan of action. Significance of the 40 Compound Number is shown in the 40 days and nights of the Great Flood in the Old Testament before Noah and the Ark found land upon which to start the race anew, and the 40 days and nights that Jesus Christ spent in the wilderness completing the final testing of his resolve and his spiritual faith before moving on to fulfill his mission. (See the meaning and description of the Number 18 and the Number 9 which were the vibrations of Jesus Christ's Purpose Number.)

Number 41 Compound Number

The Compound Number 41 has the root vibration of the Number 5, setting the tone for freedom, change, action, and communications. And, although the Number 41 seems similar in nature to the Number 14, the flow of the 41 vibrational patterns are reversed. With the Number 4 coming first and therefore the dominant vibration, it reduces the risk and uncertainty of the 14 energies. As a result, the 41 provides a favorable environment for success within the influences of the 5 energies. The structure, discipline, and foundation of the 4 maintain a disciplined and stable environment in which the vibrational influences of the 1, such as individuality, independence, leadership, originality, and creative and inventive ideas, are focused and channeled.

Number 42 Compound Number
The Compound Number 42 may seem similar to, but is not the "same" as, the Number 24 vibrational pattern. This is evident because with the Number 4 coming first and dominating, it implies a potentially restrictive code of values shaping the environmental patterns, particularly when blended with the patterns of the Root Number 6, which is focused on home, community, service, balance, teaching, and counseling. The 4 overshadows the Number 2 and may structure the receptivity, dampen cooperative spirit, and suppress the emotion and nervous energy of the 2. When taken in relation to the 6 patterns, it indicates a religious overtone in the sense of emphasizing dogma, creed, or an established set of values. The 42 is referenced in Matthew, the first chapter of the New Testament of the Bible, in relation to the 42 generations of history from Abraham to the birth of Jesus Christ.

Number 43 Compound Number
The Compound Number 43 vibration patterns unfold within the Root Number 7 environment— introspection, faith, intellect, perfection, and aspects of mysticism. The vibrational energy of the 7 sets the overtone of the environment in which the 43 functions, combining the discipline, detail, and loyalty aspects of the Number 4 with the aggressive and forceful patterns within the Number 3, self-expression, ambition, and drive, and tends to influence activities connected with upheavals of any kind, challenges to rigid dogma, the status quo, and conditions that are out of balance.

Number 44 Compound Number
The Compound Number 44 emphasizes and magnifies the importance of practicality, loyalty, discipline, and stick-to-itiveness. These attributes in connection with the Root Number 8, which emphasizes power, energy, and judgment, govern success in pursuit of a military career, within a corporate environment, and in undertaking judicial endeavors, as well as success in any practical undertaking.

Number 45 Compound Number
The Compound Number 45 is a success-oriented number which governs the helping of others and involvement in the upliftment of the race consciousness (from the Root Number 9). The Number 4, ruled by structure, discipline, hard work, detail, and loyalty, dominates and establishes a framework within which the freedom, action, and versatility of the Number 5

takes shape. The 4 and 5 patterns blend and unfold within an overall environment of the Root 9—universality, healing, force, and energy. The 4 provides determination and focus for the 5 which implies that "communications" skills will play an important part in the success of any action taken.

Number 46 Compound Number

The Compound Number 46 combines the practicality and discipline of the Number 4 with the idealism of the service-oriented Number 6, within an environment in tune with the attributes of the Compound Number 10 (success potential) and the Root 1—pioneering spirit, leadership abilities, originality, and creative ideas. The 46 stands for framework, foundation, and the builder, operating in an environment of balance, harmony, family, service, community, truth, and beauty. When "foundation" rules "idealism," great works are accomplished.

Number 47 Compound Number

The Compound Number 47 is a combination of the discipline, methodology, and routine of the Number 4 and the intellectual and analytical abilities of the Number 7, which gives this compound number special significance in scientific and "logical" endeavors. Inherent within the 47 are the vibrational patterns of the Compound Number 11 and the Root Number 2. The 47 creates an interweaving vibrational environment of discrimination (4), cooperation (2), visionary ideas (11), and analysis (7).

Number 48 Compound Number

The Compound Number 48 combines the practicality, hard work and framework aspects of the Number 4 which dominates, supported by the vibrational energies of the Number 8, power, intuition and strong judgment which magnify the psychic and prophetic aspects of experiencing. The 48 also contains both a compound number within a compound number, the Number 12 and the Root Number 3. The tone of the environment in which the 48 operates is set by the vibrational patterns of self-expression, integration, sociability, and public activities of the Root 3, and the underlying patterns of the 12. The 12 brings with it the pioneering spirit and creativity of the 1 and the cooperative spirit and sensitivity of the 2. Success is generated through the wise use of the power and judgment of the 8, with the practicality and determination of the 4.

Number 49 Compound Number

The Compound Number 49 generates the patterns of discipline, foundation, and framework (the builder or Number 4), operating in an environment of healing, high energy, emotion, and universality (9). Inherent within the 49 are the "power" of the Compound Number 13 and the force of the Number 9. These highly active and aggressive numbers are balanced and contained by the fact that the 4 is the dominant (lead) Number of the 49 which also has the Root Number 4, as such giving added structure and form to the 49 environment. The 49 governs the laying of a foundation in areas related to the healing of body, mind, and spirit.

Number 50 Compound Number

The Compound Number 50 is the Root Number 5 raised in potential. The zero (0) magnifies and intensifies the impact of the Root 5 vibrational patterns—freedom, action, change, movement, and versatility. The presence of the 50 implies accelerated action, major changes, rapid movement, broadened freedom, multiple experiences and associations, and perhaps extensive travel.

Number 51 Compound Number

The Compound Number 51 is communications (words in action)—movement, action, change, and freedom of the Root Number 5 vibrational patterns "rule" the Compound Number 51, influenced and supported by the pioneering spirit (new ideas, new associations), leadership, individuality and creative originality of the Number 1. The 51 operates within the Root Number 6 vibrational patterns of harmony, beauty, balance, calmness, and truth, providing a protective umbrella over actions which occur under the influence of the 51. The 51 governs such areas as investigative reporting, detective work, evangelism, and travel agencies.

Number 52 Compound Number

The Compound Number 52 has contained within it the freedom and action of the Number 5 vibration in combination with the creative imagination and the ability to see both sides of the issues of the Number 2, operating within the environment of the Root Number 7, intellectuality, analytical abilities, and desire to seek the truth behind reality. This blending of energies makes this compound number a favorable influence for understanding and resolving problems, finishing up tasks, tying up loose ends, and completing projects. We see the Number 52 in the 52 weeks in a year, the 52 playing cards in a standard card deck, and the number of white keys (notes in C major scale) on the piano.

Number 53 Compound Number

The Compound Number 53 is similar to the Number 35, in that they both have the Root Number 8—power, sound judgment, and business patterns. However, the similarity stops there. Where the Number 3 dominated the 35, the dominating vibration of the 53 is the Number 5. The 5 represents changeability, movement, freedom of action, and versatility, a number of words in action. Being first in place, its vibrations prevail and dominate the overarching patterns of the 53. The Number 3, self-expression, verbal arts, and ambition, supports the 5 vibrations. The Number 53 Compound Number is also very "literary" in nature, but governs in such arenas as TV documentaries, promotional endeavors, public relations, sales, playwriting, shorts stories, etc. Be aware that the dominant 5 combined with the ambitious 3 can create a scattering effect on your energy and efforts. Allow the energy of the Root 8 to influence the direction of the 53 by using the inherent "good judgment" of the 8 in all your decisions.

Number 54 Compound Number

The Compound Number 54 is similar to the Number 45, in that they both have the Root Number 9—universality, healing, force, and energy. Where the similarity stops is that the dominating vibration of the 54 is the Number 5. However, the Number 4, which includes the patterns of discipline, foundation, structure, and hard work, gives stability to the changeability of the 5. The 54 favors communications operating from a strong foundation and structure. Success can be achieved in promoting compassion and healing (Root 9) to the world.

###

Chapter 10:
Beyond Numerology

Introducing the Essence Numerology Master Chart

In this chapter, we will show you just how powerful numbers really are by sharing the revelations that the Essence Numerology Master Chart presents to you. The Essence chart is a major, newly discovered enhancement that takes Numerology to the next level. It is an advancement of Numerology in both technique and understanding that is far beyond anything that is currently provided by numerologists anywhere. It was virtually a family secret developed by Numbers R U in the early 1980s and was not revealed to the general public until the year 2004—and is still only available through NumbersRU.com today. It is the Essence Numerology Master Chart that will take you beyond Numerology by allowing the process of self-acceptance and self-advocacy to begin to heal your mind and heart.

The Essence Numerology chart takes an accurate, in-depth, and far-reaching look at what you are working through inwardly (emotionally and intellectually) year-by-year, and is a combination of your Essence numbers, Personal Year numbers, and Universal Year numbers, which represent the differing physical, mental, and spiritual elements that influence each year of your life. The Essence chart reveals the setting, the nature, and the duration of the inner experiences that you must work through each year to attain personal and spiritual growth and awareness that this journey through life demands. Since the Essence numbers are calculated from the letters of your name, this vibration is deeply personal to you.

The Personal Year is a most important tool in understanding and preparing you for the true nature of the events you are to experience during that year and is very personal to you because it is calculated from your birthdate. The Personal Year clearly defines what to expect, what to avoid, and the nature of your personal affairs to be experienced. How you respond to these experiences will be influenced by your free will and the choices you make as you attract the experience.

The Universal Year (also known as a calendar year) is the only vibrational pattern that's not personal to you, since this is the vibration everyone will be affected by, at the same time, as we go into each new calendar year. We have no control over the universal vibrational patterns coming from a particular year, but we do have control over how we respond to them. The Universal Year indicates how the affairs of the world will tend to influence the attitude of humanity. For example, take the year 2005 which calculated to be a 7 Universal Year. The focus or emphasis for that year was on completions, endings, and education, so 2005 would not have been a social year in the manner we know it. In fact, 2005 was a year for mental housecleaning and growth which required more individual solitude or downtime than normal. Universal Years are measured from January 1 through December 31.

The Essence and Personal Years begin on your birthday. If your birthday falls in the "last" half of the calendar year, your Personal Year will come under the vibration of the "following" year. You will begin to feel the following year vibration pull on you during the months leading up to your birthday. It is easier to flow with the stream of life once you know what to expect on a yearly basis. Knowing what the year will bring can add spice and excitement to life. This awareness will also enhance your ability to live in grace rather than suffer from the pangs of resistance and fear of uncertainty that "not knowing" often brings. If you were given a warning that an earthquake was coming, would you want to have this information in advance so you could prepare for it? The information contained in the Essence Numerology Master Chart is just that, a heads up, look ahead, road map, or guide to prepare the way for you.

Going Beyond Numerology

What makes this Essence Numerology Master Chart so unique is the healing strategy that has been designed and programmed into the chart. Here's how the Essence chart works. The chart takes you from Age "1" to your "Current" Age, and out "5" years into the future. By capturing your Essence number and Personal and Universal Year numbers in the chart, we are able to forecast the type of experiences that you are likely to attract each year based on the vibrational patterns from each of those numbers. In addition, we can track the highs and lows in your life through the information captured in this chart, that is, through the integration of all three numbers, whose combined information forms a total picture of your experiences—whether they are good or bad.

The healing process begins as we start to discuss each of the areas in the chart that indicate disruptions or crises in the individual's life by going back in time. By asking the individual if they remembered what happened in a specific year or age, either they could not remember or if they did, would generally start telling a story of what was going on with them during that time.

Initially, it was startling to discover how many people were in denial over a traumatic incident that happened to them which they chose to block from their memory due to the painful nature of the circumstances. By walking the individuals through their charts year-by-year, and pointing out specific number combinations that would indicate some troubled times, they actually became ready to talk about their stories, one right after the other, throughout their chart readings, finding it unbelievable that the Essence chart could accurately track such events throughout time on a personal level.

We don't know what their personal stories are from looking at the charts but we do know what the number combination would indicate. Something just seems to trigger a memory jolt and people are then able to remember the incident that had been blocked or forgotten. More importantly, they became able to share their secrets with someone at last, if they couldn't before. An example would that of an individual who was assaulted at an earlier age and suddenly remembered the details of the incident. Many people tend to carry forward unfinished business that still affects them because they couldn't find a way to release it at the time. The chart becomes a form of release, in that the patterns described by the numbers in their charts allow the individuals to talk about their stories if they choose, acknowledge the trauma and grief of past experiences, and then let them go.

The purpose of this chart then is simply to provide you with valuable information not ordinarily found about your life anywhere else, including a holistic look at your entire life. Having the ability to view your experiences and then having the opportunity to look five years into the future definitely has its advantages in helping you to build and maintain a lifetime of good choices, right decisions, and prosperous experiences because you will have advance notice of the type of vibrations you will be going into.

We use numbers consciously and unconsciously on a daily basis and in every aspect of our lives but most people have no idea just how powerful numbers really are or the role they play in our lives. In the financial world, many stock charting programs exist for the sole purpose of providing factual details that are considered bulletproof from the viewpoint of the accuracy of how the information is obtained and reported. This is done so that a potential investor can make an informed decision on whether to buy or sell a stock or even to get involved in the financial transaction in the first place. Charting programs are not a secret and it's certainly not rocket science on how they can greatly influence your decision-making process. Of course, if we were to compare that type of charting system to the Essence chart, the results would be similarly based on the nature of each product. Both would serve as road maps or guidelines in providing the information needed for you to make the best possible decisions.

The amount of personal information that is gleaned from the Essence chart and the accuracy far exceeds any type of reading available today. Many venues profess to allow you the opportunity to connect with your higher self, such as with Psychic, Tarot, and Astrology readings, meditation, and many others. What makes Chaldean Numerology so accurate is that it is based on an exact, proven mathematical formula that is by far the most valuable tool in helping you gain insight into various aspects and areas of your life, whether they are personal or business-related. The information contained in this chart can also tell you if and when it is likely that you may enter into a relationship, go through major changes, experience some health problems, go into a strong financial year, or encounter a Karmic lesson while at the same time, showing the patterns of various different experiences leading up to your current age.

A good numerologist will know exactly how to draw out the details of your story through interaction. A story is the actual experience you went through during a specific year such as a divorce, marriage, birth, major move, disruption in your life, etc. Depending on what your numbers calculate out to be, the result shows up in the form of a root (single-digit) or compound (double-digit) number.

If there is a special compound number in your chart, it is shown in combination with the single-digit "root" number. There are eight special compound double-digit number combinations. These number combinations are shown in table 10–1. Two of these are considered to be Master Numbers, the 11/2 and 22/4. The others are 19/1, 13/4, 14/5, 23/5, 16/7, and 18/9, all of which have a more intensified meaning or influence over your life experiences since these compound numbers, in particular, have more of a diverse impact on the type of experiences you will draw.

These following compound numbers provide significant additional information about the vibrational patterns of those particular numbers, and therefore, those numbers are not reduced down to a single-digit number because they provide a more in-depth interpretation of the actual meaning of the patterns of the characteristic. If the numbers were reduced down, you would get a partial reading of what the numbers truly mean versus not reducing the numbers down, and getting the full meaning from that compound number.

Double-Digit Compound Number Conversion Table

When the Final Number Adds Up To	The Number Converts To	Final Number Becomes
19	19/1	19/1
11	11/2	11/2
13	13/4	13/4
22	22/4	22/4
14	14/5	14/5
23	23/5	23/5
16	16/7	16/7
18	18/9	18/9

Table 10–1

These compound numbers do not get reduced down in the Essence chart because they represent the full meaning of the vibration that you are to experience and the arrangement of the numbers is critical to understanding your experiences. If you were to reduce that number down to a single-digit number, then the reading would not provide the complete picture that is required to get all of the available information from the chart, nor would the interpretation be as accurate.

Imagine the number of stories you will have to tell, starting from Age "1" to your "Current" Age. You may say, "Now how would I ever remember what I was doing at age 1?" of course, for the obvious reasons. However, amazingly enough for those earlier years, the numbers may indicate that you were ill as a baby, a parent might have died, parents divorced, or there were disruptions in the home due to many other reasons. As you were growing up, your parents or grandparents relayed stories of family circumstances when you were younger so you would have been aware of the earlier years. At some point in time, however, you will remember your own stories along with those passed on to you.

So how do the stories show up in your chart? How can numbers possibly show that kind of information to you? The answer to those questions is that numbers alone do not provide those stories but rather it's the Numerologist zeroing in on specific dates, focusing on the combination of certain numbers that stand out, interpreting the language of those numbers, and asking questions based on the description of the vibrational patterns in your chart. The Essence charts are done this way so that you can receive the best possible results. Many people make the mistake of thinking they can simply buy a "how to" book on the subject, prepare the chart, understand what the chart is saying to them, and then try to interpret it. We strongly caution you not to take the reading of the Essence Numerology Master Chart lightly. We want to make it quite perfectly clear that the process of interpreting your Essence numbers is complex, and it is exceptionally important that the meaning of your numbers accurately portrays the stories that will show themselves to you.

Sample Essence Numerology Master Chart and Process of Interpretation

The graphical representation of the data provided in a sample Essence chart is depicted in table 10–2. The written explanation, the sample chart, and the process of interpretation are shown in table 10–3 (representing six different examples of time periods in a person's life). This will show you a picture of the numerical data, that is, show you what the data looks like in chart form. And then, we will talk about the process used to interpret some of the numbers in the chart, that is, show you how to read the chart. The great value of this chart will become obvious, not only for bringing hidden insights to you, for providing clarity, understanding, and acceptance of where you've been in your life cycles, but also by giving you the opportunity to free yourself to move forward in your life. You will also become more aware of the magnitude of what is needed to understand the language of your Essence Numerology Master Chart and the importance of being a participant in the reading—talking out the reality of your stories.

The sample chart shown in table 10–2 will provide data for the interpretation of some of the number combinations that have been extracted for demonstration purposes. The Numerologist will typically start reading your chart from Age "1" and cover your entire chart interpreting primarily only those years that appear to have been, are now, or may become challenging. The years that were selected—1957, 1975, 1976, 1980, 2005, and 2007—are what we call challenging years as indicated in the Essence chart for that particular year. It's the past and current difficult years that we seek to flush out, while interpreting what the future five years will bring. The process of the selection of which years to read first starts with viewing the chart by looking across the top row to find the years, i.e., 50 = 1950, etc.

Next, you will want to run your finger down the column vertically, to locate the Essence, Personal, and Universal Year numbers for the example years selected for the demonstration. To recap again, the Essence number is personal to you since it is calculated using your full name and is valid from birthday to birthday. It is what you are working through emotionally and intellectually. The Personal Year is also personal to you and is calculated using your birthdate, also valid from birthday to birthday. It is like an assignment from the Universe and is the physical attraction of experiences (this tells you what patterns and events are being set up for the year in question). The Universal Year, which is not personal to you, is measured on a calendar year (January 1 through December 31), is a universal vibration that everyone is subject to collectively, and drives the activities of the world from the vibration that number represents.

The process and interpretation are discussed in the table 10–3 examples. Since these example charts are a static reading and there is no interaction (no live consultation), we can only demonstrate the process we go through, to draw out the details of the incident you have experienced. Obviously, in a live consultation with immediate feedback, we will get to know the individual's story and patterns fairly quickly and be able to confirm the accuracy of our reading while we search for answers with the individual to determine how the numbers apply to him or her. Because of the personal nature of this chart, some clients may not wish to tell their story, which is fine, since it is their journey and their life to experience. The Essence information is brought forth and documented during the reading. And now that this information has come to the surface and been addressed, the person may not wish to actively participate in the telling of their stories. They may wish, as is their right, to discover, on their own, what does or does not make sense to them. In either case, a healing process will have begun whether the individual chooses to confront and tackle the conflict now, or later, because his or her entire life from Age "1" was just examined detail by detail on a holistic level.

Most people have been through troubling times in their life. That just happens to be the norm. No one should feel embarrassed to talk about an incident that has happened or feel ashamed in any way for a situation they got into. The more you participate in this process, the more effective the chart becomes for you. After all, this is your journey to work out. And regardless of what your stories are, you are no different from the next person. Most people have already been there and done that too. For the most part, it's really hard to escape living through a diverse set of life experiences, since challenges are the opportunity for personal growth, as opposed to the exception of having a perfect life, which is rare and far between. The stories may have different characters, different events, and different causes, but the trauma is still there for the individual. At the culmination of your experiences, you can become a more integrated and adjusted person, which is critical to you in finding happiness and harmony in life. Sometimes it takes a lifetime to get to that point. (Following table 10–2 are number interpretations from the specific years and ages noted in each chart.)

See Tables 10–2 and 10–3 on the Following Pages.

Example of an Essence Numerology Master Chart Years 1950–1989

Essence Numerology Master Chart

Holistic Look of Your Life From
Age "1" to Current Age + 5 years into the Future

Joanne Marie Justis
Birthdate: March 4, 1949

1950–1969

Birth Year 1949	50	51	52	53	54	55	56	57	58	59	60	61	62	63	64	65	66	67	68	69
Age	1	2	3	4	5	6	7	8	9	10	11	12	13	14	15	16	17	18	19	20
First Name	J	O	O	O	O	O	O	O	A	N	N	N	N	N	N	N	N	N	N	E
Middle Name	M	M	M	M	A	R	R	I	E	E	E	E	E	M	M	M	M	A	R	R
Last Name	J	U	U	U	U	U	U	S	S	S	T	T	T	T	I	S	S	S	J	U
Essence	6	8	8	8	14/5	6	6	11/2	9	13/4	14/5	14/5	14/5	13/4	1	3	3	9	8	13/4
Personal Year	13/4	14/5	6	16/7	8	9	1	11/2	3	13/4	14/5	6	16/7	8	9	1	11/2	3	13/4	14/5
Universal Year	6	7	8	9	1	2	3	22/4	5	6	7	8	9	1	2	3	22/4	5	6	7

1970–1989

Birth Year 1949	70	71	72	73	74	75	76	77	78	79	80	81	82	83	84	85	86	87	88	89
Age	21	22	23	24	25	26	27	28	29	30	31	32	33	34	35	36	37	38	39	40
First Name	E	E	E	E	J	O	O	O	O	O	O	O	A	N	N	N	N	N	N	N
Middle Name	A	R	R	Y	M	M	M	M	A	R	R	Y	M	M	M	M	A	R	R	Y
Last Name	U	U	U	U	U	S	S	S	T	T	T	T	I	S	S	S	J	U	U	U
Essence	3	16/7	16/7	16/7	3	6	14/5	14/5	6	6	3	13/4	4	9	13/4	13/4	11/2	16/7	16/7	6
Personal Year	6	16/7	8	9	1	11/2	3	13/4	14/5	6	16/7	8	9	1	11/2	3	13/4	14/5	6	16/7
Universal Year	8	9	1	2	3	22/4	5	6	7	8	9	1	2	3	22/4	5	6	7	8	9

Table 10–2
1 of 2

Example of an Essence Numerology Master Chart Years 1990–2011

Essence Numerology Master Chart

Holistic Look of Your Life From

Age "1" to Current Age + 5 years into the Future

Joanne Marie Justis

Birthdate: March 4, 1949

1990–2009

Birth Year 1949	90	91	92	93	94	95	96	97	98	99	00	01	02	03	04	05	06	07	08	09
Age	41	42	43	44	45	46	47	48	49	50	51	52	53	54	55	56	57	58	59	60
First Name	N	N	N	E	E	E	E	E	J	O	O	O	O	O	O	O	A	N	N	N
Middle Name	M	M	M	A	R	R	I	E	E	E	E	E	M	M	M	M	A	R	R	I
Last Name	U	U	U	S	S	S	T	T	T	T	I	S	S	S	J	U	U	U	U	U
Essence	6	6	6	9	1	1	1	14/5	1	16/7	13/4	6	14/5	14/5	3	8	8	13/4	13/4	3
Personal Year	8	9	1	11/2	3	13/4	14/5	6	16/7	8	9	1	11/2	3	13/4	14/5	6	16/7	8	18/9
Universal Year	1	2	3	22/4	5	6	7	8	9	1	2	3	4	5	6	7	8	9	1	11/2

2010–2011

Birth Year 1949	010	011
Age	61	62
First Name	N	N
Middle Name	A	E
Last Name	U	S
Essence	3	13/4
Personal Year	1	11/2
Universal Year	3	22/4

Table 10–2

2 of 2

Example of an Essence Chart Static Reading for Year 1957

Example #1	Explanation of Numbers	What's Your Story
In **1957/Age 8**, the numbers displayed in the chart are: Essence = 11/2 Personal Year = 11/2 Universal Year = 22/4	The 11/2 Essence is a Master Number and indicates a sudden shock, very emotional, and electrical in nature. The Personal Year of an 11/2 could be a year to develop your intuitive side but the combination of the double 11/2 Essence and 11/2 Personal Year would more likely be a big shake up in your life, e.g., parents that fought and did not get along causing disruption in the family dynamics or an illness in the family. There could be many different scenarios depending on the environment you were growing up in which shapes your beginning in life. The 22/4 Universal Year is also a Master number and a year for stability and foundation.	After seeing the three number combinations, the numbers would indicate 1957 was probably a troubling year. Can you recall that year? The person either can/cannot remember that particular year. If they did remember, they would start telling their story, if they wished to do so. Keep in mind that in 1957, Joanne was only 8 years old. The chart is being read during her adult years, so she either could/could not remember the incident, or maybe her parents might have told her later on what was going on during that time frame. And that's why she could pass on the story.

Table 10-3
1 of 6

Example of an Essence Chart Static Reading for Year 1975

Example #2	Explanation of Numbers	What's Your Story
In **1975/Age 26**, the numbers displayed in the chart are: Essence = 6 Personal Year = 11/2 Universal Year = 22/4	The 6 Essence is a domestic number so this year is going to be all about what you personally want in relationship to a partner, family, or friends. The Personal Year of an 11/2 is also very emotional and electrical in nature, highly charged, like a sudden surprise or jolt. The Universal Year of 22/4 is a year for hard work, getting your affairs in order and building your foundation.	Because you are in a 6 Essence (this is your emotional state of mind) and a 11/2 Personal Year (highly charged), your chart would indicate that this year could mean that you were ending a personal relationship, divorcing, or there was a death in the family since the combination of the 6 and 11/2 generally indicates an emotional ending on a personal level. Do you recall what you were experiencing in 1975? Did you end a relationship or was there a death in the family or of a friend?

Table 10–3
2 of 6

Example of an Essence Chart Static Reading for Year 1976

Example #3	Explanation of Numbers	What's Your Story
In **1976/Age 27**, the numbers displayed in the chart are: Essence = 14/5 Personal Year = 3 Universal Year = 5	The 14/5 Essence represents emotional changes or disruptions. The Personal Year of a 3 is very social, magnetic, romantic, and successful. The 5 Universal Year is a year of <u>unexpected</u> changes such as winning a trip, getting in a car accident, changing jobs, moving to a different location, etc.	The numbers would indicate that you were going through emotional changes but they may have been on the positive side. Since the Personal Year is one of joy and of a social nature and the 5 Universal Year is one of unexpected changes, this may have been a year that you traveled and were not expecting to. Do you recall what was going on in 1976? Since the 3 and 5 are exciting vibrations, this was probably an exciting year for unexpected travel.

Table 10–3
3 of 6

Example of an Essence Chart Static Reading for Year 1980

Example #4	Explanation of Numbers	What's Your Story
In **1980/Age 31** the numbers displayed in the chart are: Essence = 3 Personal Year = 16/7 Universal Year = 9	The 3 Essence would indicate that this year you will be more social and joyful since the Essence is your emotional state of mind and the 3 is the entertainer who likes to have fun. This is a 16/7 Personal Year. The 16 is known to be the bringer of a Karmic lesson(s) to be learned during this year. The 9 Universal Year is a year of completions and endings, which may include romance and anything emotional by nature.	Since the Essence is how you are feeling emotionally, this should have been a good year for you; however, although you might have been happy, you were in a 16/7 Personal Year which represented a Karmic lesson and you might have made a decision that got you off track. Do you recall if anything comes to mind about a particular experience or lesson that was troubling or considered to be a challenge for this year? In addition to being in a 3 Essence and 16/7 Personal Year, you were in a 9 Universal Year, a year of completions and endings so you probably were housecleaning on many levels. You may have completed an educational course, changed jobs, moved from another location, or ended a relationship, etc. The 7 in the 16/7 and 9, both are endings and completions of some kind, so this might have been another difficult year for you.

Table 10–3
4 of 6

Example of an Essence Chart Static Reading for Year 2005

Example #5	Explanation of Numbers	What's Your Story?
In **2005/Age 56** the numbers displayed in the chart are: Essence = 8 Personal Year = 14/5 Universal Year = 7	The 8 Essence is a good vibration to be in since it represents feeling mentally and emotionally confident in all of your affairs. You take control and work toward your goals. The 14/5 Personal Year would indicate a year of disruption brought about by a possible move by location, career change, of any type of major change. A 7 Universal Year brings about completions and endings and is a less social year than others.	Being in an 8 Essence you are more likely to become more focused and goal-driven during this year with a desire to put your affairs in order. With that said, you are in a Personal Year of a 14/5 that brings about disruption and changes on any level because the 5 brings about unexpected changes. That means, you could move, change jobs, or make decisions that involve changes in your life. If you are investing in a 14/5 year, be aware that the 14/5 can mean risky business from a financial standpoint. It would be hard not to remember what type of experience you attracted with the 14/5 and 7 combination.

Table 10–3
5 of 6

Example of an Essence Chart Static Reading for Year 2007

Example #6	Explanation of Numbers	What's Your Story?
In **2007/Age 58** the numbers displayed in the chart are: Essence = 13/4 Personal Year = 16/7 Universal Year = 9	The 13/4 Essence can mean that you are moving forward in your life, and having fun, while at the same time putting your affairs in order. Remember not to scatter your forces but to focus on your priorities. On the flip side of things, you should watch your health since the 13/4 can also mean a potential health problem. The 16/7 Personal Year is known to be the bringer of a Karmic lesson(s) to be learned during this year, while the 7 of the 16/7 is more of a loner time, requiring time to yourself. The 9 Universal Year is a year of completions and endings, which may include romance and anything emotional by nature.	The year 2007 may be more difficult for you because you may have health issues (13/4), or deal with a Karmic lesson (16/7), while entering into completions and endings (7 and 9). The 9 Universal Year tends to be more emotional and may include a romance or an affair.

Table 10–3
6 of 6

Continuing the process of asking questions and getting answers throughout your entire life is very healing and often times becomes a teary-eyed session. The Essence Numerology Master Chart is so accurate that it will reinforce the predictions calculated from the chart, and astound you with the amount of available information about you and your experiences that can't be found by anyone else. This information will help to guide you in keeping your life on track, if you live your life making informed choices and decisions, instead of living a life of uncertainty.

Conclusion

Self-knowledge is the key to your freedom, while self-advocacy is your key to success. Your journey starts with taking the first step, the desire to bring about change. If you are at the crossroads of life or going through transitions because of yourself, family, or friends, personal or business relationships, career or finances, issues about health or well-being, then you may need a "jump" start to put your life back on track, especially if you are not satisfied with your life or specific areas in your life. You have the power to create different outcomes and it's all about making the right choices and having the courage to make the necessary changes that will better serve you. There is much knowledge in the world as well as valuable tools such as these Essence charts that will lead you on your journey's path, and ultimately, to the happiness and success that you seek.

###

Chapter 11:
Naming For Business Ventures, Companies, Products, Pets, Pedigrees, and Babies

I. Introduction

A spiritual master plan is woven into "every" name that has existed and which will exist—whether the name is for a business venture, company, product, pet, pedigree, or baby. And only Numerology, the Science of Numbers, through a mathematical formula, can identify and interpret that master plan, reveal what lies at the heart of a selected name, and tell you exactly what that means to you. The "chosen" name can influence the vibrational patterns that will directly affect your baby, your business, or your animal in a positive or negative way. Simply put, you can now learn how to decode the name you've picked before finalizing it through reverse engineering, converting the letters of the name into numbers, and then applying a mathematical formula to arrive at a very specific, personalized blueprint for that particular name.

This chapter will focus on providing you with examples and case studies, and specific step-by-step instructions on how to calculate the names for a company, a pedigree racehorse, and two babies, and to understand the hidden meaning within each name. So, if you are interested in discovering how life's experiences will take shape with the specific name you select, you would want to generate what is called a "Chord" Numerology Master Chart. The Chord Numerology Master Charts are named as such because only the primary characteristics of the name can be determined, since there are no birthdates to factor into the formula calculations. The Chord provides you with the vibrational patterns of three unique "core" characteristics, the Soul/Heart's Desire, the Personality, and the Purpose as described below:

The Soul/Heart's Desire reflects the emotional aspect and inner motivations;
The Personality forms the first real impressions made on the outside world;
The Purpose reveals what the mission in life will be.

Except for baby naming, the different types of naming being discussed in this chapter only require you to find out what the above characteristics reveal. In the case of baby naming, there are eight soul qualities (lessons to be learned) derived from the name, in addition to the three core characteristics. This is the only case where the soul qualities would apply because naming for a "human being" is slightly more complex than for the rest of the names.

You may ask yourself why you would want to know this type of information. For instance, in a business venture or any kind of naming for financial purposes, it is presumed that you would want to choose a "winning" name that brings ambition, success, and prosperity energies versus a name that may attract less desirable outcomes, such as negative and distracting vibrational patterns attached to the name, other vibrational patterns that bring disruptions, or constant undesirable changes or obstacles shown in the patterns revealed by the numbers calculated from the name. This is true for business ventures, companies, products, and pedigree naming. Although the same information is revealed for pets and babies, the results are applied differently. The goal for selecting "winning" names is generally financially driven for investment reasons such as for a pedigree animal, company, and product naming. In the case of pet and baby naming, whatever name you finally select brings with it a unique, core set of personal characteristics. If you change the name, you change that set of characteristics, giving you the ability to affect the traits of an animal or baby by virtue of changing the name. The information and knowledge you receive from the name you have picked will be very surprising to say the least, once you've learned exactly how much information can be extracted from the Chord Numerology Master Chart.

Before beginning this chapter, we need to make a distinction between generating charts for people (with birthdates) versus a baby (not yet with a birthdate) and for the other naming possibilities just mentioned. In the case of a baby, generally the parents select a name prior to birth. So, for the exercise in this chapter, no birthdate would be factored into the formula, since the birthdate is not required to determine the vibrational patterns of the name selection. Since we do not yet have a birthdate, which is required to generate the full Numerology chart, we can only generate a partial chart. This is also true about the name you give your pets and all your animals. Therefore, the name you pick forms a unique numerical blueprint for each of their lives.

The following examples and instructions show you how to calculate the Chord Numerology Master Chart for a Business name, a Pedigree racehorse, and two Baby names. All the vibrational patterns of three unique core characteristics are calculated the same way except, as mentioned above, for baby naming which is the exception to the rule.

II. Selecting a Name for a Business Venture, Company, or Product

This section addresses calculating the numbers of the Chord Numerology Master Chart, including the three core characteristics of a name—Soul/Heart's Desire, Personality, and Purpose—for a Business Venture, Company, Corporation, and Product Naming. (Note: Abbreviations such as Inc., LLC, Ltd., and PC, are <u>not</u> considered in the Naming process, since they are standard legal connotations and do not contribute to your intent in selecting a

Name to use.) It has long been recognized throughout time, that names play a vital part in directing and influencing the experiences and outcomes in the world. Numerology applies numbers to the "sounds" within names. Those numbers represent vibrational patterns that determine the experiences drawn to the entity bearing a particular name. The full name of a Business Venture, Company, or Product forms a unique numerical blueprint. The language of numbers is the key that unlocks the door and reveals the hidden meaning of the vibrational patterns. The name that is selected for such an entity can influence the vibration of the entity in either a positive or negative way.

The following is general information on choosing a Chord for a business name in addition to an explanation of what each position number means that is personalized to the name you selected. This information will allow you to determine whether you have chosen a "winning" name or not. Case Study #1 will research a business name, Numbers R U, to determine the blueprint for that name or the vibrational patterns the name calculates to be.

II.A Business Naming Case Study #1: Name Researched–Numbers R U

The Chord or vibration of this name is made up of the following core characteristics with the calculated number for each shown in figure 11–1.

Example of Calculated Chord Numbers for Numbers R U

Core Characteristics	Calculated Numbers
Soul/Heart's Desire	8
Personality	18/9
Purpose	8

Figure 11–1

II.A.1 What the Chord Numbers Mean (Soul/Heart's Desire, Personality, and Purpose)

Following is a brief written explanation of the meaning of the number assigned to each of the three core characteristics that make up the Chord or vibration of the business name Numbers R U that were shown in figure 11–1. The three numbers outlined in the chart are unique only to the name selected. The descriptions are written to explain the meaning on an ideal level, then you apply that meaning to this name in context for a Business Venture, Company, or Product Naming. Numbers R U is a very "successful" business name in that it brings with it the vibrational patterns of leadership, ambition, and service to mankind. This is the type of Chord you want in picking a winning business name. The Chord of the Number 8, 18/9, and 8, is one of the few most desirable Chords or vibrational patterns for your business venture. The 1s, 8s, and 9s and combinations of those numbers together are very successful numbers.

Below are the descriptions of the three "core" characteristics.

Number 8 Soul/Heart's Desire
Ambition, Success

The Soul/Heart's Desire is the emotional aspect and is the innermost desire to seek to express itself in this world. The innermost desire of the Number 8 is to gain power and success on all levels, for this is an aggressive, materialistic vibration. This vibration has all the stamina, courage, and talents needed to be successful in any business venture. This is also a very successful money number.

Number 18/9 Personality
Ambition, Leadership, Service to Mankind

The Personality is the physical aspect of the entity. This is the first impression that the Name of the Business will give to others. The Number 9 Personality is sincere, well-balanced, truthful and noble, and dedicated to the service of mankind. The 18/9 Personality is a powerful combination of the leadership of the Number 1 and the sound judgment and efficiency of the Number 8. The 18 has its Root Number in the 9, combining the vibrational force and energy of all the numbers and humanitarian spirit.

Number 8 Purpose
Ambition, Success

The Purpose number reveals what the mission in life will be. The 8 Purpose in life is to attain financial recognition and success that brings with it all of the materialism associated with being financially successful.

Numbers to avoid because they bring less than desirable results are the 7, 14/5, and 16/7, while winning Numbers are the 1, 8, 18/9, or combinations using those numbers. There are many other number combinations that could bring you a Chord or vibration that would range from ok to good, but it is advisable to find a business name that will bring you the most successful number combinations possible.

Following is another real-time case study involving the selection of a business name from a list of potential names.

II.B Business Naming Case Study #2: Researching Multiple Names for a New Business Venture

A client wanted a successful name for her business and suggested three names that she liked best. The names were lengthy and difficult to pronounce but she thought they described her business to a tee. So, the charts were generated. None of the names were a successful vibration therefore we had to come up with more names to run until we were able to pick the most successful vibration of all for a business name, in addition to shortening the name and pleasing the client. It took running ten names before the perfect combination of characteristics could be attained to achieve that "winning" name with a successful vibration.

We will now explore the development of the specific calculations and interpretation of the language of numbers for the core characteristics of Case Study #1 Business Name Numbers R U (see figure 11–1).

II.B.1 Calculating a Business Name Soul/Heart's Desire Number (From the Vowels of the Full Name)

The definition and explanation of the Soul/Heart's Desire are include in chapter 6, section B. The description and meaning of the Soul/Heart's Desire numbers are included in chapter 8, section 8.B.

Soul/Heart's Desire Number
Two-Step Process on How to Calculate the Number of the Business Name
Step 1

> To find the number of the Vowels of the Business Name, lay out the full Name on a sheet of paper with room to place numbers below the letters (see figure 11–2 in illustration 11a). Using the values shown in table 11–1, assign the correct value to the letters of the Vowels. (Note: Table 11–1 is a standard table used throughout this chapter whenever the "Vowels" of a name are being calculated.)

Step 2

To arrive at the Soul/Heart's Desire number of the Business Name, you will need to add the Vowel numbers together as indicated in illustration 11a. The final calculation number can add up to either be a single-digit root number or a double-digit compound number such as shown in table 7–3. If the final calculation number adds up to be one of the special compound numbers as shown in table 11–2, then you would not reduce that compound number down to a single-digit number. However, if the calculated compound number is not listed in table 11–2, then you would reduce that number down to a single-digit root number. These particular compound numbers provide significant additional information about that characteristic and that is why it is important to get a more in-depth interpretation of the actual meaning of the characteristic's patterns. (Note: Table 11–2 is an extraction of table 7–3.)

Chaldean Alphabet/Formula
Assigned Numbers Letters Identified
Vowels Only

1	2	3	4	5	6	7	8
A				E	U	O	
I							
Y							

Table 11–1

Double-Digit Compound Number Conversion Table

When the Final Number Adds Up To	The Number Converts To	Final Number Becomes
19	19/1	19/1
11	11/2	11/2
13	13/4	13/4
22	22/4	22/4
14	14/5	14/5
23	23/5	23/5
16	16/7	16/7
18	18/9	18/9

Table 11–2

Soul/Heart's Desire Number

Illustration 11a: Calculating the Numbers of the Vowels of the Business Name (Add only the Numbers of the Letters A, E, I, O, U, Y)

Example of Calculating the Soul/Heart's Desire Number of the Business Name

N	U	M	B	E	R	S		R	U
	6			5					6

6+ 5+ 6

Addition = 17* (Compound Number)

Reduced to 1+ 7 = 8

Soul/Heart's Desire Number **= 8**** (Root Number)

Figure 11–2

* See chapter 9 for Compound Number meanings.

** See chapter 8, section 8.B for the definition and explanation of the Soul/Heart's Desire numbers.

II.B.2 Calculating a Business Name Personality Number (From the Consonants of the Full Name)

The definition and explanation of the Personality are included in chapter 6, section 6.C. The description and meaning of the Personality numbers are included in chapter 8, section 8.C.

Personality Number

Two-Step Process on How to Calculate Number of the Business Name

Step 1

To calculate the Consonant numbers of the Business Name, lay out the full Name on a sheet of paper with room to place numbers below the letters (see figure 11–3 in illustration 11b.) Now, using the numerical values shown in table 11–3, assign the correct number value to the letters of the Consonants.

Step 2

To arrive at the Personality number of the Business Name, you will need to add all of the Consonant numbers together as indicated in illustration 11b. The final calculation number can add up to either be a single-digit root number or a double-digit compound number such as shown in table 7–3. If the final calculation number adds up to be one of the special compound numbers as shown in table 11–2, then you would not reduce that compound number down to a single-digit number. However, if the calculated compound number is not listed in table 11–2, then you would reduce that number down to a single-digit root number. These particular compound numbers provide significant additional information about that characteristic and that is why it is important to get a more in-depth interpretation of the actual meaning of the characteristic's patterns. (Note: Table 11–2 is an extraction of table 7–3.)

Chaldean Alphabet/Formula
Assigned Numbers with Letters Identified

Consonants Only

1	2	3	4	5	6	7	8
	B	C	D				F
	K	G	M	H	V	Z	P
J	R	L	T	N	W		
Q		S		X			

Table 11–3

Double-Digit Compound Number Conversion Table

When the Final Number Adds Up To	The Number Converts To	Final Number Becomes
19	19/1	19/1
11	11/2	11/2
13	13/4	13/4
22	22/4	22/4
14	14/5	14/5
23	23/5	23/5
16	16/7	16/7
18	18/9	18/9

Table 11–2

Personality Number

Illustration 11b: Calculating the Numbers of the Consonants of the Full Name (Add the Numbers of all of the Letters Except A, E, I, O, U, Y)

Example of Calculating the Personality Number of the Business Name

N	U	M	B	E	R	S		R	U
5		4	2		2	3		2	

5+ 4+ 2+ 2+ 3+ 2

Addition = 18* or 18/9
(Compound Number)

(Do Not Reduce the 18/9 Down to a Root Number)

Personality Number = 18/9**

Figure 11–3

* See chapter 9 for Compound Number meanings.
** See chapter 8, section 8.C for the definition and explanation of Personality numbers.

II.B.3 Calculating a Business Name Purpose Number (From the Letters of the Full Name)

The definition and explanation of the Purpose are included in chapter 6, section 6.D. The description and meaning of the Purpose numbers are included in chapter 8, section 8.D.

Purpose Number
Two-Step Process on How to Calculate the Number of the Business Name
Step 1

To calculate the Purpose number of the Business Name, lay out the full Business Name on a sheet of paper with room to place numbers below the letters (see figure 11–4 in illustration 11c). Now, using table 11–4, assign the correct number value to all of the letters of the full name. (Note: Table 11–4 is a standard table used throughout this chapter whenever the "Full Name" is being calculated.) Place the number of each letter underneath each corresponding letter as shown in figure 11–4.

Step

To arrive at the Purpose number of the Business Name, you will need to add the numbers of all of the letters of the Business Name together as indicated in illustration 11c. The final calculation number can add up to either be a single-digit root number or a double-digit compound number such as shown in table 7–3. If the final calculation number adds up to be one of the special compound numbers as shown in table 11–2, then you would not reduce that compound number down to a single-digit number. However, if the calculated compound number is not listed in table 11–2, then you would reduce that number down to a single-digit root number. These particular compound numbers provide significant additional information about that characteristic and that is why it is important to get a more in-depth interpretation of the actual meaning of the characteristic's patterns. (Note: Table 11–2 is an extraction of table 7–3.)

Chaldean Alphabet/Formula
Assigned Numbers with Letters Identified

1	2	3	4	5	6	7	8
A	B	C	D	E	U	O	F
I	K	G	M	H	V	Z	P
J	R	L	T	N	W		
Q		S		X			
Y							

Table 11–4

Double-Digit Compound Number Conversion Table

When the Final Number Adds Up To	The Number Converts To	Final Number Becomes
19	19/1	19/1
11	11/2	11/2
13	13/4	13/4
22	22/4	22/4
14	14/5	14/5
23	23/5	23/5
16	16/7	16/7
18	18/9	18/9

Table 11–2

Purpose Number
Illustration 11c: Calculating the Numbers of the Complete Business Name (Add the Numbers of all of the Letters of the Full Name)

Example of Calculating the Purpose Number of the Business Name

N	U	M	B	E	R	S		R	U
5	6	4	2	5	2	3		2	6

5+ 6+ 4+ 2+ 5+ 2+ 3+ 2+ 6

Addition = 35* (Compound Number)

Reduce to 3+ 5 = 8

Purpose Number = 8** (Root Number)

Figure 11–4

* See chapter 9 for Compound Number meanings.
** See chapter 8, section 8.D for the definition and explanation of Purpose numbers.

III. Pets and Pedigree (Animal) Naming

Before addressing the calculation of the Chord Numerology Master Charts for pets or pedigrees, we will first discuss some general information on animal naming. You may simply want to know the vibration of the name you have picked for your pet as everyone wants to share a happy and fulfilled life with their animals—or, you may want to understand what the name means that's already been assigned and how that name affects your pet. Numerology gives you the ability to test how a name affects your pet and the environment in which you live before you make a final decision.

If your intent is to name pedigrees (i.e., animals associated with a business), such as racehorses, you would probably want to select a name with as "successful" a vibration as possible. You can now test the name (or names) you have chosen by following some easy steps on how to calculate the name you have picked to determine what the vibration of that name is.

It should be mentioned that the vibrational patterns that shape the animal's life experiences will also be greatly affected by how the animal is treated. This is no different when caring for and raising a child. No matter what their vibrational patterns are, the outcomes from life experiences will most definitely be influenced by the way they are nurtured. The combined effect of environment, the care they are given, and training will determine how well, or not so well, the pedigree animal will respond to the people around them, and the "successful" environment created by the vibrational patterns of their name. As in the case of a racehorse, you may have the most successful vibration from a naming standpoint, but if the horse is mishandled or abused, and as a result its "will" or "spirit" is broken, you have compromised the full potential of influence the name offered the animal. Failure to care for and nurture any animal will drain the energy from the "winning" vibration of a pedigree or the "loving" vibration of a pet.

The Chord or vibration of a name is made up of three core characteristics with a calculated number assigned to each—Soul/Heart's Desire, Personality, and Purpose. The Soul/Heart's Desire reflects the emotional aspect and inner motivation, the Personality forms the first real impressions made, and the Purpose reveals what the mission in life will be. Following is a step-by-step process for how to calculate the three core characteristic numbers of the name of your Pet or Animal (Pedigree), and the meaning of the Chord Numbers. These three numbers are outlined in the chart and are unique only to the name you have selected for your pet with the descriptions written to specifically explain the meaning of this name. The descriptions are written to explain the "potential" of the name on an "ideal" level, and then you need to determine how to go about bringing that potential into the life and experiences of your Pet or Pedigree.

III.A Pedigree Naming Case Study #1: Name Researched B. Hoedown, Thoroughbred Racehorse

We will illustrate this calculation by running the name of "B. Hoedown," a well-known thoroughbred racehorse. The owner wanted to know what the numbers say about B. Hoedown's destiny. This information has been provided with the permission of the owner.

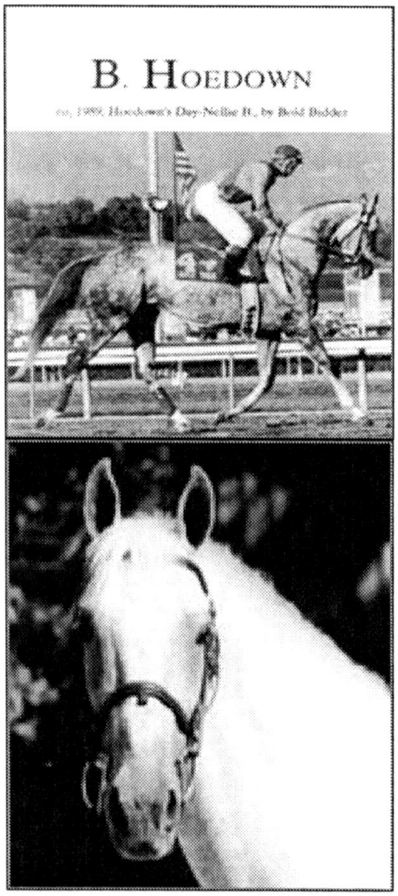

B. Hoedown, Thoroughbred Racehorse

The Chord or vibration of the name is made up of the following core characteristics with the calculated number for each characteristic:

Example of Calculated Chord Numbers for B. Hoedown

Core Characteristics	Calculated Numbers
Soul/Heart's Desire	19/1
Personality	22/4
Purpose	5

Figure 11–5

As shown in figure 11–5, B. Hoedown's name calculates out to be a Chord of (19/1, 22/4, and 5). He has a Number 19/1 Soul/Heart's Desire, a Number 22/4 (Master Number) Personality, and a Number 5 Purpose. The combination of the Chord numbers forms a successful vibration or a "winning" name. He has the best of all the number combinations (19/1) for Soul/Heart's Desire, the Master Number (22/4) for strong foundation, durability, and the endurance of a leader, and the speed and freedom of the (5).

Listed below is a description of each of the "core" Characteristics.

Number 19/1 Soul/Heart's Desire

Success-Oriented Vibratory Force

The Number 1 brings with it all of the characteristics of a leader, individual, and pioneer with the desire to seek to express itself in the world, always in a forward motion. The Number 9 represents the compassionate humanitarian. And, the Number 19/1 is the most success-oriented vibratory force that exists because it operates under the veil of universality, with the 9 in this vibration being a protected number.

Number 22/4 Personality

Hard Worker, Service to Mankind

The Number 4 Personality gives the impression of being conservative, orderly, and self-reliant. The Number 22/4 is a Master Number that raises the Root 4 to a much higher energy level. The 2s bring emotional energy, tact, detail, diplomacy to the vibration. The Root Number 4 adds discipline, structure, foundation, and a less emotional aspect. This is the number of the Master builder. The Number 22 Master Number represents the intensity of the 4.

Number 5 Purpose

Action, Freedom, Speed

The Number 5 Purpose is to promote freedom and change and it's all about movement, speed, and action. This involves bringing forth new ideas for the purpose of expansion and progress to pass on to others.

Based on the numbers in B. Hoedown's chart, he clearly was born to be magnificent, especially because of his spectacular "blueprint" or numbers with which he was born. B. Hoedown draws a Master Number of a 22/4 in his Personality, a 19/1 Soul/Heart's Desire or strong foundation, and a 5 Purpose for being in the public arena and racing. The combination of these numbers makes him a very powerful and confident horse and a true gentleman. These attributes have been witnessed by so many from the standpoint that this stallion has a beautiful temperament, is well-bred, with manners well beyond the norm—and is clearly recognized as an unusual and striking creature. All these things came about through a wonderful combination of a very powerful and "winning" name, and a loving and nurturing owner.

III.A.1 Calculating the Soul/Heart's Desire Number of the Pedigree Name (From the Vowels of the Full Name)

The definition and explanation of the Soul/Heart's Desire are included in chapter 6, section 6.B. The description and meaning of the Soul/Heart's Desire numbers are included in chapter 8, section 8.B.

Soul/Heart's Desire Number
Two-Step Process on How to Calculate the Number of the Pedigree Name
Step 1

To find the number of the Vowels of the Pedigree Name, lay out the full Name on a sheet of paper with room to place numbers the letters (see figure 11–6 in illustration 11d). Using the values shown in table 11–1, assign the correct number value to the Vowels of the Pedigree Name.

Step 2

To arrive at the Soul/Heart's Desire number of the Pedigree Name, you will need to add the Vowel numbers together as indicated in illustration 11d. The final calculation number can add up to either be a single-digit root number or a double-digit compound number such as shown in table 7–3. If the final calculation number adds up to be one of the special compound numbers as shown in table 11–2, then you would not reduce that compound number down to a single-digit number. However, if the calculated compound number is not listed in table 11–2, then would reduce that number down to a single-digit root number. These particular compound numbers provide significant additional information about that characteristic and that is why it is important to get a more in-depth interpretation of the actual meaning of the characteristic's patterns. (Note: Table 11–2 is an extraction of table 7–3.

Chaldean Alphabet/Formula
Assigned Numbers with Letters Identified
Vowels Only

1	2	3	4	5	6	7	8
A				E	U	O	
I							
Y							

Table 11–1

Double-Digit Compound Number Conversion Table

When the Final Number Adds Up To	The Number Converts To	Final Number Becomes
19	19/1	19/1
11	11/2	11/2
13	13/4	13/4
22	22/4	22/4
14	14/5	14/5
23	23/5	23/5
16	16/7	16/7
18	18/9	18/9

Table 11–2

Soul/Heart's Desire Number

Illustration 11d: Calculating the Numbers of the Vowels of the Full Name (Add Only the Numbers of the Letters A, E, I, O, U, Y)

Example of Calculating the Soul/Heart's Desire Number of the Pedigree Racehorse

B		H	O	E	D	O	W	N
			7	5		7		

7+ 5+ 7

Addition = 19* or 19/1 (Compound Number)

(Do Not Reduce the 19/1 Down to a Root Number)

Soul/Heart's Desire Number = 19/1**

Figure 11–6

* See chapter 9 for Compound Number meanings.
** See chapter 8, section 8.B for the definition and explanation of the Soul/Heart's Desire numbers.

III.A.2 Calculating the Personality Number of the Pedigree Name (From the Consonants of the Full Name)

The definition and explanation of the Personality are included in chapter 6, section 6.C. The description and meaning of the Personality numbers are included in chapter 8, section 8.C.

Personality Number
Two-Step Process on How to Calculate the Number of the Pedigree Name
Step 1

To calculate the Consonant numbers of the full Pedigree Name, lay out the Name on a sheet of paper with room to place numbers below the letters (see figure 11–7 in illustration 11e). Now, using the numerical values shown in table 11–3, assign the correct number value to the letters of the Pedigree's Consonants.

Step 2

To arrive at the Personality number of the Pedigree Name, you will need to add all the numbers of the Consonants in the name together as indicated in illustration 11e. The final calculation number can add up to either be a single-digit root number or a double-digit compound number such as shown in table 7–3. If the final calculation number adds up to be one of the special compound numbers as shown in table 11–2, then you would not reduce that compound number down to a single-digit number. However, if the calculated compound number is not listed in table 11–2, then you would reduce that number down to a single-digit root number. These particular compound numbers provide significant additional information about that characteristic and that is why it is important to get a more in-depth interpretation of the actual meaning of the characteristic's patterns. (Note: Table 11–2 is an extraction of table 7–3.)

Chaldean Alphabet/Formula
Assigned Numbers with Letters Identified
Consonants Only

1	2	3	4	5	6	7	8
	B	C	D				F
	K	G	M	H	V	Z	P
J	R	L	T	N	W		
Q		S		X			

Table 11–3

Double-Digit Compound Number Conversion Table

When the Final Number Adds Up To	The Number Converts To	Final Number Becomes
19	19/1	19/1
11	11/2	11/2
13	13/4	13/4
22	22/4	22/4
14	14/5	14/5
23	23/5	23/5
16	16/7	16/7
18	18/9	18/9

Table 11–2

Personality Number

Illustration 11e: Calculating the Numbers of the Consonants of the Full Name (Add the Numbers of all of the letters Except A, E, I, O, U, Y)

Example of Calculating the Personality Number of the Pedigree Racehorse

B		H	O	E	D	O	W	N
2		5			4		6	5

2+ 5+ 4+ 6+ 5

Addition = 22* or 22/4
(Compound Number)

(Do Not Reduce the 22/4 Down to a Root Number)

Personality Number = 22/4**

Figure 11–7

* See chapter 9 for Compound Number meanings.

** See chapter 8, section 8.C for the definition and explanation of Personality numbers.

III.A.3 Calculating the Purpose Number of the Pedigree Name (From all of the Letters of the Full Name)

The definition and explanation of the Purpose are included in chapter 6, section 6.D. The description and meaning of the Purpose numbers are included in chapter 8, section 8.D.

Purpose Number

Two-Step Process on How to Calculate the Number of the Pedigree Name

Step 1

To calculate the Purpose number of the Pedigree Name, lay out the full Pedigree Name on a sheet of paper with room to place numbers below the letters (see figure 11–8 in illustration 11f). Now, using table 11–4, assign the correct number value to all of the letters of the full name. Place the number of each letter underneath each corresponding letter as shown in figure 11–8.

Step 2

To arrive at the Purpose number of the Pedigree Name, you will need to add the numbers of all of the letters of the full Name together as indicated in illustration 11f. The final calculation number can add up to either be a single-digit root number or a double-digit compound number such as shown in table 7–3. If the final calculation number adds up to be one of the special compound numbers as shown in table 11–2, then you would not reduce that compound number down to a single-digit number. However, if the calculated compound number is not listed in table 11–2, then you would reduce that number down to a single-digit root number. These particular compound numbers provide significant additional information about that characteristic and that is why it is important to get a more in-depth interpretation of the actual meaning of the characteristic's patterns. (Note: Table 11–2 is an extraction of table 7–3.)

Chaldean Alphabet/Formula
Assigned Numbers with Letters Identified

1	2	3	4	5	6	7	8
A	B	C	D	E	U	O	F
I	K	G	M	H	V	Z	P
J	R	L	T	N	W		
Q		S		X			
Y							

Table 11–4

Double-Digit Compound Number Conversion Table

When the Final Number Adds Up To	The Number Converts To	Final Number Becomes
19	19/1	19/1
11	11/2	11/2
13	13/4	13/4
22	22/4	22/4
14	14/5	14/5
23	23/5	23/5
16	16/7	16/7
18	18/9	18/9

Table 11–2

Purpose Number

<u>Illustration 11f:</u> Calculating the Numbers of your Pedigree's Full Name (Add the Numbers of all of the Letters of the Full Name)

Example of Calculating the Purpose Number of the Pedigree Racehorse

B		H	O	E	D	O	W	N
2		5	7	5	4	7	6	5

2+ 5+ 7+ 5+ 4+ 7+ 6+ 5

Addition = 41*
(Compound Number)

Reduce to 4 + 1 = 5

Purpose Number = 5** (Root Number)

Figure 11–8

* See chapter 9 for Compound Number meanings.

** See chapter 8, section 8.D for the definition and explanation of Purpose numbers.

Following is another real-time case study summary involving the selection of pedigree names from a list of potential names.

III.B Pedigree Naming Case Study #2: Researching Names of Racehorses

A client has racehorses and selects each name for her foals based on the numerical vibration for speed that she seeks for the potential of that horse. Once the name is registered, the vibrational patterns of that name stay with the horse its entire life. So from the client's standpoint, naming is critical since she has an understanding of the magnitude of Numerology and how this system of numbers can impact her horses.

Picking a "winning" name is so very important when you are selecting a name for a baby, a person, pets, pedigrees, or a business venture because it can bring about either a positive or negative vibration to the entity—the difference between a "successful" name and one that's less desirable. See chapter 8 for a list of meanings to all of the possible special number combinations for root and compound numbers. This list has been provided so that you can look up the meaning of the numbers assigned to the Soul/Heart's Desire, Personality, and Purpose of the Chord chart.

IV. Baby Naming

The naming convention influences the vibrational patterns assigned to the name of the baby and plays a vital part in directing and influencing the baby's purpose and mission in life. Numerology applies numbers to names that determine the experiences drawn to that human being coming into the world bearing a particular name.

Before we begin, we would like to share some general information on selecting what is called a Chord or Vibration to reveal the characteristics of the vibrational patterns that flow in and through the chosen name. If you have already picked a name for your baby, you can now determine what vibrational patterns will be revealed by the numbers of that name's characteristics. Or, if you have not yet chosen a baby name and have a list of "finalist" names, you can calculate the numbers of each name and choose that name whose numbers you feel will generate the most appropriate and correct set of vibrational patterns to shape the experiences of your baby. The advantage here is the opportunity to learn, through the numbers of the baby name, about the potential design and blueprint of the patterns that will form the experiences of your baby's life, prior to their conception and birth.

What would you say if you were told that you have the power to pick the three top "core" characteristics of your child's "design" prior to birth by virtue of a name selection process? Can you imagine that! The name you assign to your baby's Birth Certificate along with the Birthdate will determine your child's foundational blueprint and the potential experiences he or she will experience throughout his or her entire lifetime.

There are many ways to select baby names, especially when you investigate all of the resources available on the Internet, which includes people who specialize in the naming process as well as the many published baby naming books on the market today. Parents may select a Baby Name through:

Intuition/Process of Elimination Some parents just know intuitively what they will call their newborn; not always knowing why, but having very strong feelings that the name they selected will be the perfect fit for their baby.
Culture Some cultures will dictate the naming convention that's traditionally driven. Since most of us have ethnic pride and want to connect and preserve our ethnic roots, the names common to our culture are the obvious choice. Some names carry information about our roots, such as family or clan names. They are generally inherited.
Prior Selection of a Name Picking a name you always loved and wanted to name your child is, of course, the simplest way to name a baby since it is a name that appeals most to you.
Honoring Someone Special The name is chosen to remember someone special, such as a parent or relative that may have died, to honor that person by carrying on their name.
Inventing a Non-Traditional Name There are those parents who are independent and non-traditional and want to select a Baby Name that's very different, a name that no one could normally relate to, such as the name "Venus," "Clover," or "Charisma."

You will notice that Numerology was not listed as one of the above methods for selecting a name. That's because most people are not familiar with Numerology or how this science of numbers works. According to this science, which is both theosophical and metaphysical, all numbers give off vibrational energy which shapes the potential attitudes, talents, traits, and environment of an individual. However, Numerology can be much more complex than that. Numerology is in fact a valuable tool that is not only a method for researching a Name but can also provide the true meaning of the name you have selected. Here's how the process works. Your Name and Birthdate together form your "foundational" blueprint (Basic Numerology Master Chart) at birth, which remains with you your entire life or until you legally change your name.

In the baby naming process, since we do not have a Birthdate to work with yet, the next best thing we can do is to research the name. The name reveals the "core" personal characteristics, plus the eight soul qualities or lessons to be learned in this lifetime. By generating the Chord chart we can discover the three primary characteristics that determine the design that the infant will grow into and play a significant role in determining the most important characteristics of that individual. Even though we can only generate a partial blueprint, knowing the "core" characteristics will enable parents to choose a name based on the primary traits the characteristics calculate to be. It doesn't matter whether we are running a Chord Numerology chart for an infant or a Basic Numerology Master Chart for an adult, every blueprint has those three characteristics—and more—which will always remain the same until there is a legal name change, at which time the foundational blueprint may be altered slightly or greatly depending on the name change.

It is highly recommended that sometime after the birth of and before your child enters Kindergarten, that you have a Basic Numerology Master Chart generated based on the baby's name and birthdate. This will allow you to become aware of your child's foundational design and blueprint revealed by the numbers generated in the Numerology Chart, including your child's destiny, all of the personal characteristics, vibrational growth cycles and challenges, pinnacles, strengths and weaknesses, and soul lessons for his or her lifetime.

The type of personal information that you will receive about your child will be very surprising to say the least, once you've learned just how much information can be extracted from the chart. The information gleaned will empower you as a parent to guide your child with more exact clarity, insight, and understanding into the areas where you can help him or her the most because of the foresight you have received through the knowledge presented to you. Learn your child's Destiny, Soul/Heart's Desire, Personality, Purpose, Life Goal, Birthdate Cycles, Challenges, Pinnacles, and Soul Qualities (lessons to be learned or developed) and guide him or her accordingly by knowing each need, strength, and weakness.

The general information added in this section on baby naming was meant to provide enlightened parents on the importance of naming their baby that is not a part of our standard educational process or culture per se and how knowing your baby's design will enable parents to have a better insight into raising their child.

Check the Chord of the name you have chosen to see what the vibrational patterns calculate to be, and whether the outcome is a match for what you had in mind, for instance, your child's Personality. For example, if you come from a highly intellectual family, you may want your child to mirror the rest of the family's intelligence and follow in their footsteps. On the other hand, maybe you want your child to be more outgoing, expansive, and self-expressive as a contrast to and compliment to the "bookworm" type. To illustrate the Chord chart, we have provided you with two case studies using different baby naming examples, which will include the meaning of the Chord Numbers for the three core characteristics of the name—Soul/Heart's Desire, Personality, and Purpose.

The next section will show you (1) how to calculate the Chord numbers in addition to an explanation of the number combinations and what they mean for the name we are researching and (2) the steps in learning how to calculate the soul qualities revealed by the name after we have first explained their importance.

The Chaldean Alphabet/Formula tables will provide you the key to converting the name from letters into the "assigned" numbers as shown, followed by the explanation of the number meaning. It should be noted that the numbers will either convert to a single-digit number called a root number or to a double-digit compound number. The compound numbers that appear in the name have a special significance due to the high energy and intensity that are generated by these compound numbers. There are eight compound number combinations that contribute significant important in-depth information to the meaning of names. These Numbers are the 19/1, 11/2, 13/4, 22/4, 14/5, 23/5, 16/7, and 18/9.

IV.A Baby Naming Case Study #1: Baby Name Researched–Jennifer Marie Jones

IV.A.1 The Numbers of the Chord

Before describing the calculation process for the numbers of the Chord, we have given a brief explanation of the meaning of the numbers assigned to each of the three core characteristics that make up the Chord or vibrations (see figure 11–9) of the baby name. The three numbers outlined in the chart are unique only to the name you have selected. The descriptions are written to explain the meaning to this name.

Example of Calculating the Chord Numbers for Jennifer Marie Jones

Core Characteristics	Calculated Numbers
Soul/Heart's Desire	3
Personality	9
Purpose	3

Figure 11–9

Listed below are the descriptions for each of the three "core" characteristics:

Number 3 Soul/Heart's Desire

Creative, Enthusiastic, Inspirational

This is the emotional aspect and generates the innermost desire of how to express oneself in this world. The 3 Soul/Heart's Desire represents self-expression and creativity which form the keynote of this joyful and social vibration. This success can be enhanced with discipline and purpose.

Number 9 Personality

Compassionate Humanitarian, Multitalented

The Personality is the physical aspect of the entity, what others will see them as. The 9 Personality is sincere, well-balanced, truthful, noble, and dedicated to the service of mankind.

Number 3 Purpose

Create, Entertain, Inspire

The Purpose number reveals what the mission in life will be. The 3 Purpose is to bring inspiration through self-expression along with the talent for creativity and entertaining.

IV.A.2 Calculating the Soul/Heart's Desire Numbers (From the Vowels of the Baby Name)

The definition and explanation of the Soul/Heart's Desire are included in chapter 6, section 6.B. The description and meaning of the Soul/Heart's Desire numbers are included in chapter 8, section 8.B.

Soul/Heart's Desire Number
Two-Step Process on How to Calculate the Number of the Baby Name
Step 1

To find the number of the Vowels of the Baby Name (First, Middle, Last Name) under consideration, lay out each Name on a sheet of paper with room to place numbers below the letters (see figure 11–10 in illustration 11g). Using the values shown in table 11–1, assign the correct value to the letters of the Vowels of the Baby Name.

Step 2

To arrive at the Soul/Heart's Desire number of the Baby Name, you add the Vowel numbers together as indicated in illustration 11g. The final calculation number can add up to either be a single-digit root number or a double-digit compound number such as shown in table 7–3. If the final calculation number adds up to be one of the special compound numbers as shown in table 11–2, then you would not reduce that compound number down to a single-digit number. However, if the calculated compound number is not listed in table 11–2, then you would reduce that number down to a single-digit root number. These particular compound numbers provide significant additional information about that characteristic and that is why it is important to get a more in-depth interpretation of the actual meaning of the characteristic's patterns. (Note: Table 11–2 is an extraction of table 7–3.)

Chaldean Alphabet/Formula
Assigned Numbers with Letters Identified
Vowels Only

1	2	3	4	5	6	7	8
A				E	U	O	F
I							
Y							

Table 11–1

Double-Digit Compound Number Conversion Table

When the Final Number Adds Up To	The Number Converts To	Final Number Becomes
19	19/1	19/1
11	11/2	11/2
13	13/4	13/4
22	22/4	22/4
14	14/5	14/5
23	23/5	23/5
16	16/7	16/7
18	18/9	18/9

Table 11–2

Soul/Heart's Desire Number
<u>Illustration 11g</u>: Calculating the Numbers of the Vowels of the Full Baby Name (Add Only the Numbers for A, E, I, O, U, Y)

Example of Calculating the Soul/Heart's Desire Number of the Baby Name

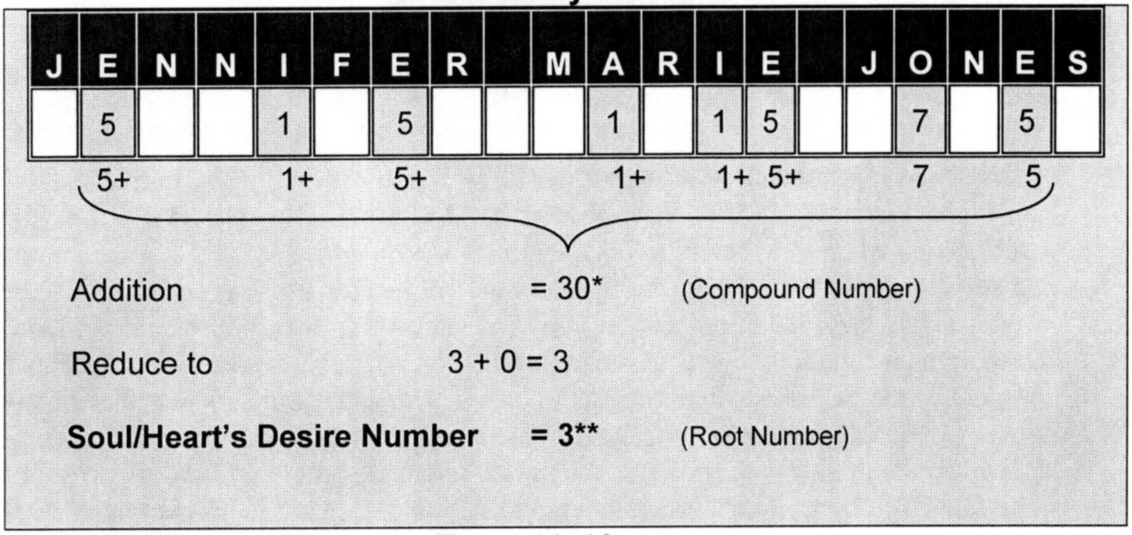

Figure 11–10

* See chapter 9 for Compound Number meanings.
** See chapter 8, section 8.B for the definition and explanation of Soul/Heart's Desire numbers.

IV.A.3 Calculating the Personality Number (From the Consonants of the Baby Name)

The definition and explanation of the Personality are included in chapter 6, section 6.C. The description and meaning of the Personality numbers are included in chapter 8, section 8.C.

Personality Number

Two-Step Process on How to Calculate the Number of the Baby Name

Step 1

To calculate the Consonant numbers of the full Baby Name, lay out the Name on a sheet of paper with room to place numbers below the letters (see figure 11–11 in illustration 11h). Now, using the numerical values shown in table 11–3, assign the correct number value to the letters of the consonants of the Baby name.

Step 2

To arrive at the Personality number of the Baby Name, you will need to add all of the Consonant numbers together as indicated in illustration 11h. The final calculation number can add up to either be a single-digit root number or a double-digit compound number such as shown in table 7–3. If the final calculation number adds up to be one of the special compound numbers as shown in table 11–2, then you would not reduce that compound number down to a single-digit number. However, if the calculated compound number is not listed in table 11–2, then you would reduce that number down to a single-digit root number. These particular compound numbers provide significant additional information about that characteristic and that is why it is important to get a more in-depth interpretation of the actual meaning of the characteristic's patterns. (Note: Table 11–2 is an extraction of table 7–3.)

Chaldean Alphabet/Formula
Assigned Numbers with Letters Identified
Consonants Only

1	2	3	4	5	6	7	8
	B	C	D				F
	K	G	M	H	V	Z	P
J	R	L	T	N	W		
Q		S		X			

Table 11–3

Double-Digit Compound Number Conversion Table

When the Final Number Adds Up To	The Number Converts To	Final Number Becomes
19	19/1	19/1
11	11/2	11/2
13	13/4	13/4
22	22/4	22/4
14	14/5	14/5
23	23/5	23/5
16	16/7	16/7
18	18/9	18/9

Table 11–2

Personality Number
Illustration 11h: Calculating the Numbers of the Consonants of the Baby Name (Add the Numbers of all the Letters Except for A, E, I, O, U, Y)

Example of Calculating the Personality Number of the Baby Name

J	E	N	N	I	F	E	R		M	A	R	I	E		J	O	N	E	S
1		5	5		8		2		4		2				1		5		3

1+ 5+ 5+ 8+ 2+ 4+ 2+ 1+ 5+ 3

Addition = 36* (Compound Number)

Reduce to 3 + 6 = 9

Personality Number = 9** (Root Number)

Figure 11–11

* See chapter 9 for Compound Number meanings.

** See chapter 8, section 8.C for the definition and explanation of Personality numbers.

IV.A.4 Calculating the Purpose Number (From the Letters of the Full Baby Name)

The definition and explanation of the Purpose are included in chapter 6, section 6.D. The description and meaning of the Purpose numbers are included in chapter 8, section 8.D.

Purpose Number

Two-Step Process on How to Calculate the Number of the Baby Name

Step 1

To calculate the Purpose number of the Baby Name, lay out the full Baby Name on a sheet of paper with room to place numbers below the letters (see figure 11–12 in illustration 11i). Now, using table 11–4, assign the correct number value to each of the letters of the Baby Name. Place the number of each letter underneath each corresponding letter as shown in figure 11–12.

Step 2

To arrive at the Purpose number of the Baby Name, you will need to add the numbers of all of the letters of the full Name together as indicated in 11i. The final calculation number can add up to either be a single-digit root number or a double-digit compound number such as shown in table 7–3. If the final calculation number adds up to be one of the special compound numbers as shown in table 11–2, then you would not reduce that compound number down to a single-digit number. However, if the calculated compound number is not listed in table 11–2, then you would reduce that number down to a single-digit root number. These particular compound numbers provide significant additional information about that characteristic and that is why it is important to get a more in-depth interpretation of the actual meaning of the characteristic's patterns. (Note: Table 11–2 is an extraction of table 7–3.)

Chaldean Alphabet/Formula
Assigned Numbers with Letters Identified

1	2	3	4	5	6	7	8
A	B	C	D	E	U	O	F
I	K	G	M	H	V	Z	P
J	R	L	T	N	W		
Q		S		X			
Y							

Table 11–4

Double-Digit Compound Number Conversion Table

When the Final Number Adds Up To	The Number Converts To	Final Number Becomes
19	19/1	19/1
11	11/2	11/2
13	13/4	13/4
22	22/4	22/4
14	14/5	14/5
23	23/5	23/5
16	16/7	16/7
18	18/9	18/9

Table 11–2

Purpose Number

Illustration 11i: Calculating the Numbers of the Full Baby Name (Add the Numbers of all of the Letters of the Full Name)

Example of Calculating the Purpose Number of the Baby Name

J	E	N	N	I	F	E	R		M	A	R	I	E		J	O	N	E	S
1	5	5	5	1	8	5	2		4	1	2	1	5		1	7	5	5	3

1+ 5+ 5+ 5+ 1+ 8+ 5+ 2+ 4+ 1+ 2+ 1+ 5+ 1+ 7+ 5+ 5+ 3

Addition = 66

Reduce to 6+ 6+ = 12* or 1 + 2 = 3

Purpose Number = 3** (Root Number)

Figure 11–12

* See chapter 9 for Compound Number meanings.

** See chapter 8, section 8.D for the definition and explanation of Purpose numbers.

IV.A.5 Calculating the Soul Quality Numbers (From the Letters of the Full Baby Name)

The birthname also reveals the Soul Qualities (SQ#) or growth areas for your infant that need to be developed in order to bring about balance, harmony, and equilibrium in his or her life. There are eight Soul Qualities and each is assigned a numerical value based on a formula used to calculate the Soul Qualities.

The definition and explanation of the Soul Qualities are included in Chapter 6, section 6.I. The description and meaning of the Soul Quality numbers are included in chapter 8, section 8.I.

There is a "rating" system associated with the Soul Qualities that will help you gauge just what areas your infant will need to develop. The numbers indicate if the particular Soul Quality has already been developed and to what degree, or if it is an area that must be developed in order to achieve his or her highest potential in this lifetime. The Chord chart for baby naming is unique in that it's the only entity in this chapter where the Soul Qualities apply.

The Soul Quality rating system is as follows: #1 (Leadership/Pioneer), #3 (Creativity/Social), and #5 (Freedom/Change), will have a normal value of 3, while Soul Qualities #2 (Partner/Sensitivity), #4 (Structure/Foundation), #6 (Domestic/Cosmic Parent), #7 (Teacher/Intellect), and #8 (Ambition/Balance), will have a normal value of 1. A zero (0) value on any Soul Quality means the person has a Karmic lesson to learn. A Soul Quality assigned a number value with a plus sign (+) means that the person has been developing this quality and exceeds the normal value indicated. A Soul Quality assigned a number value followed by a minus sign (–) means the person has not yet reached the particular level of understanding for that Soul Quality and has more work to do in that area in order to achieve balance and full potential.

The Soul Qualities are areas that need development and are found by discovering which vibrational patterns are "lacking" in the letters of the full name. Before describing the calculation process for the Soul Qualities, we are giving a brief explanation of the meaning of the numbers assigned to each of the eight development areas that make up the Chord of the baby name. For this exercise we will calculate the Soul Qualities for the name Jennifer Marie Jones.

Soul Quality Numbers

Three-Step Process on How to Calculate the Numbers of the Baby Name

Step 1

> Make a table to show how many of each of the Soul Quality values you have in your full Baby Name by writing the full Name on sheet of paper, as shown in table 11–5. Table 11–4 will be used to convert the letters of the baby name into numbers.

Step 2

> By using the following example in table 11–5, convert the letters in the Baby Name to numbers using the numbers assigned to letters in table 11–4.

Step 3

Count how many total 1s, 2s, 3s, 4s, 5s, 6s, 7s, and 8s there are in the Baby Name and create a matrix that shows the total number for each. Table 11–6 will give you the numerical value count for each Soul Quality.

Chaldean Alphabet/Formula
Assigned Numbers with Letters Identified

1	2	3	4	5	6	7	8
A	B	C	D	E	U	O	F
I	K	G	M	H	V	Z	P
J	R	L	T	N	W		
Q		S		X			
Y							

Table 11–4

Example of Calculating the Soul Quality Numbers of the Baby Name

Full Name	J	E	N	N	I	F	E	R		M	A	R	I	E		J	O	N	E	S
Conversion Numbers	1	5	5	5	1	8	5	2		4	1	2	1	5		1	7	5	5	3

Table 11–5

Example of the Soul Quality Numerical Value Count for the Name Jennifer Marie Jones

Soul Qualities & Development Areas 3 is Normal for SQs #1, 3, and 5 1 is Normal for SQs #2, 4, 6, 7, and 8 Plus Sign (+) is Above Normal Minus Sign (–) is Below Normal Zero (0-) is a Karmic Lesson	**Breakdown of Numbers in the Name**
SQ#1 Leadership/Pioneer	5+ (There are five 1s) – More than three
SQ#2 Partner/Sensitivity	2+ (There are two 2s) – More than one
SQ#3 Creativity/Social	1- (There is one 3) – Less than three
SQ#4 Structure/Foundation	1 (There is one 4) – Normal
SQ#5 Freedom/Change	7+ (There are seven 5s) – More than three
SQ#6 Domestic/Cosmic Parent	0- (There are "no" zeros) – Karmic lesson
SQ#7 Teacher/Intellect	1 (There is one 7) – Normal
SQ#8 Ambition/Balance	1 (There is one) – Normal

Table 11–6

Now you will need to apply the rating system to the numbers indicated in the breakdown of numbers column in table 11–6. In the table you will see either a minus sign (–), a plus sign (+), or a zero (0-) assigned instead of a number. Using the rating system you can determine if the development areas are underdeveloped (indicated by a minus sign [–]), overdeveloped (indicated by a plus sign [+]), developed (normal), or a Karmic lesson, which would be indicated by a zero minus [0-]). All you would need to do is to add the minus sign (–) or plus sign (+) sign to those numbers that apply using the standard rating system.

The standard number (normal) for Soul Qualities 1, 3, and 5 is 3. Therefore, if you have a number assigned to those Soul Qualities that exceeds 3, then the sign shown next to those numbers will be a plus sign (+). Less than 3 will show a minus sign (–). The standard number (normal) for Soul Qualities 2, 4, 6, 7, and 8 is 1. Therefore, if you have a number assigned to those Soul Qualities that exceeds 1, then the sign shown next to those number values, will be a plus sign (+). Less than 1 will show a minus sign (–). A zero (0-) indicates a Karmic lesson for this lifetime. Using the rating system helps determine a starting point and understanding where the baby's development may begin, based on generating the Chord chart.

Table 11–7 will take you through the process of interpreting the meaning and impact of the Soul Quality numerical values count shown in table 11–6. This will allow you to see the nature and importance of the information given to you through determining the effect of the Soul Qualities that you have already experienced, and those Soul Qualities that you still have to develop.

In the case example shown in table 11–7, the SQ#6 = 0- which would mean that there are "no" 6s in the name being tested; therefore, the zero (0-) represents a Karmic lesson in this lifetime. SQ#2 = 2+ which would mean that the sensitivity level of this baby is higher than normal and an area of development to overcome; hence, 2+ since the number should be a 1. The SQ#5 = 7+ is overdeveloped and may require balance because that number is four times higher than the norm.

Example of the Soul Quality Numbers Counted and Explained for the Name Jennifer Marie Jones

Represents Soul Qualities 1–8	Converting Letters into Numbers from the Full Name: Total Number of 1s, 2s, 3s, 4s, 5s, 6s, 7s, and 8s in the Name	Standard Rating System Number	What The Standard Rating System Means to You
1 Leader Pioneer Independent	5+ You have more than learned the lessons of leadership, pioneering, creative originality, and independence.	5+ Exceeds the standard 3	The 5 count indicates you are highly developed as a leader/pioneer and have the potential to be just that, wherever you are.
2 Diplomat Peacemaker Cooperative Spirit	2+ You have more than developed the ability to see both sides of the issues. You are balanced and wish to bring peace, harmony, cooperation, and sensitivity into the process of living.	2+ Exceeds the standard 1	The 2 indicates that the traits of this Soul Quality have been fully developed with the potential to become a diplomat, mediator, and peacemaker, promoting goodwill and cooperation wherever you are.
3 Self-Expression Sociability Entertainer	1- You need to continue to develop yourself socially, verbally, as well as in a creative, self-expressive manner, for these traits are either lacking or need to be improved.	1- Is less than the standard 3	The 1 count indicates you must work to improve your social skills as well as communication skills, and your ability to express your talents and ambition.
4 Structure Foundation Loyalty	1 You have developed the traits of a builder/carpenter who likes structure, discipline, foundation, and commitment.	1 Is equal to the standard 1	The 1 count indicates you have learned to put your affairs in order, are loyal, and know how to lay down a strong foundation.
5 Freedom Change Action	7+ You are more than capable of responding, adapting, and working to be part of the world while keeping your life in balance—balancing your "freedom" with your "responsibilities."	7+ Exceeds the standard 3	The 5 indicates you possess an investigative spirit and you fully understand the meaning of movement, change, travel, progress, communication, and curiosity.
6 Cosmic Parent Counselor Community	0- There are no 6s in this name therefore it's a "zero," a Karmic Lesson to be learned in this lifetime.	0- Is less than the standard 1	You must strive for a good balance between your emotions and intellect, the giving of service, and fulfilling domestic

			and community responsibilities.
7 Intellect Educator Loner	1 You have developed technical and intellectual skills, while at the same time, have the ability to understand what real "Faith" is all about.	1 Is equal to the standard 1	The 1 count indicates intellectual strength being reserved, aloof, selective, and analytical. You understand the mysteries of this Universe, and can share this gained knowledge with others as an educator.
8 Judgment Ambition Balance	1 You have developed compassion, sound judgment, ambition, and a desire for fame and success.	1 Is equal to the standard 1	The 1 count indicates that you have learned the meaning of responsibility, the making and proper use of money, and balance in spiritual and material pursuits.

Table 11–7

IV.B Baby Naming Case Study #2: Baby Name Researched–Grayson David Jones

Before describing the calculation process for the numbers of the Chord, we are giving a brief explanation of the meaning of the numbers assigned to each of the three core characteristics that make up the Chord (see figure 11–13) or vibrations of the baby name. The three numbers outlined in the chart are unique only to the name you have selected. The descriptions are written to explain the meaning to this name.

Example of Calculated Chord Numbers for Grayson David Jones

Core Characteristics	Calculated Numbers
Soul/Heart's Desire	23/5
Personality	9
Purpose	14/5

Figure 11–13

Below are the descriptions of each of the three "core" characteristics.

Number 23/5 Soul/Heart's Desire

Creative, Desire for Freedom and Change, Social

This is the emotional aspect and generates the innermost desire of how to express oneself in this world. The Number 5 Soul/Heart's Desire represents freedom, change, progress, movement, action, and variety—is highly enthusiastic, resourceful, and creative, and has a strong intuitive power from within, in addition to having fast mental and physical reflexes. The 23/5 Soul/Heart's Desire is the best vibration of all the Number 5 combinations. The 2 emphasizes peace, diplomacy, and receptivity, and complements the creative and joyful 3. The 23 has its root in the 5 which needs complete freedom, variety, and change. Combined together, these numbers create both a pleasant and lively vibration.

Number 9 Personality

Humanitarian, Noble, Sincere, Truthful, Well-Balanced

The Personality is the physical aspect of the being which is sincere, well-balanced, truthful, noble and dedicated to the service of mankind. The Personality is the physical aspect of the being which is sincere, well-balanced, truthful, noble and dedicated to the service of mankind.

Number 14/5 Purpose

Builder, Leader, Risk Taker

The Purpose number reveals what the mission in life will be. The Number 5 Purpose in life is to promote freedom. This involves bringing forth new ideas for the purpose of expansion and progress to pass these concepts on to others. The 14/5 Purpose represents the Root 5 which is the number of change, variety, and communication. The Number 1 represents creative and original leadership and individual freedom similar to the 5. Between them is the Number 4, which demands foundation, discipline, structure, and detail. This is known to be a vibration of change, disruption, and risk taking.

The practice of naming has probably been around since the beginning of time. Although all cultures and races use names, naming customs vary greatly from people to people. Using Numerology to decipher the hidden secrets that the name reveals prior to naming your baby will enable you to give your child an advantage in life by selecting his or her three core characteristics prior to birth. The second example of a Chord chart shown for Grayson David Jones is calculated exactly the same way as the chart for Jennifer Marie Jones.

IV.B.1 Calculating the Soul/Heart's Desire Number (From the Vowels of the Baby Name)

The definition and explanation of the Soul/Heart's Desire are included in chapter 6, section 6.B. The description and meaning of the Soul/Heart's Desire numbers are included in chapter 8, section 8.B.

Soul/Heart's Desire Number
Two-Step Process on How to Calculate the Number of the Baby Name
Step 1

To find the number of the Vowels of the Baby Name (First, Middle, Last Name) under consideration, lay out each Name on a sheet of paper with room to place numbers below the letters (see figure 11–14 in illustration 11j). Using the values shown in table 11–1, assign the correct value to the letters of the Vowels of the Baby Name.

Step 2

To arrive at the Soul/Heart's Desire number of the Baby Name, you add the Vowel numbers together as indicated in illustration 11j. The final calculation number can add up to either be a single-digit root number or a double-digit compound number such as shown in table 7–3. If the final calculation number adds up to be one of the special compound numbers as shown in table11–2, then you would not reduce that compound number down to a single-digit number. However, if the calculated compound number is not listed in table 11–2, then you would reduce that number down to a single-digit root number. These particular compound numbers provide significant additional information about that characteristic and that is why it is important to get a more in-depth interpretation of the actual meaning of the characteristic's patterns. (Note: Table 11–2 is an extraction of table 7–3.)

Chaldean Alphabet/Formula
Assigned Numbers with Letters Identified
Vowels Only

1	2	3	4	5	6	7	8
A				E	U	O	
I							
Y							

Table 11–1

Double-Digit Compound Number Conversion Table

When the Final Number Adds Up To	The Number Converts To	Final Number Becomes
19	19/1	19/1
11	11/2	11/2
13	13/4	13/4
22	22/4	22/4
14	14/5	14/5
23	23/5	23/5
16	16/7	16/7
18	18/9	18/9

Table 11–2

Soul/Heart's Desire Number
Illustration 11j: Calculating the Numbers of the Vowels of the Full Baby Name (Add Only the Numbers for A, E, I, O, U, Y)

Example of Calculating the Soul/Heart's Desire Number of the Baby Name

G	R	A	Y	S	O	N		D	A	V	I	D		J	O	N	E	S
		1	1		7				1		1				7		5	

1+ 1+ 7+ 1+ 1+ 7+ 5

Addition = 23* or 23/5
(Compound Number)

(Do Not Reduce the 23/5 down to a Root Number)

Soul/Heart's Desire Number = 23/5**

Figure 11–14

* See chapter 9 for Compound Number meanings.
** See chapter 8, section 8.B for the definition and explanation of Soul/Heart's Desire numbers.

IV.B.2 Calculating the Personality Number (Consonants of the Baby Name)

The definition and explanation of the Personality are included in chapter 6, section 6.C. The description and meaning of the Personality numbers are included in chapter 8, section 8.C.

Personality Number

Two-Step Process on How to Calculate the Number of the Baby Name

Step 1

To calculate the Consonant numbers of the Baby Name, lay out the Name on a sheet of paper with room to place numbers below the letters (see figure 11–15 in illustration 11k). Now, using the numerical values shown in table 11–3, assign the correct number value to the letters of the Consonants.

Step 2

To arrive at the Personality number of the Baby Name, you will need to add all of the Consonant numbers together as indicated in illustration 11k. The final calculation number can add up to either be a single-digit root number or a double-digit compound number such as shown in table 7–3. If the final calculation number adds up to be one of the special compound numbers as shown in table 11–2, then you would not reduce that compound number down to a single-digit number. However, if the calculated compound number is not listed in table 11–2, then you would reduce that number down to a single-digit root number. These particular compound numbers provide significant additional information about that characteristic and that is why it is important to get a more in-depth interpretation of the actual meaning of the characteristic's patterns. (Note: Table 11–2 is an extraction of table 7–3.)

Chaldean Alphabet/Formula
Assigned Numbers with Letters Identified
Consonants Only

1	2	3	4	5	6	7	8
	B	C	D				F
	K	G	M	H	V	Z	P
J	R	L	T	N	W		
Q		S		X			

Table 11–3

Double-Digit Compound Number Conversion Table

When the Final Number Adds Up To	The Number Converts To	Final Number Becomes
19	19/1	19/1
11	11/2	11/2
13	13/4	13/4
22	22/4	22/4
14	14/5	14/5
23	23/5	23/5
16	16/7	16/7
18	18/9	18/9

Table 11–2

Personality Number

Illustration 11k: Calculating the Numbers of the Consonants of the Full Baby Name (Add the Numbers of all the Letters Except for A, E, I, O, U, Y)

Example of Calculating the Personality Number of the Baby Name

G	R	A	Y	S	O	N		D	A	V	I	D		J	O	N	E	S
3	2			3		5		4		6		4		1		5		3

3+ 2+ 3+ 5+ 4+ 6+ 4+ 1+ 5+ 3

Addition = 36* (Compound Number)

Reduce to 3+ 6 = 9

Personality Number = 9** (Root Number)

Figure 11–15

* See chapter 9 for Compound Number meanings.

** See chapter 8, section 8.C for the definition and explanation of Personality numbers.

IV.B.3 Calculating the Purpose Number (From the Full Baby Name)

The definition and explanation of the Purpose are included in chapter 6, section 6.D. The description and meaning of the Purpose numbers are included in chapter 8, section 8.D.

Purpose Number

Two-Step Process on How Calculate the Number of the Baby Name

Step 1

To calculate the Purpose number, lay out the full Baby Name on a sheet of paper with room to place numbers below the letters (see figure 11–16 in illustration 111). Now, using table 11–4, assign the correct number value to each of the letters of the Baby Name. Place the number of each letter underneath each corresponding letter as shown in figure 11–16.

Step 2

To arrive at the Purpose number of the Baby Name, you will need to add the numbers of all of the letters of the full Baby Name together as indicated in illustration 111. The final calculation number can add up to either be a single-digit root number or a double-digit compound number such as shown in table 7–3. If the final calculation number adds up to be one of the special compound numbers as shown in table 11–2, then you would not reduce the compound number down to a single-digit number. However, if the calculated compound number is not listed in table 11–2, then you would reduce that number down to a single-digit root number. These particular compound numbers provide significant additional information about that characteristic and that is why it is important to get a more in-depth interpretation of the actual meaning of the characteristic's patterns. (Note: Table 11–2 is an extraction of table 7–3.)

Chaldean Alphabet/Formula
Assigned Numbers with Letters Identified

1	2	3	4	5	6	7	8
A	B	C	D	E	U	O	F
I	K	G	M	H	V	Z	P
J	R	L	T	N	W		
Q		S		X			
Y							

Table 11–4

Double-Digit Compound Number Conversion Table

When the Final Number Adds Up To	The Number Converts To	Final Number Becomes
19	19/1	19/1
11	11/2	11/2
13	13/4	13/4
22	22/4	22/4
14	14/5	14/5
23	23/5	23/5
16	16/7	16/7
18	18/9	18/9

Table 11–2

Purpose Number
Illustration 111: Calculating the Numbers of the Full Baby Name (Add the Numbers of all of the Letters of the Full Baby Name)

Example of Calculating the Purpose Number of the Baby Name

G	R	A	Y	S	O	N		D	A	V	I	D		J	O	N	E	S
3	2	1	1	3	7	5		4	1	6	1	4		1	7	5	5	3

3+ 2+ 1+ 1+ 3+ 7+ 5+ 4+ 1+ 6+ 1+ 4+ 1+ 7+ 5+ 5+ 3

Addition = 59 or 5+ 9 = 14* or 14/5
(Compound Number)

(Do Not Reduce the 14/5 Down to a Root Number)

Purpose Number = 14/5**

Figure 11–16

* See chapter 9 for Compound Number meanings.
** See chapter 8, section 8.D for the definition and explanation of Purpose numbers.

IV.B.4 Calculating the Soul Quality Numbers (From the Letters of the Baby Name)

As stated in IV.A.5, the birthname reveals the Soul Qualities or growth areas for your infant that need to be developed in order to bring about balance, harmony, and equilibrium in his or her life—and, the eight Soul Qualities are each assigned a numerical value. The "rating" system associated with the Soul Qualities, which helps parents to gauge what areas the infant will need to develop, is also discussed.

The definition and explanation of the Soul Qualities are included in chapter 6, section 6.I. The description and meaning of the Soul Quality numbers are included in chapter 8, section 8.I. For this exercise we will calculate the Soul Qualities for the name Grayson David Jones.

Soul Quality Numbers

Three-Step Process on How to Calculate Numbers of the Baby Name

Step 1

Make a table to show how many of each of the Soul Quality values there are in the full Baby Name by writing the Baby Name on sheet of paper, as shown in table 11–4. Table 11–8 will be used to convert the letters of the Baby Name into numbers.

Step 2

By using the following example in table 11–8, convert the letters in the Baby's Name to numbers using the numbers assigned to letters in table 11–4.

Step 3

Count how many 1s, 2s, 3s, 4s, 5s, 6s, 7s, and 8s there are in the Baby Name and create a matrix that shows the total number for each (see table 11–9). This gives you the numerical value count for each Soul Quality.

Chaldean Alphabet/Formula
Assigned Numbers with Letters Identified

1	2	3	4	5	6	7	8
A	B	C	D	E	U	O	F
I	K	G	M	H	V	Z	P
J	R	L	T	N	W		
Q		S		X			
Y							

Table 11–4

Example of Calculating the Soul Qualities of the Baby Name

Full Name	G	R	A	Y	S	O	N		D	A	V	I	D		J	O	N	E	S
Conversion Numbers	3	2	1	1	3	7	5		4	1	6	1	4		1	7	5	5	3

Table 11–8

Example of the Soul Quality Numerical Count for the Name Grayson David Jones

Soul Qualities & Development Areas 3 is Normal for SQs #1, 3, and 5 1 is Normal for SQs #2, 4, 6, 7, and 8 Plus (+) is Above Normal Minus (–) is Below Normal Zero (0-) Represents a Karmic Lesson	**Breakdown of Numbers in the Name**
SQ#1 (Leadership/Pioneer)	5+ (There are five 1s) – More than three
SQ#2 (Partner/Sensitivity)	1 (There is one 2) – Normal
SQ#3 (Creativity/Social)	3 (There are three 3s) – Normal
SQ#4 (Structure/Foundation)	2+ (There are two 4s) – More than one
SQ#5 (Freedom/Change)	3 (There are seven 5s) – Normal
SQ#6 (Domestic/Cosmic Parent)	1 (There is one 6) – Normal
SQ#7 (Teacher/Intellect)	2+ (There are two 7s) – More than one
SQ#8 (Ambition/Balance)	0- (There are "no" zeros) – Karmic lesson

Table 11–9

Interpreting the Meaning and Impact of the Soul Quality Number Count

In the case of the Baby Name Grayson David Jones shown in table 11–9, the SQ#8 = zero (0-) means that there are "no" 8s in the name being tested; therefore, the zero (0-) represents a Karmic lesson in this lifetime. The SQ#1 = 5+ indicates an area that is overdeveloped, and alerts you to be aware of a potential domineering aspect of the Number 1, and to work to bring that influence into balance. SQ#2 = 1, which means that the sensitivity level of this baby is normal. Using the rating system helps determine a starting point and understanding where the baby's development may begin based on generating the Chord chart.

For a more complete understanding of the process of interpreting the meaning and impact of the Soul Quality numerical values count, refer to section IV.A.5, subsection b., where the process shown in table 11–7 takes you through the breakdown of numbers for the Baby Name Jennifer Marie Jones. This will allow you to see the nature and importance of the information given to you by determining the effect of the Soul Qualities revealed in the baby name that have been developed and those Soul Qualities that have yet to be developed.

When you think about it, a baby name selection is a significant and serious decision. Choosing the right name for your infant is one of the first and most important things you will ever do for your new baby. Remember, you and your newborn will have to live with the name for a lifetime whether he or she will like the name you have selected or not. And it's how the world will identify your child. The more insight you have into the powerful influence of a name before assigning it, the greater the opportunity to enjoy the success your child is capable of achieving based on the vibrational patterns inherent in the name you choose. Chaldean Numerology can help you choose the best possible name.

###

Chapter 12: The Numbers of Addresses, Street Names, and Apartment Numbers

I. Defining the Influence of Addresses and Street Names

Through the information presented in this chapter, we are laying the groundwork for determining what the numbers of your home address, and street name, and place of business reveal, and understanding the very real importance of selecting a residence or place of business with an address that is in tune with the numbers of your core characteristics—your Destiny, Soul/Heart's Desire, Personality, and Purpose. If your personal numbers match the vibrational patterns of the numbers of the home or business address, you are more likely to be happy living and working in that particular environment.

Sometimes you take the "places" that you experience, where you live and move and take part in the action, for granted. If it is a city, well, you have no control over that environment, right? Wrong! You have the right to choose which city, state, country, etc., in which you are going to reside—even if you believe that you don't. You have the right to choose the neighborhood in which you wish to live, and to select where your home will be—whether it's a single-family house, a duplex, an apartment, a condominium, or a townhouse, etc. You also have the right to select the address (which includes the street name and number, and "suite" number) which will be the home of your business. And, it seems that it would also be in your best interest to know the vibrational patterns of the place of business where you are employed and how they affect and impact the patterns of your "personal" design and blueprint.

If, and this is a big if, you somehow find yourself in the uncommon situation where you have no choices, you can still allow yourself to become aware of what to expect in whatever environment you find yourself in. By understanding the language of the "names" and "numbers"—which shape the environments around you—you can become informed with information available to you through the interpretation of the vibrational patterns behind the numbers which are a part of such environments.

We cannot emphasize enough the importance of consciously selecting the street name and numbers of any place in which you find yourself, to be assured that the vibrations of that place are (1) primarily in tune with the numbers and vibrational patterns of your major characteristics, or (2) if not in tune, that you make yourself aware of any potential conflicting vibrations so that you can prepare for any contingency actions or decisions which you may need to make with confidence and knowing. For if your numbers match the vibrational patterns of the numbers of the addresses at which you find yourself as you move through life, you are more likely to be happy and content living or working in that particular environment.

Now, whatever city, state, or country you find yourself in, your focus is always concentrated on, "Where am I going to live or work or play?"—it is personal and immediate.

So, instead of taking it for granted that an address is an address is an address, or one house or apartment or building is the same as another house or apartment or building, you now have the opportunity to make informed choices and decisions through the information that the Numerology of the addresses which affect your personal life and concerns can provide you.

Note here that we are not talking about style, design, blueprints, or personal preferences in architecture or view or class of location. We are talking about the space (environment) in which you move and live. Your "home" is the place where your family, personal possessions, and sacred space is centered, where your private story takes shape, and where quiet joys, plans, and hopes are imagined and experienced. Your business or employment environment is the place where you spend hours using your energy, expressing yourself creatively, and developing disciplines which you hope will lead to success and achievement.

Would you be surprised to learn that the numbers of your home and work address reveal the vibrational patterns inside your home or office, and the combination of the street numbers and the street name reveal the vibrational patterns of the local area surrounding these places? Your home and office have a location marker, an address, which is an identifier made up of street names and numbers. Well, the "names and numbers" of these places do indeed give off particular vibrational patterns based on the Numerology of those addresses. You shouldn't be surprised to learn that the street numbers and name of your address (including the apartment number where you live, the suite number of your business or place of employment, etc.) reveal the energy and potential patterns of the environment within your home and within the place you work, as well as the potential environment "outside" of your home and place of doing business in the area (neighborhood) around your home and work place.

What's the purpose of knowing this information? How would this information benefit you? Now, you don't have to wonder where you can get this information, the answer is simple. Numerology! It provides you with another unique tool that can reveal definitive information not found anywhere else that may save you from uncertainty, confusion, heartache, and potential financial loss in the near term. And this requires very little effort on your part. Wouldn't it be useful to know prior to moving into a new residence—whether renting or buying—if the dwelling is a match for your personality, the patterns of your life, your desires, or your potential future? Wouldn't it be of value to you to understand the vibration patterns and your reactions to the patterns that move in and through your work or business environment? This may sound a little far out to those not aware of Numerology and what can be gleaned from numbers. However, those who accept the truths of this age-old science know the importance and value of a quick calculation to determine the vibrational patterns of that residence before making the move.

The address numbers are more important than the street name in that the vibrational patterns of the "numbers" of the address foretell the potential experiences that will be attracted to the environment within your home or place of work. The street name represents the influence of the neighborhood (outside), so its importance is not as "personal" or immediate as the effects of the patterns "inside" your work and living space. Ultimately, the combination of both the street numbers and name will define your living environment and surroundings. Provided is an example of how to calculate the numbers of the address number and street name of a house to reveal the vibrational patterns of a residence using the address of 5248 Pope Street. We will first calculate the house address numbers in figure 12–1. The calculation of the numbers of the street name and numbers is a three-step process. Also, if the address contains an apartment number such as #B12, or unit number #25, you would not factor those additional numbers or letters into this calculation; however, if you wanted to know the vibrational patterns of your apartment/unit number, then you would calculate that number independent of the street number and name. For this particular exercise, we are only looking to discover the vibrational patterns of the street "address" number and street "name." If an address contains "Drive," "Street," "Boulevard," or "Lane," then those names would be considered a part of the formal street name.

II. Calculating the Street Address (The Number and Name)

Street Address Number

Three-Step Process on How to Calculate Number and Name of the Street Address

Step 1

Lay out the Street Address (Number and Name) on a sheet of paper (in this case, the house address of 5248 Pope Street). Then add up the street numbers and reduce to a single-digit.

Step 2

Now you will convert the letters of the street Name into numbers using the Chaldean Alphabet formula in table 12–1. The letters of the street name are represented by numerical values (numbers) as shown in figure 12–2; so we reverse engineer the letters of the street name to convert them into numbers, then calculate the street name number.

Step 3

To calculate the "final" number of your address (the sum of the address number and street name) add the number from Step 1 to the number in Step 2, as shown in figure 12–3.

Example of Calculating the Number of the Street Address

	5 + 2 + 4 + 8 **Pope Street**	
	=19	
Addition	1 + 9 = 10	(Compound Number)
Reduce to	1 + 0 = 1	
Number of the Address	**= 1***	(Root Number)

Figure 12–1

* The 1 represents independence, creative originality, new beginnings, and paving new roads for others to follow. This is a home with a positive vibration, good energy, and progressive influence. The 19 is a special compound number and is explained in chapter 9.

Chaldean Alphabet/Formula Number Assignment with Letters Identified

1	2	3	4	5	6	7	8
A	B	C	D	E	U	O	F
I	K	G	M	H	V	Z	P
J	R	L	T	N	W		
Q		S		X			
Y							

Table 12–1

Example of Calculating the Street Name into Numbers

Street Name	P	O	P	E		S	T	R	E	E	T
Conversion Numbers	8	7	8	5		3	4	2	5	5	4

8+ 7+ 8+ 5+ 3+ 4+ 2+ 5+ 5+ 4

Addition = 51* (Compound Number)

Reduce to 5+ 1 = 6

Street Name Number = **6**** (Root Number)

Figure 12–2

* See chapter 9 for Compound Number meanings.
** The 6 indicates that the street neighborhood has a domestic and warm vibration representing a family/community environment.

Example of Calculating the Final Number of the House Address

	Number (Numerical Value) of the Address Number		Number (Numerical Value) of the Street Name
Addition	(from Step–1)		(from Step–2)
	1	+	6

Number of the Home Address
Street Name and Number = 7*

Figure 12–3

* The 7 is the number of self-preservation. This is known as the caretaker vibration, indicating the neighbors would be family-oriented (from the Number of the street name = 6) and watchful of their neighborhood.

If you want to know what the vibrational patterns are of your apartment/unit number you live in or will be moving into, then you would calculate that number independent of the street number and name. In the following two exercises, we will show you how to calculate the apartment/unit number using the Chaldean Alphabet/Formula to turn letters into numbers then apply a formula resulting in a single-digit root number or a compound number.

Chaldean Alphabet/Formula
Number Assignment with Letters Identified

1	2	3	4	5	6	7	8
A	B	C	D	E	U	O	F
I	K	G	M	H	V	Z	P
J	R	L	T	N	W		
Q		S		X			
Y							

Table 12–2

III. Calculating Apartment Building/Unit Numbers

Example of Calculating an Apartment/Unit Number
Apartment Building/Unit #B12

Apartment Building/Unit #B12
This is Building B, Apartment #12

Add Only the Apartment Numbers together

1 + 2 = 3

The Apartment/Unit Number calculates to be a "3" or an environment keyed to self-expression and creativity, keynotes of a social vibration.

Figure 12–4

Example of Calculating an Apartment/Unit Number
Apartment Building/Unit #CC49

Apartment Building/Unit #CC49
This is Building CC, Apartment #49

Add Only the Apartment Numbers together
4 + 9 = 13 or 13/4

This Apartment/Unit Number calculates to be a "13/4" or an environment surrounding joy and stability.

Figure 12–5

Double-Digit Compound Number Conversion Table

When the Final Number Adds Up To	The Number Converts To	Final Number Becomes
19	19/1	19/1
11	11/2	11/2
13	13/4	13/4
22	22/4	22/4
14	14/5	14/5
23	23/5	23/5
16	16/7	16/7
18	18/9	18/9

Table 12–3

Apartment/Unit Number
Two-Step Process on How to Calculate the Number
Step 1

> Lay out the Apartment Building/Unit Number on a sheet of paper. Then convert all of the letters using the Chaldean Alphabet/Formula (see table 12–3) to convert letters into numbers.

Step 2

> Lay out the Apartment Building/Unit Number on a sheet of paper. Then convert all letters using the Chaldean Alphabet/Formula to convert letters into numbers. Add all of the numbers together. If the number calculates to be a Compound Number, as shown in table 12–3 (such as 13/4), then the number would not be reduced down. The 13/4 Compound Number represents the whole vibrational pattern of the apartment/unit.

Calculating the potential energy and patterns around and within a home will obviously be different than an apartment/unit since the apartment/unit will have a unique number assigned to it as opposed to a house that's only assigned the street number and name.

For instance, if 5248 Pope Street were an apartment building instead of a house and the apartment number was #141, the numerical value of the apartment "home" would be 6 (1+ 4+ 1 = 6), which defines the vibrational patterns within the apartment. This is a pattern favorable to family and community living, and along with the Number 6 patterns of the "neighborhood," makes this an ideal family environment. Now, if that environment is in tune with you and your family's personal numbers, you would have found an excellent place to live in.

If you are looking for a happy and peaceful home, avoid specific numbers, such as the 11/2, 14/5, 16/7, etc., that represent disruption, risky business, emotionally charged patterns, or a Karmic vibration. You can greatly benefit on all levels by understanding the meaning of numbers, how they affect your life, and how you use that knowledge to make better decisions

The following case studies are just two examples of how Numerology was used to decipher the code that showed what was wrong with these particular homes. What other resource on the market do you know of that could compare with this type of analysis in determining a logical explanation of this situation?

IV. Case Studies

a. Illness that Stemmed from Moving into the Wrong Home–Case Study #1

Jane and her family were being transferred to California on short notice and had to find a new residence within a week. A quick trip to California proved successful and Jane purchased a home during that week and felt confident that she had selected the perfect home. After moving in, Jane discovered many things wrong with the house that she had not noticed before. Strange things were happening in the home that could not be explained, and the family was feeling ill since moving in. She was at a loss to figure out a solution to this expensive mistake.

Jane explained her dilemma at a gathering and asked about having a chart generated to determine whether or not the vibrational patterns stemming from her home address were compatible with her characteristics, in the hope of discovering answers to the strange, unexplained occurrences. The street numbers indicated that the vibrational patterns coming from the home were emotionally charged, shocking, and highly volatile, while the neighborhood revealed risky business and was highly disruptive. In asking a few questions about the exact location of the home, we learned that her house was directly in the path of carbon monoxide fumes coming from busy intersections close to her home which we had to assume was causing the illnesses in the family, since there were no medical reasons for their symptoms. Intuitively Jane knew the explanation given to her was correct and she decided to sell the house.

b. Purchase of a Highly Volatile Versus Peaceful Home–Case Study #2

A client and her partner bought a home in a particular area without really checking out the neighborhood first. After living there for a couple of months, both noticed they were continually agitated. They wanted a Numerology chart generated based on the house numbers to see what they revealed. The house numbers indicated that the home itself was very electrical in nature, emotional, and highly charged, in addition to the surrounding area being disruptive and noisy. When the verdict was in, both were surprised to learn what the vibrational patterns for this house were. Instead of living in a peaceful home, it was just the opposite. They were amazed at how accurate the reading was which confirmed their worst fears that the purchase of this house was an impulsive buy. A decision was made to live there for another six months while looking for a home with harmonizing vibrational patterns to match theirs—they now realized the importance of the meaning behind address numbers and street names.

###

Chapter 13:
The Numbers of the Personal Years

I. Defining the Influence of the Personal Year Numbers

The influence of the Personal Year, which is calculated from your Birthdate, defines and explains the nature of the vibrational patterns that will appear in your upcoming Personal Years, and, if you are interested, can show you the patterns of past years, which perhaps may clear up the reason or reasons that a particular year was extraordinarily good or not so good. This information will help you understand the patterns of those things that are happening "now," within the current year, or soon to be happening later. When you enter a particular year, you will find that year's experiences developing in a certain way within vibrational patterns specific to you. Your Personal Year patterns are set up to form or take the shape of, if you will, the "potential" events, situations, and associations that resonate to a particular environment defined by your Personal Year numbers. By knowing these things, you can prepare for the coming events, conditions, or situations that will be possibilities in that year. You will be given a "heads up" look at the coming year's happenings, an early warning description of things to come. By knowing the potential experiences reflected in the vibrational patterns of the Personal Year, you can use your resources to your greatest advantage.

Each Personal Year's vibrational patterns gives you a mini-blueprint within your "larger" blueprint, like reference pages in your "owner's manual." The information becomes available to you anytime you wish to see it—now, a month from now, a year from now, or ten years from now. You can take advantage of all the things written upon the pages of your "owner's manual," which lay out a mini-blueprint of each specific Personal Year that you want to "read" about. And, you can move the activities that interest you in the direction you want to take them, change the approach or strategy for experiencing them, or take action to minimize or avoid any potential discomfort or disadvantage. The important thing to know about your Personal Year vibrational patterns is that the more you prepare to take advantage of them, the greater your success and satisfaction will be.

What if you could find out the best years (and the best times during the year) to start a business, change careers, take a trip, or take a vacation, before you even planned it? What if you could learn what kinds of patterns and experiences were going to prevail in a particular year? You could develop a stronger business plan, investigate potential career changes without being rushed, and craft your vacation, business trip, or special event to get maximum enjoyment for the potential patterns that are taking shape for that year. You could become aware of and make maximum preparations for potential conditions that will influence the experiences in which you may want to participate. What are the favorable times for doing these special things? Would it be best to know or to just get potluck?

Knowing about and understanding the language of the numbers of your Personal Years can help you enjoy each year's contribution to your life experiences even more.

II. Calculating the Numbers of the Personal Years

A Personal Year number is found by adding the number of your Birth Month to your Birth Day, then adding that sum to the number of the Universal Year (calendar year) in which you are interested. (Note: This chapter will introduce you to the use of the "Universal Year" number in the calculation of Personal Year numbers. However, chapter 16 will contain a more definitive discussion of Universal Years, Months, and Days.) The other interesting thing about determining the numbers of your Personal Years is the fact that it is important to note the "time" of the year in which your Birthday falls, since that fact has an essential part to play in selecting the correct Universal Year number included in the formula. If your Birthday falls in the "first" half of the year, the "current" calendar (Universal) year number is used to calculate your Personal Year. If your Birthday falls in the "last" half of the year, the "following" calendar (Universal) year number is used to calculate your Personal Year. The calculations of the Personal Year numbers are shown in two examples in II.A and II.B.

The selection and use of the Universal Year numbers in the formulas will be included in the calculations in II.A and II.B. That is, one example will show you the process for calculating your Personal Year number when your Birthday falls in the First Half of the Universal (calendar) Year. And another example will show you the process for calculating your Personal Year number when your Birthday falls in the Last Half of the Universal (calendar) Year.

As mentioned above, and as shown in the examples, the calculation of your Personal Year numbers is dependent on Universal Year numbers. As such, your Personal Year's patterns will be shaped from the overarching vibrational patterns of the Universal (calendar) Year which affect everyone and everything in the same way. The Universal Year patterns, in and of themselves, are "beyond" your control, until the Numerology formula translates the Universal Year patterns into patterns of "your" Personal Year. This is especially true in regard to shaping the environmental patterns of the physical world around you. For it is the world you live in, such as it is.

There are potential events unfolding in your Personal Year, as well as multiple conditions and situations occurring simultaneously. People of all walks of life, cultures, religions, political views, and more, are interacting and reacting to those events. Since the formula for calculating the Personal Year number includes your Birth Month and Day numbers, this inclusion "personalizes" the Universal Year vibrational patterns to reveal those potential experiences that are a part of only your design and blueprint.

Your primary concern and question should be "How am I going to respond to what is revealed to me?" The best response is to determine what events you want to participate in, when you want to participate, for how long, with whom, etc., thereby choosing the nature and timing of your actions. What you choose or decide to do (or not do) will affect the direction and shape of these Universal Year vibrational patterns within your blueprint, to a larger degree than you may think. Again, the reminder of what is unique and unusual about this calculation process is that the Universal Year Number *may or may not* be exactly the same number as the current calendar year, since the calculation depends on which part of the Universal Year your birthday falls in.

For instance, if you were born *before* June 30 of the year (in the First Half of the calendar year), the overarching vibrational patterns of the "current" calendar year influence your Personal Year patterns. That is, the current calendar year number will be the number of the Universal Year that you use in the calculation of your Personal Year. However, if you were born *after* June 30 of the year, the overarching vibrational patterns of the next calendar year, that is, the Universal (calendar) Year number "following" your birthday, bring your Personal Year under the influence of the next Universal Year patterns. Examples 1 and 2, shown in illustration 13a, will discuss the differences in formulas and calculation of the Personal Years. This will be discussed and shown to you in the instructions and calculations for illustration 13a.

Within illustration 13a, we will first take you through a three-step process for calculating the numbers of your Personal Years in Example 1, where the Birthday falls in the First Half of the calendar year. This will be followed by instructions for a three-step process in Example 2, where the Birthday falls in the Last Half of the calendar year. Then, you will be shown the actual calculations in illustration 13a (figure 13–1 and figure 13–2) for determining the numbers of your Personal Years. Once you have written down the "dates" of the Birthdays as shown in Example 1 and Example 2, you can follow the calculation process as laid out in the illustration.

To support the calculation of Personal Year numbers, we are providing a list of the "numbers" of the Universal Years in table 13–1.

Example of Universal (Calendar) Year Numbers Reduced Down

2006 = 8	2015 = 8	2024 = 8
2007 = 9	2016 = 9	2025 = 9
2008 = 1	2017 = 1	2026 = 1
2009 = 2	2018 = 2	2027 = 2
2010 = 3	2019 = 3	2028 = 3
2011 = 4	2020 = 4	2029 = 4
2012 = 5	2021 = 5	2030 = 5
2013 = 6	2022 = 6	2031 = 6
2014 = 7	2023 = 7	2032 = 7

Table 13–1

II.A Example #1–Personal Year Birthdays in the First Half of the Year

Personal Years
Three-Step Process on How to Calculate the Numbers for Birthdays in the First Half of the Calendar Year
Step 1

Lay out the Birth Month, Day, and Calendar Year (for the year you are interested in) on a sheet of paper. Then select the appropriate Universal Year number from table 13–1. The Birthday in Example 1, March 4, 2006, falls in the First Half of Calendar Year 2006 (between January 1 and June 30). Therefore, the Universal Year closest to the Birthday to use in the calculation of the Personal Year is the "current" calendar year (2006). The Universal Year number to be included in the Personal Year calculation formula for this example is taken from table 13–1 (2006 = 8).

Step 2

Next, you add the numbers of the Birth Month and Birth Day and the appropriate Universal Year number. The number of the month (March) is 3. The Number of the day is 4. The Universal Year (2006) Number is 8. You now add 3 + 4 + 8 = 15 = 1 + 5 = 6.

Step 3

The Personal Year number for Birthdays in the First Half of the Year can add up to either be a single-digit root number or a double-digit compound number such as shown in table 7–3. If the final calculation number adds up to be one of the special compound numbers as shown in table 13–2, then you would not reduce that compound number down to a single-digit number. However, if the calculated compound number is not listed in table 13–2, then you would reduce that number down to a single-digit root number. These particular compound numbers provide significant additional information about that characteristic and that is why it is important to get a more in-depth interpretation of the actual meaning of the characteristic's patterns. (Note: Table 13–2 is an extraction of table 7–3.)

Double-Digit Compound Number Conversion Table

When the Final Number Adds Up To	The Number Converts To	Final Number Becomes
19	19/1	19/1
11	11/2	11/2
13	13/4	13/4
22	22/4	22/4
14	14/5	14/5
23	23/5	23/5
16	16/7	16/7
18	18/9	18/9

Table 13–2

Figure 13–1 is a graphic representation of the calculation process in Example 1.

Example of Finding a Personal Year Number in the First Half of the Calendar Year

March 4, 2006*

3+ 4+ 8

Addition = 15**

Reduce to 1 + 5 = 6

Personal Year Number = 6

Figure 13–1

* 2006 is the Universal Year Number 8; see table 13-1.
** See chapter 9 for Compound Number meanings.

Here is a brief summary write-up of the figure 13–1 Personal Year calculation process for a birthday that falls in the First Half of the calendar year (between January 1 and June 30). The number of the Universal Year that is used in the calculation of the Personal Year is the current calendar year. Since the birthday, March 4, 2006, is in the first 6 months of calendar year 2006, the "Universal Year" Number of 2006 (8) is used in calculating your Personal Year. A restatement of the calculations in figure 13–1 is as follows. You add 3 (the Number of the month of March) to 4 (the Number of the Birth Day) to 8 (the Number of the Universal Year that is the closest to your Birthday, that is, 2006 which is the current year). This sum, 3 + 4 + 8, is equal to the Compound Number 15. Since this Compound Number is not listed in table 13–2, it is reduced down to its Root Number 6 (1 + 5). Therefore, the final "numerical value" (number) of the Personal Year for March 4, 2006 is 6.

II.B Example #2–Personal Year Birthdays in the Last Half of the Year

Personal Years
Three-Step Process on How to Calculate the Numbers for Birthdays in the Last Half of the Calendar Year

Step 1

Lay out the Birth Month, Day, and Calendar (Universal) Year (for the year you are interested in) on a sheet of paper. Then select the Universal Year closest to the birthday from table 13–1 as follows. The Birthday, September 21, 2006, in example 2 falls in the Last Half of calendar year 2006 (between July 1 and December 31). Therefore, the Universal Year to use in the calculation of the Personal Year is the "following" calendar year, 2007. The Universal Year number for the calculation formula for this example is taken from table 13–1 (2007 = 9).

Step 2

Add the numbers of the Birth Month and Birth Day, and the appropriate Universal Year number. The Number of the month (September) is 9. The Number of the day is 3 (2 + 1). The Universal Year (2007) Number is 9. You now add 9 + 3 + 9 = 21 = 2 + 1 = 3.

Step 3

The Personal Year number for birthdays in the last half of the year can add up to either be a single-digit root number or a double-digit compound number such as shown in table 7–3. If the final calculation number adds up to be one of the special compound numbers as shown in table 13–2, then you would not reduce that compound number down to a single-digit number. However, if the calculated compound number is not listed in table 13–2, then you would reduce that number down to a single-digit root number. These particular compound numbers provide significant additional information about that characteristic and that is why it is important to get a more in-depth interpretation of the actual meaning of the characteristic's patterns. (Note: Table 13–2 is an extraction of table 7–3.)

Double-Digit Compound Number Conversion Table

When the Final Number Adds Up To	The Number Converts To	Final Number Becomes
19	19/1	19/1
11	11/2	11/2
13	13/4	13/4
22	22/4	22/4
14	14/5	14/5
23	23/5	23/5
16	16/7	16/7
18	18/9	18/9

Table 13–2

Example of Finding a Personal Year Number in the Last Half of the Calendar Year

	September 21, 2007* ~~2006~~
Addition	9+ 3+ 9
	21**
Reduce to	2 + 1 = 3
Personal Year Number	**= 3**

Figure 13–2

* 2007 is the Universal Year Number 9; see table 13-1.
** See chapter 9 for Compound Number meanings.

Here is a brief summary write-up of the figure 13–2 Personal Year calculation process for a birthday that falls in the Last Half of the calendar year (between July 1 and December 31). Since the birthday, September 21, 2006, is in the last 6 months of calendar year 2006, the following calendar year, 2007, becomes the Universal Year used in the Personal Year formula. This occurs because the vibrational pattern of the following year pulls you (or brings you) forward under its influence. The vibrational patterns of that Universal Year become a magnet which draws you toward the following year's influences. A restatement of the calculations in figure 13–2 is as follows. You add 9 (the Number of the month of September) to 3 (the Number of the Day, 2 + 1) to 9 (the Number of the Universal Year closest to your Birthday which in this case is 2007, the following calendar year). This sum, 9 + 3 + 9, is equal to the Compound Number 21. Since this particular compound number is not listed in table 13–2, it is reduced down to its Root Number 3 (2 + 1). Therefore, the "numerical value" (number) of the Personal Year for September 21, 2006 is 3.

III. Interpreting the Language of the Personal Year Numbers

In understanding the language of the numbers of your Personal Years, you must always stay aware of the flow of the energy of each year's vibrational patterns. An overview (short version) of the flow of patterns is as follows. In a Number 1 Personal Year, you create the idea and plan to put it into action. You begin things—for example, a new position at work, a new job, a new book, or a new association. In a Number 2 Personal Year you build on the idea by developing partnerships, working in cooperation with others, developing the chapters of a book, etc. In a Number 3 Personal Year, you experience a cycle of fruition, by expressing the idea. That is, you express yourself—in writing, in lecturing, in singing, etc. In a Number 4 Personal Year you give form to implementing your ideas—go about your business by detailing plans to build a foundation, framework, or basis from which you can expand your activities. Following the 4 Personal Year of applying hard work, the upcoming Number 5 Personal Year is one of action, change, movement, variety and expansion; the time to promote the idea.

From the action of the 5 Personal Year, you move into a 6 Personal Year, which is a year of adjustment, balance, and harmony. You can take a well-deserved break from the hectic pace of the 5 Personal Year. You can bring things into focus by taking advantage of the calming effect of the Number 6 Personal Year. From the calm, outward enjoyment of the Number 6 Personal Year, you move under the influence of the vibrational patterns of the Number 7 Personal Year, which are intellectual in nature. The 7 Personal Year is a year of introspection, self-evaluation, and self-analysis. You bring things together on an inner level, knowing that a table is already prepared before you, and nothing can stop you from finding fulfillment in your upcoming experiences. Rest and meditation will build your reservoir of energy which you will put to great use in your Number 8 Personal Year, when ambition is served. Devote the Number 8 Personal Year to planning, organization, and action. You can sign business contracts with confidence (as long as you guide the writing of it). It is a business/finance/commercial activity year. If you prepare for it, it can be very materially rewarding. This will allow you to prepare for the move into your Number 9 year. The Number 9 Personal Year represents the closing out of a 9-year cycle, preparing for a new cycle to begin. It can be a very exciting and highly emotional year. You may become emotionally sensitive. It is a year in which the more objective you are and the more universal your outlook, the more you will find satisfaction.

It is important for you to understand the importance of the flow of each year's patterns and the relationship and effect of one upon the other. You don't want to hang on or stay tuned into the prior years' patterns. If you are not ready to put the new into action and continue to do old things in the new environment, you will be confused, and most likely stifled, by the fact that things seem out of synchronization. When the new Personal Year is upon you, you will want to be ready to take full advantage of what it is presenting to you.

Below are the meanings and descriptions of the language of the root numbers (single-digit) and special compound numbers (double-digit) of the Personal Years. The special Compound Numbers are 19/1, 11/2, 13/4, 22/4, 14/5, 23/5, 16/7, and 18/9.

Number 1 Personal Year

The Number 1 Personal Year is the beginning of a new 9-year cycle and moving forward in your life. Anything that you did not complete last year, you are likely to finish this year as the 1 Personal Year is a step forward with renewed energy for accomplishments. You are at a crossroad in your life, so to speak, and need to stay on target. Making new plans and taking action are the keynotes of the Number 1 Personal Year. What you set in motion this year creates the basis and catalyst for the rest of the 9-year cycle. Since it is the 1, your creative and inventive powers will be at their peak. This is the time to initiate necessary changes for your future success, and to determine the nature of the plan and strategy you want to activate for the upcoming 9-year cycle. Therefore, you will want to be sure that you are as clear as possible in regard to your intent and desires, and maintain persistence and courage, since your success over the next nine years will depend a great deal upon what you do now. The Number 1 Personal Year begins as a time of work, organization, and clear thinking. Be aware that there may be some emotional turmoil in the first few months of this new year, due to the waning influences of and your connection to the prior Number 9 year which was a year of endings and the clearing out of the old no longer of value. As you move into the second half of the year you should see the decisions you've made begin to materialize, and by the end of the year you will see the fruits of your labors begin to manifest. If you wish to start something new, the Number 1 Personal Year is an excellent time to do so. When you meet new associates, lasting friendships should develop.

Number 19/1 Personal Year

The Number 19/1 Personal Year is considered to be the most fortunate of all of the numbers for it brings with it the Number 1 for new beginnings and creativity, the Number 9 for an ending, completion, or transformation, and another 1 for your leadership ability to pave new roads, for planting seeds, and for additional high energy. This is a very powerful, electrical vibration, and a "blessed" number, so no matter what may seem to go wrong, the outcome's effect is to always move in a positive direction. This could result in a successful outcome or tend to lessen the effect of consequences, even if it does not appear to be so. (Note: Be cautious when operating within the influence of the 19/1. The overall mixture of the patterns within your environment may bring about what is called a test of character when too great a feeling of or dependence on safety causes you to take things for granted. If this feeling of safety or protection lulls you into a false perception of your circumstances, you could make a decision to do something that could place you in a situation that will be detrimental to you. Always maintain your responsibility to stay awake and aware, and use discretion and right action, no matter what it may seem like around you.)

Number 2 Personal Year

The Number 2 Personal Year is the year that tact, diplomacy, and cooperation will bring you your greatest success and reward. It requires a sense of balance, understanding both sides of the issues, and a willingness to go around obstacles, without losing sight of your goals. Because your sensitivity and openness are heightened, many people find their soul mates in this year. So, the focus for the 2 Personal Year is on relationships, partnerships, and the home. If you are not in a relationship, a meaningful one can begin, and be long-lasting. Business partnerships are often important, and can grow. Strengthen friendships, and be patient, as new opportunities can drop in your lap unexpectedly. This year deals with emotional health and maintaining balance, but will be one of growth and advancement through gentle means. Be aware that important matters on an emotional plane may be exaggerated. You may feel moody, experience nervous energies, and cry or feel like crying. It is not advisable to make big changes this year, but rather remain in the status quo. Don't launch any new major projects. Patience and timing are the keynotes of this Personal Year.

Number 11/2 Personal Year

The Number 11/2 Personal Year is a Master Number, making this Personal Year a Master Year. It is the Root Number 2, enhanced, lifted up, and intensified by the vibration of the 11 (double 1s) which is endowed with an elevated power of creativity, originality, and leadership. Spiritual growth and inspiration are the keynotes of this vibration. Since it is a time of increased emotional and nervous energy, there is a need to listen to your own intuition for guidance. Stay focused and balanced, for this increased emotional and nervous energy may involve a disruption in either personal or business relationships. Your increased psychic and creative abilities will reach an all-time high and be an inspiration to others. If you permit yourself to go with your intuition and act on your "hunches," it can be a year of limelight and fame.

Number 3 Personal Year

The Number 3 Personal Year is for self-expression, expansion, and growth. It is a time of heightened personal expression such as taking up art, writing, music, or speaking, but for sure, moving successfully forward with your goals. This can be a good selling period. You should be able to market whatever you put into words. The 3 Personal Year is known as the cycle of fruition or success, when your ideas become a reality, borne of your energies, talents, and your actions in your 1 and 2 Personal Years. The Number 3 Personal Year is highly dynamic and charismatic, and you should find popularity with friends, large groups, and in the public. At the same time, you may choose to release friendships that have caused a drain of your energy or those who take but do not give to the relationship. This will be a busy year for you, with opportunities for travel, making many new friends, finding a new romance, and strong, supportive relationships. This should also be a happy and outgoing year, as well as a good financial year, particularly if your creativity is well-directed. Share your talents and joy with others. Health is generally good. The opportunities for success before you will be dependent on your being cheerful and optimistic; so it would be wise to surround yourself with upbeat and positive people. Try not to scatter your energies, money, or emotions. Either start or finish a project, but take caution to finish one project at a time for the best results.

Number 4 Personal Year

The Number 4 Personal Year is for building a new foundation. This is a building year in the sense of detailing out concrete plans, and organizing and developing a practical framework for future action. Hard work, personal discipline, and overcoming obstacles and limitations are the focus of this Personal Year. This is a period of consolidation and retrenching, for soon you will be very active. However, don't let the feeling of restriction keep you from growing. Although expansion will be slow, it will be positive. This is a good cycle for firming up friendships, bringing balance in family relationships, and for engagement or marriage. You desire a partner who has the same goals as you do. This is a good year to buy real estate, relocate, or remodel your home, in addition to selling and trading. However, use common sense and be wise on how you spend your money, because this may be a slow period for your finances. Another important aspect of the 4 Personal Year is that it is a practical year which requires you to "keep" very focused whether you want to or not. Organization, order, efficiency, and a systematic approach are essential in all that you do, particularly business and legal matters. Your success will come through being economical and practical rather than by depending on luck. In this year of hard work, not only is it important to have good health habits, but to always be aware of emotional, medical, and dental health issues. Be sure that you get the needed rest to maintain good health. You must also accept all responsibilities of the Number 4 Personal year with grace, if you want to enjoy the freedom and richer life the upcoming Number 5 Personal Year promises.

Number 13/4 Personal Year

The Number 13/4 Personal Year is a more powerful expression of the Number 4 Personal Year, because it combines the aggressive and masculine energy of the Numbers 1 and 3, and includes the individuality and leadership of the 1, and the ambitious and creative self-expressive energy of the 3. Their Root Number 4 adds the vibrational patterns of detail, hard work, discipline, and the desire for establishing a foundation in life. The right and successful use of this power will allow you to form various foundations to benefit mankind.

Number 22/4 Personal Year

The Number 22/4 Personal Year is a Master Number, bringing to this 22/4 Personal Year a vibration where the emotional and nervous energy of the Number 2 is magnified. The double 2s bring increased emotion and sensitivity to the 22/4 vibration, while the Root Number 4 emphasizes detail, hard work, discipline, and foundation. This vibration is the Number 4 (a time of building) elevated to a Master level. You will find great rewards through working in the name of humanity and the world, and should find yourself drawn toward deep involvement in humanitarian organizations and foundations. You may even have an opportunity to help build and become a part of an organization or foundation whose goal is to serve humanity. This is a year when your dreams can be "actualized" and brought into form. Concentrate on taking time to get your affairs in order during this vibration.

Number 5 Personal Year

The Number 5 Personal Year is a dynamic change after last year's hard work and discipline. It is a time of release, a time to get out of a rut, by resolving old issues and adopting the new ideas. Freedom and change are the keynotes of this exciting year, bringing opportunity for new growth, expansion, variety, and the possibility for travel. Accept this change in the spirit of progress and excitement. The 5 Personal Year is known as a cycle of "words in action"—possible career paths are in the areas of investigative reporting, singing, radio, television, and the communications industries (public relations, advertising, telephone, etc.). You will want to seek and find new people, new places, and new situations continually. However, make the most of this energetic period. Avoid overindulgences and don't scatter yourself by dividing your energy between too many things at once, or you risk falling into a rut. If challenges or feelings of restlessness present themselves during the year, you must proceed with grace. Make the necessary required changes, wisely and prudently establish goals of freedom, and then quickly act on them.

Number 14/5 Personal Year

The Number 14/5 is a Personal Year vibration that may bring some dissatisfaction and friction. That's because you have two action-oriented, masculine Numbers (the 1 and 5) on the outside and the disciplined, feminine structure of the 4 on the inside. The Number 1 desires to express leadership of its creative and original ideas. The Number 5 Personal Year is the vibration of freedom, change, and variety. Between these two numbers is the 4 which stands for detail, hard work, discipline, routine, and the importance of a solid foundation. In this case, the Root Number 5 of the 14/5 suggests change and action with uncertainty in money matters, particularly those dealing with speculation or investment. Be very cautious, since this could a risky year involving finances.

Number 23/5 Personal Year

The Number 23/5 Personal Year, like the Number 5 Personal Year, brings freedom and change, and opportunities for growth, expansion, variety, and travel. However, the number 23/5 vibration is the best of all of the 5 number combinations. It contains the patterns for peace, cooperation, and harmony of the Number 2 Personal Year, mingled with the social vibrations, creative expression, charisma, and joy of the Number 3 Personal Year. Combined with the Root Number 5 Personal Year, which brings an energy of freedom and action, the 23/5 Personal Year generates pleasant, creative, and lively vibrational patterns of excitement. Since the "lead" Number is the 2, any restlessness, challenge, and conflicting energies are held in balance. Changes under a 23/5 Personal Year are easier to accept and new ideas are easier to adopt and incorporate into your experiences.

Number 6 Personal Year

The Number 6 Personal Year is the year to focus on creating and maintaining harmony, balance, and adjustment—in business, community, and domestic affairs. This will be a period of calming and harmonious patterns. It is a good time for getting married, establishing a home, or engaging in a community project. It is a year of responsibility, with all aspects of home, family, relationships, and career at the forefront. You will always attract a soul mate, for the desire to love and be loved is vital to your health and happiness. It is also a time for relaxing and enjoying the arts. You can cement great friendships and find new and lasting ones during this year. The strong desire to establish order should bring great satisfaction to you and may require that you listen to the advice of others. Strive to keep your ideals high in spite of what may appear to be an unfair situation. Family members will require much of your energy, and they may also need material help, especially financial. Regardless of the circumstances, you will always accept your responsibility with grace. Be sure to complete all business and domestic obligations. Even if progress seems slow, your ultimate goal will be attained if you react in a constructive and conscientious way. You can buy, sell, or redecorate a new home, as this is a year of progress and financial advancement.

Number 7 Personal Year

The Number 7 Personal Year is a time to seek greater inner understanding, pursue intellectual interests, establish peace of mind, and to spend more time alone. It is also the time for mental housecleaning, and increasing spiritual enlightenment through meditation. This will be a slow period where you could experience delays, but it will pass. The desire to withdraw and the feeling of aloneness may come over you, but this too will pass. This is not a time for social activities nor is it a year to reach goals on a material level. Your metaphysical interests will expand your awareness of things beyond third-dimensional reality. The desire to be alone to escape from normal pressures of life may prevail. Take advantage of this time to build up your health and improve your mind. You are actually laying the foundation for future plans and goals, which will be of great importance to you. Consider this time as a period of waiting. You don't have to push for things to happen. Just let them happen. You will sense decreased physical energy, so be aware to avoid the feeling of depression that this could bring. Follow your hunches and flow with the slower pace of this year. There will be a reward of some sort in the offing at the end of the year.

Number 16/7 Personal Year

The Number 16/7 Personal Year vibration brings a year of introspection, mental housecleaning, meditation, and spiritual growth. Be alert to the potential lessening of physical energy because of the increased mental activity. During the 16/7 Personal Year, there may be patterns of confusion and disruption. This may happen for two reasons. The first being the potential effect of the masculine, aggressive aspects of the Number 1 (ego) coming into conflict with the feminine, receptive aspects of the Number 6 (community). The 1 is the desire for leadership, individuality, and creative originality, versus the 6 which is a team/family-oriented vibration dedicated to family, home, and community service. The other potential conflict comes from the desire of the Root Number 7 to withdraw and be alone, which is essentially the opposite desire of the 1 and 6. The 16/7 year is considered a Karmic year with lessons to be learned. So, it is important to live through any disruptive experience or conflict with grace and tolerance. To avoid the feeling of being depressed while going through this time, know that it is for your higher self and inner growth. The vibrational patterns of this Personal Year are not favorable for marriage.

Number 8 Personal Year

The Number 8 Personal Year brings great opportunities for business and financial success. Your power is visible and strong, your mental creativity is high, you can avail yourself of energy, discipline, and sound judgment, and your vision and intuition will guide you while you become more efficient and focused. Planning, organizing, and putting new ideas into action follow naturally. Money, power, business, and career are the keynotes of this year.

However, you should be cautioned that this could be a year of financial loss, unless you remain focused and motivated. Since this is a business year, control your emotions and face the real facts in order to bring improvement in your financial situation. It's very important to your success and satisfaction to balance your business drive with volunteering your services and taking the time to join worthwhile organizations. Also during this time, you may want to buy a new car or travel—just to avoid boredom. You will find that greater freedom will be yours this year than you have had for quite a long time.

Number 9 Personal Year

The Number 9 Personal Year is for completion and endings that come before the beginning of a new 9-year cycle. It is an energetic, forceful, and highly charged year that can cause you to become highly emotional. As a result, you may end up taking things entirely too personal, when you shouldn't. This is the time to move on from old relationships, things that no longer work, and things that are no longer valid for you by unburdening yourself of the old. It is a time to cast off old attitudes and non-constructive habits to get ready for your new experiences. This can be a very difficult year, particularly if you do not like change.

Number 18/9 Personal Year

The Number 18/9 Personal Year is an even more powerful expression of the Number 9 vibrational patterns. The 18/9 Personal Year is associated with social, political/military, financial, religious, and/or medical arenas. It forms a magnetic force to do good works benefiting mankind. The Number 1 represents leadership, originality, and creative ideas along with the desire for independence, combined with the 8, which brings power, sound judgment, and efficiency to the equation. Along with these elements, their Root 9 has the vibrational energy of all the numbers, and represents completion, force, energy, healing, universality, and compassion. Their combined energy suggests completion on corporate or management levels, and could include business, medicine, religious endeavors, military, or political and social organizations.

###

Chapter 14:
The Numbers of the Personal Months

I. Defining the Influence of the Personal Month Numbers

The influence of the Personal Month, which is calculated by adding the number of the Universal (calendar) Month to the number of your Personal Year (see chapter 13), defines and explains the nature of the vibrational patterns that will appear in your upcoming Personal Months. For instance, your Personal Month vibrational pattern for the month of August is found by adding the number of your Personal Year to the number of August (Universal/Calendar Month) which is Number 8. When you read the language of the Number 8 month, you will be given insight to the most likely patterns unfolding in that month. This information will help you become aware of events, conditions, and potential situations that are very quickly unfolding in your current Personal Month and will be unfolding in future months.

As you enter a particular month, you will find that your environment is being filled by vibrational patterns specific to you. Your Personal Month is being rapidly set up to form or take the shape of, if you will, the "potential" experiences and associations that resonate to a particular environment defined by your Personal Month's numbers. By knowing this potential, you can prepare for these experiences that are forming around you. You will be able to effectively plan major personal events, appointments, interviews, etc., that can be experienced with maximum success within the patterns unfolding in the Personal Month. In this way, you can take advantage of "inside" information available to you, which was not available to you before.

The Personal Month is a mini-blueprint within the mini-blueprint of your Personal Year's vibrational patterns. This allows you to become more focused on smaller areas of major concern to you. In addition, this information is available to you ahead of time, so to speak, for the upcoming month (or months) in the current year, the following year, and in future years. You can take advantage of all the things written within these sections and sub-sections of your "owner's manual," which lays out the mini-blueprints for the months of your Personal Years. And you can plan your strategies for "future" events to take place in more opportune environments shown to you in the patterns of your Personal Months. The important thing to know about your Personal Month vibrational patterns is that the more you take advantage of them, the greater are your chances for successful and satisfying experiences.

As stated above, and as shown in figure 14–1, the calculation of your Personal Month is dependent on the effect of the Universal (calendar) Month vibrational pattern. The number of the Universal (calendar) Month generates an umbrella effect over your Personal Month patterns, i.e., you function within your vibrations, but within the overtone of the Universal

Month vibrations. This occurs in the same manner, albeit a smaller envelope of influence, that the Universal Year number affects your Personal Year patterns. The greater your participation in your experiences, the greater your influence on the unfolding events. This is because of the fact that you find your Personal Month when you take the Universal Month number and personalize it by adding it to your Personal Year, thereby drawing upon and modifying the universal vibrations to create a set of events that are personal and specific to you. Now, the meanings of your Personal Month vibrational patterns must be understood in relation to the span of time available.

When compared to the Personal Year, the Personal Month time period moves very quickly. Therefore, you must take advantage of the aspects you wish to use, and events you wish to take part in, by preparing for them before they occur, or at least planning for them. You will begin to feel the influence of the next month as you move into the last week of the current month. And, although the vibrational pattern of your current personal month still governs, you will begin to react to some of the following month's personal vibrations.

When we work with the language of the vibrational patterns of our Personal Years and Months, we are simply getting in tune with the action of the coming periods of experiences (not periods of time, but periods of action, participation, and experiencing). In using the information that's available to you through the language of your numbers, you do not want to get caught in the trap of living your life by your numbers, no more than you should live your life by your stars or by the words of your teachers, or counselors, or any other framework of concepts, ideas, or creeds. However, you can take advantage of the unfolding events to your benefit by familiarizing yourself with the general pattern of your personal numbers. Then you allow yourself to be flexible in taking part in the unfolding experiences that present themselves to you. For events or happenings which are special or of great importance to you, you can get more "specific" in the information you wish to use from the personal vibrations of your numbers. You will find that the event or happening will occur with greater ease and result in greater satisfaction to you when you use the language of your numbers. (Note: The calculation of the Personal Month numbers are shown in chapter 14, figure 14–1, while the meaning and description of the Personal Month numbers are provided after figure 14–1.)

II. Calculating the Personal Month Numbers

A Personal Month number is found by adding the number of your Personal Year to the calendar month in which you are interested (see chapter 13.) A list of Universal Year numbers is provided table 14–1. The calendar month numbers are known as *Universal Month* numbers. To support the calculation of Personal Month numbers, we are providing a list of the "numbers" of the Universal (calendar) Months in table 14–2.

Example of Assigned Universal Year Numbers Reduced Down

2005 = 7	2014 = 7	2023 = 7
2006 = 8	2015 = 8	2024 = 8
2007 = 9	2016 = 9	2025 = 9
2008 = 1	2017 = 1	2026 = 1
2009 = 2	2018 = 2	2027 = 2
2010 = 3	2019 = 3	2028 = 3
2011 = 4	2020 = 4	2029 = 4
2012 = 5	2021 = 5	2030 = 5
2013 = 6	2022 = 6	2031 = 6

(For purposes of calculation, use the numbers shown in this table.)
Table 14–1

Example of Assigned Universal Month Numbers

Month	Assigned Number	Month	Assigned Number
January	1	July	7
February	2	August	8
March	3	September	9
April	4	October	10 reduced to 1
May	5	November	11 reduced to 2
June	6	December	12 reduced to 3

(For purposes of calculation, use the numbers shown in this table.)
Table 14–2

Before showing you the actual calculations of your Personal Month (figure 14–1), we will first take you through a three-step written process for calculating the numbers of your Personal Months.

Personal Months

Three-Step Process on How to Calculate the Numbers

Step 1

Lay out the selected Universal (calendar) Month (in this case, August 2007) alongside the Personal Year in which you are interested on a sheet of paper. Use the appropriate Universal Month number from the table 14–1 listing above, August = 8. To get the Personal Year number for this case, we are using the Birthday of September 21, 2006 (taken from example 2 in chapter 13). Therefore, the Personal Year number is 9 + 3 + 9 = 21 = 3 which is the Birth Month number (9), plus the Birth Day number (3), plus the Universal Year number 2007 (see table 14–2). Example 2 in chapter 13 uses 2007 because September falls in the Last Half of the calendar year 2006.

Step 2

Calculate the Personal Month number by adding the number of the Universal Month, which is 8, to the Personal Year Number, which is 3. In this case, when you add the number of the Universal Month (8) to the Personal Year number (3), 8 + 3, it equals the Compound Number 11. When comparing the 11, a Master Number, against the list of compound numbers in table 14–3, you will find that the Number 11 is, in fact, one of the special combination final numbers. This means that the 11 will not be reduced down any further and will be designated as the 11/2, making it the Personal Month Number for August 2007.

Step 3

The Personal Month number can add up to either be a single-digit root number or a double-digit compound number such as shown in table 7–3. If the final calculation number adds up to be one of the special compound numbers as shown in table 14–3, then you would not reduce that compound number down to a single-digit number. However, if the calculated compound number is not listed in table 14–3, then you would reduce that number down to a single-digit root number. These particular compound numbers provide significant additional information about that characteristic and that is why it is important to get a more in-depth interpretation of the actual meaning of the characteristic's patterns. (Note: Table 14–3 is an extraction of table 7–3.)

Double-Digit Compound Number Conversion Table

When the Final Number Adds Up To	The Number Converts To	Final Number Becomes
19	19/1	19/1
11	11/2	11/2
13	13/4	13/4
22	22/4	22/4
14	14/5	14/5
23	23/5	23/5
16	16/7	16/7
18	18/9	18/9

Table 14–3

The actual calculations are shown in figure 14–1. To find the Personal Month number for the month of August 2007, add the Personal Year number to the Universal (calendar) Month number.

Example of Calculating the Personal Month Number for September 21, 2006

Personal Year Number			**Universal (Calendar) Month Number**
September 21, 2007 ~~2006~~*			August 2007
9+ 3+ 9 = 21			(From table 14–2)
Reduce to	2 + 1 = 3	+	8 = 11 or 11/2
Personal Month Number		**= 11/2****	(Compound Number)

Figure 14–1

* Use next calendar year vs. 2006; 2007 is the Universal Year Number 9; see table 13-1.
** See chapter 9 for Compound Number meanings.

Here is a summary of the Personal Month calculation process (figure 14–1) for September 21, 2006, which falls in the Last Half of the calendar year. Therefore, the following calendar year, 2007, becomes the Universal Year (9). A restatement of the calculations is as follows. You add 9 (the Number of the month of September) to 3 (the Number of the Day, 2 + 1) to 9 (the Number of the Universal Year closest to your Birthday). This sum, 9 + 3 + 9, is equal to the Compound Number 21. Since 21 is not listed in table 14–3, it is reduced to its Root Number 3 (2 + 1) which is the Personal Year number. Now the 3 is added to the calendar month August, whose Universal Month Number is 8, resulting in the Personal Month Number 11/2.

III. The Language of the Personal Month Numbers

In working with the language of numbers of your Personal Months, you must always keep in mind how rapidly the "month" passes, perhaps not as rapidly as the "day," but significantly faster than the year. An overview of the flow of patterns of the Personal Months follows the same or similar flow as the vibrational patterns of the Personal Year numbers.

That is, in a Number 1 Personal Month, you envision the idea, the design, and create a plan to put it into action. You start things or become involved in "new" experiences. In a Number 2 Personal Month, you build on the idea through partnership and cooperation. In a 3 Personal Month, you express the idea. In a Number 4 Personal Month you give form to the idea. You detail out plans and lay out a blueprint as the basis from which you can expand. You consolidate. You prepare for a Personal Month of action in your Number 5 Personal Month. The Number 5 Personal Month is one of action, change, movement, variety and expansion, the time to promote the idea.

Then you move into a 6 Personal Month, which puts the patterns of balance and harmony into motion. You can take a break from the hectic pace of the 5 Personal Month and bring things into focus under the calming effect of the Number 6 Personal Month. You then move under the influence of the vibrational patterns of the Number 7 Personal Month which brings a desire for introspection, self-evaluation, and self-analysis. Things come together on an inner level. Rest and meditation during the 7 Personal Month patterns help you build your reservoir of energy, which you will need in your Number 8 Personal Month, when ambition is served. It is a month of planning, organization, and direction. It is a business/finance/commercial activity month. If you prepare for it, it can be materially rewarding. This allows you to prepare for your Number 9 month, which represents the closing out of a cycle of completion. It can be a very exciting and highly emotional month, since you will be phasing out a familiar, but no longer appropriate view of things, while preparing for the "new" start of the next Number 1 month.

Because the time passes so quickly, you must stay alert and not hang on or stay in tune with the prior month's patterns. If you are not ready to put the new month's cycle into motion, you may become confused, and most likely stifled, by the fact that "old" things seem out of synchronization. When the next cycle of Personal Months begins, you will want to be ready to take full advantage of all opportunities.

Following are the meanings and descriptions of the language of the root numbers (single-digit) and special compound numbers (double-digit) of the Personal Months. The special Compound Numbers are 19/1, 11/2, 13/4, 22/4, 14/5, 23/5, 16/7, and 18/9.

Number 1 Personal Month

The Number 1 Personal Month emphasizes new beginnings, such as starting new projects, meeting new associates, getting a promotion at work, etc. And it enhances your ability to make progress. This is a favorable period for associations and/or work with men (because of the masculine/aggressive nature of the 1). This could also be a good time for expressing your ambitions or asking for a raise. This cycle could be signified by you becoming the main figure in an organization, if you take the first step.

Number 19/1 Personal Month

The Number 19/1 Personal Month is considered to be the most fortunate of all of the numbers for it brings with it the Number 1 of new beginnings, the 9 for completion or transformation and energy, and another 1 for confidence, individuality, and courage. This is a very powerful, inspiring vibration, and is a "blessing" to any environment, so that the possibility of things going wrong is minimized, favoring an outcome that moves in a positive and successful direction. (Note: When operating within the influence of the "19/1," we must caution you to stay aware of your surroundings. The mixture of the patterns that flow within your environment may bring you a test of character in regard to letting your guard down because of feeling protected by the vibrations of the "19," or letting your attention become diverted because you are taking things for granted. You do not want to be lulled into a false perception of your circumstances and make a decision that will put you at risk.)

Number 2 Personal Month

The Number 2 Personal Month is keynoted by cooperation, coordination, partnership, and receptivity. Associations and work with women are emphasized. This is a time for practicality as well as follow-through effort. Your creative imagination is active; use it.

Number 3 Personal Month

The Number 3 Personal Month is a time of self-expression, lightheartedness, socialization, and public events. This should be a period when you have a happy, positive, and uplifting outlook. Social popularity is emphasized in both private and public environments, as well as interactions with and in clubs and organizations. If your talents and energies are not scattered, it could be a very successful time for you. It is a time of heightened personal expression such as taking up art, writing, music, or speaking. Watch your desire to spend money—be wise.

Number 4 Personal Month

The Number 4 Personal Month is a number of being down-to-earth, having discipline, establishing a foundation, working hard, and showing loyalty. You may feel restricted this month, and may need to pay attention to detail. Be patient, for this is a time of building for future success. It is a time of busyness. Discipline yourself and work with determination. Success will follow you more easily if you develop and express tolerance, mercy, and compassion.

Number 13/4 Personal Month

The Number 13/4 Personal Month has more power than the Number 4 Personal Month, because it combines the forceful and aggressive energy of the Numbers 1 and 3, including the independence and individuality of the 1, and the highly dynamic and self-expressive energy of the 3. Their Root Number 4 provides structure, hard work, discipline, and foundation, which helps to focus and concentrate the power of the 13. The right and successful use of this power will allow you to form various foundations to benefit mankind.

Number 22/4 Personal Month

The Number 22/4 Personal Month is a Master Number and magnifies the cooperative spirit, sensitivity, creative imagination and intuition, and ability to see both sides of the issues of the Number 2, while standing upon the foundation and framework vibrational patterns of the Number 4. This Master vibration is good for laying the foundations for humanitarian activities. International and worldly affairs are emphasized during this cycle. Under the influence of the 22, you can make your dreams a reality.

Number 5 Personal Month

The Number 5 Personal Month brings with it freedom, action, and versatility. This is a period of change, travel, and movement. You should experience many new and varied situations, and people and events, including new associations and acquaintances. There may be an opportunity for evangelical (religious and spiritual work through "words in action") type of events. This is an excellent time for speaking, writing and salesmanship, including promoting your own ideas. Be aware. During this time, it would be best not to make decisions hastily.

Number 14/5 Personal Month

The Number 14/5 Personal Month vibration may bring uncertainty, along some dissatisfaction. That's because you have two active and versatile, masculine Numbers (the 1 and 5) on the outside, and the disciplined and structured feminine 4 on the inside. The Number 1 expresses individuality, independence, and creative and original ideas. The Number 5 vibrational patterns flow from the expression of freedom, change, movement, and variety—while between these two numbers stands the 4 whose patterns activate the vibrations of hard work, discipline, routine, and structure. In this case, the Root Number 5 of the 14/5 suggests change, action, and uncertainty when dealing in money matters, particularly activities which involve speculation or investment. Be careful to be very watchful in regard to how you manage and use your resources and money.

Number 23/5 Personal Month

The Number 23/5 Personal Month sets up an environment of freedom, change, opportunities for growth, expansion, variety, and travel. The 23/5 vibration is the best of all of the 5s. It contains vibrational patterns of cooperation, harmony, and receptivity of the Number 2, supported by the social vibrations, creative expression, charisma, and joy of the Number 3. The 2 and 3 combined with the Root Number 5, which brings an energy of freedom and action, brings a month of pleasant, creative, and lively vibrational patterns of excitement. Since the "lead" Number is the 2, any restlessness, impatience, and conflicting energies are held in balance. Changes under a 23/5 month are more easily accepted, while new ideas and associations are easier to incorporate into your experiences.

Number 6 Personal Month

The Number 6 Personal Month will emphasize the law of balance and responsibility. It is the number of home, family, and community affairs. You should have opportunities to earn good money, but may be required to share it with many others. Married life and romance are highlighted. You will find great enjoyment in things revolving around rhythm, beauty, culture, and fine arts.

Number 7 Personal Month

The Number 7 Personal Month is a good period for intellectual pursuits (quiet pleasures of the mind). Pursue studies of a mystical nature. This cycle is one in which you can put ideas into form. And you can carry out plans in which personal contact is unnecessary. Be aware of a tendency to feel alone, withdrawn, and lonely. Although it is a good period to contact your center through meditation and introspection, do not withdraw from participating in the activities occurring around you.

Number 16/7 Personal Month

The Number 16/7 Personal Month brings a month of reflection, mental housecleaning, meditation, and intellectual pursuits. Be alert to the potential lessening of physical energy because of the increased mental activity. The challenge here is to stay focused and be aware of potentially conflicting energies between the 1, independence and individuality, the 6, family and community service provider, and the reserved and withdrawn 7. The interaction between these energies can be disruptive and unsettling, so it is important to live through this experience with grace and tolerance. The vibrational patterns of the 16/7 are not favorable for marriage.

Number 8 Personal Month

The Number 8 Personal Month brings sound judgment, energy, and power under your command during this cycle. You should now be able to avail yourself of whatever is at hand. Actions regarding money, business, and career should result in a favorable outcome, if you can take the reins of your action and participation and set your own direction. Be aware; power has been entrusted to you; use discrimination.

Number 9 Personal Month

The Number 9 Personal Month, being the number of healing energy, transformation, and completion, makes this a good month to eliminate negative influences and conditions that are no longer nurturing to you. This monthly cycle is signified by balance, growth, and gain. Cast off old (no longer valid) modes, ways, and attitudes, and cheerfully make way for the new. The best use of this vibration comes from service to others through humanitarian associations.

Number 18/9 Personal Month

The Number 18/9 Personal Month generates power, drive, and emotional energies. It is the most powerful expression of the Number 9 vibrational patterns. The envelope of energy surrounding the 18/9 encourages social, political/military, financial, religious, and/or medical change and upheaval. The 18/9 blends the Number 1, leadership, originality, and creative ideas, the 8, brings power, sound judgment, and efficiency, and the Root 9, completion, healing, universality, and compassion. This combination could suggest completion on corporate or management levels in business, medicine, religious endeavors, as well as in military, political, and social organizations.

###

Numbers–The Powerful Bridge Beyond

Chaldean Numerology for the New Millennium

Chapter 15:
The Numbers of the Personal Days and Hours

I. Defining the Influence of the Personal Day and Hour Numbers

It's been said that there is nothing new under the sun, that each day is simply an extension or a slightly different variation of yesterday. However, that is not the case. The truth is, that *everything* under the sun is new and each and every day *is a completely new experience*. If, for instance, you were to calculate the numbers of Personal Days that were special to you, and, as a result, be able to interpret and describe the specific and important vibrational patterns of each day's potential, don't be surprised to find the language of that day's patterns reveals a distinctly "new" environment which is indeed different from yesterday and any future day's environment. What a gift it would be to have the opportunity to make informed decisions and take appropriate actions that increase your potential for success within the day's events, conditions, and situations.

We have never seen or been aware of any Numerology book addressing the numbers of Personal Days and Hours. We felt that by providing you with the formulas, calculations, and meaning of the language of the numbers of the Day and Hour, invaluable detailed information can be revealed to you about the energies and patterns that surround a particular day's and/or hour's happenings. To say the least, at this level of detail, it is apparent that you could take advantage of knowing and planning for the potential that is flowing around you. So in the development of this book, we address and discuss the process and value of having access to knowledge of the patterns of those Personal Days and Hours in which you are interested.

Personal Day and Hour numbers, like the Personal Year and Personal Month numbers, are derived from the numbers of your birthdate. These numbers provide additional valuable information about the patterns forming within your design and blueprint, although in a much smaller and finer time frame of action and on a much more detailed level. In the case of Days and Hours, the "time span" passes by exceedingly fast, particularly in relation to Personal Years and Personal Months, so that the information and knowledge must be acted upon with due haste.

Each day opens with new unfolding vibrational patterns, revealing information about potential events and situations, and possible associations that could fall within the patterns of that day's environment. This is also true for the patterns of each hour of the day. Now, by knowing the potential that is reflected in the numbers and vibrational patterns of each day or hour, you can use your resources and make choices and decisions to your greatest advantage. And, although the period of your experiences flows by much quicker, the available information allows you to be better prepared for the potential experiences of the days and hours. This information is available to you for any day and hour you are interested in checking out—today, tomorrow, next week, next month, and as far into the future as you wish to go.

It must be emphasized here that using the information of the numbers of the Personal Days and Hours is best done in those arenas and environments where you, at least, have some say in picking the day and time of the situation, event, etc. The more that you participate in the making of the decision or choice, the more accurate and appropriate use of information you will get from the meaning and description of your numbers. That is, if you have control to some degree in determining the day or hour, there is greater certainty that the event or situation has a reasonable chance of occurring as expected or desired—barring any change or chance event caused by an unforeseen emergency. For instance, describing the "personal" patterns of a day or hour would be appropriate when setting up a dental or medical appointment, when making an appointment for the hairdresser/barber, when selecting the best time to take your car in for servicing, repairing, or painting, when deciding the timing for classes or workshops, when taking an important examination (if, of course, there is more than one opportunity to take the examination, and you have the option to choose the date and time), or when setting the day and time of your wedding.

The calculation of the Personal Day numbers (figure 15–1) and Personal Hour numbers (figure 15–2) follows the same logic as used in calculating the formulas for the Personal Year (see chapter 13) and Personal Month (see chapter 14). In this example, we are using the Birth Day of March 4.

II. Calculating the Numbers of the Personal Days

Before showing you the actual calculations of your Personal Day number (figure 15–1), we will first take you through a two-step written process for calculating the numbers of your Personal Days, using the date June 8, 2006. This date could represent a day chosen for a doctor's appointment, a job interview, or perhaps a potential wedding. A list of Universal Day Numbers is shown in table 15–1. The number of the Universal Day is exactly equal to the calendar day number.

Personal Days and Hours

Two-Step Process on How to Calculate the Numbers

Step 1

First, calculate the Personal Year number by adding the Birth Month March (3) to the Birth Day (4) to the Universal (calendar) Year number for 2006 (8) (see chapter 13, illustration 13a, example 1). Then, calculate the Personal Month number for June by adding the Personal Year number to the Universal Month number for June (see chapter 14, figure 14–1). Finally, calculate the number of the Personal Day for June 8 by adding the Personal Month number to the Universal Day (8) number as shown in figure 15–1.

Step 2

The Personal Day number can add up to either be a single-digit root number or a double-digit compound number such as shown in table 7–3. If the final calculation number adds up to be one of the special compound numbers as shown in table 15–2, then you would not reduce that compound number down to a single-digit number. However, if the calculated compound number is not listed in table 15–2, then you would reduce that number down to a single-digit root number. These particular compound numbers provide significant additional information about that characteristic and that is why it is important to get a more in-depth interpretation of the actual meaning of the characteristic's patterns. (Note: Table 15–2 is an extraction of table 7–3.)

See Tables and Figure on the Following Pages.

Example of Assigned Universal (Calendar) Day Numbers

1 = 1	10 = 10	19 = 19	28 = 28
2 = 2	11 = 11	20 = 20	29 = 29
3 = 3	12 = 12	21 = 21	30 = 30
4 = 4	13 = 13	22 = 22	31 = 31
5 = 5	14 = 14	23 = 23	
6 = 6	15 = 15	24 = 24	
7 = 7	16 = 16	25 = 25	
8 = 8	17 = 17	26 = 26	
9 = 9	18 = 18	27 = 27	

(For purposes of calculation, use the numbers shown in this table.)

Table 15–1

Double-Digit Compound Number Conversion Table

When the Final Number Adds Up To	The Number Converts To	Final Number Becomes
19	19/1	19/1
11	11/2	11/2
13	13/4	13/4
22	22/4	22/4
14	14/5	14/5
23	23/5	23/5
16	16/7	16/7
18	18/9	18/9

Table 15–2

Example of Calculating the Personal Day Number

Birthdate: March 4, 1949 (First half of the year)

Selected Date: June 8, 2006

Personal Year Number for 2006

Birth Month = 3+ Birth Day = 4+ Universal/Calendar Year 2006 = 8

3 + 4 + 8+ = 15 or 1 + 5 = 6

Personal Month Number for June

Personal Year = 6 + Universal/Calendar Month of June = 6

6 + 6+ = 12 or 1 + 2 = 3

Personal Day Number Calculation for June 8

Personal Month Number for June Universal/Calendar Day Number

3 + 8

Personal Day Number = 11 or 11/2** (Compound Number)

Figure 15–1

** See chapter 9 for Compound Number meanings.

In the case of the example in figure 15–1, the calculated Personal Day Number is an 11 or 11/2, a Master Number that never gets reduced down to a root number as shown in table 15–2.

III. Calculating the Numbers of the Personal Hours

Before showing you the actual calculations of Personal Hour numbers (figure 15–2), we will first take you through a two-step written process for calculating the numbers of your Personal Hours, using the date June 8, 2006, which could be the time of your wedding, a college entrance examination, an important job interview, etc. To determine the Universal (clock) Hour, you must go to the Greenwich (Meridian) Mean Time (GMT) designation of the clock hours. The origin of "clock hours" is addressed in chapter 16. A list of the numbers of the Universal Clock hours is shown in table 15–3.

Example of Assigned Universal Clock Hour Numbers

Hour/Number	Hour/Number	Hour/Number
1 AM = 1	10 AM =10	7 PM = 19
2 AM = 2	11 AM =11	8 PM = 20
3 AM = 3	12 AM =12	9 PM = 21
4 AM = 4	1 PM =13	10 PM = 22
5 AM = 5	2 PM =14	11 PM = 23
6 AM = 6	3 PM =15	12 PM = 24
7 AM = 7	4 PM =16	
8 AM = 8	5 PM =17	
9 AM = 9	6 PM =18	

(For purposes of calculation, use the numbers shown in this table, do not reduce down.)
The Universal day is subdivided into 24–Universal Hour numbers.
Table 15–3

Personal Hour
Two-Step Process on How to Calculate the Number
Step 1

Figure 15–1 shows you the calculation of your Personal Day numbers. It is the Personal Day number that is used in calculating the number of the "Hour" in which you are interested. *The Universal Day is subdivided into 24–Universal Hour numbers.*

Step 2

You now calculate the Personal Hour number, for the particular event, appointment, etc., you are concerned with, by adding the Personal Day Number 11 from figure 15–1 to the number of the Universal "Clock" Hour in which you are interested to determine the Personal Hour number. For instance, the Personal Hour number for your wedding vows or entrance examination at 4 PM on June 8, 2006, is calculated in figure 15–2.

Example of Calculating the Personal Hour Number

Personal Hour Number for 4 PM

Personal Day Number (figure 15–1)		Universal "Clock" Hour (table15–3)
11	+	16

27** (Compound Number)

Reduce to 2 + 7 = 9

Personal Hour Number = 9* (Root Number)

Figure 15–2

* See chapter 15 for Personal Day and Hour meanings.
** See chapter 9 for Compound Number meanings.

IV. The Language of the Personal Day and Hour Numbers

For interpreting the language of the Personal Day and Hour numbers, you can refer to the descriptions shown at the end of this chapter. These descriptions are similar to those contained in the language of the Personal Month numbers in chapter 14. At this level of detail there is very little variation in the meaning of calculated "time" values (numbers) and underlying vibrational patterns for the Personal Month, Day, or Hour.

You can decide when and to what extent you want to address the meaning of your Personal Day, for such occasions as getting married, starting a job, buying a car, etc., or for events like taking an examination, submitting a job application, being interviewed, and other important actions, choices, and decisions.

For interpreting the impact of Personal Hour numbers, you can decide when and to what extent you want to use the information and knowledge that is revealed by the meaning of your Personal Hour numbers.

Although each day may seem to be virtually the same, the day does in fact reveal new patterns and environments for you to experience. Add to that the fact that each "Personal" hour generates different vibrational patterns than the previous day. You will be able to see the patterns of each day by looking at the language of the numbers that describe the patterns of the day and the patterns of the hours within the day. You get an overview of the potential for that particular day—as it relates to the particular design and blueprint of your experiences. Understanding the unfolding patterns of the day or hour should provide you with a means of becoming more aware of the myriad of changing and emerging newness that exists in each day. So, if you feel the need to examine that potential environment for an important event or the impact on potential events which may be in the offing, that avenue will be available to you for your use.

This concept of being able to define each day and hour is what gives rise to the premise the "everything under the sun is new"—the opposite of contemporary and traditional thought that "nothing is new under the sun." Although most of the things you may see will be familiar and appear to be the same—the streets you drive down, the house you live in, the office you work at, the store where you shop—in reality, the opportunity for new experiences or rather the potential for new events and situations will be waiting for you. This newness is a part of our experiencing as soon as we become aware of the day—as soon as we awaken to each day.

In the moment that you open your eyes and respond with the perception of all your senses, you have created a new pattern of experiencing in that environment. That day is the only conscious, perceptive experiencing of which you are aware, and is its own creation, its own pattern, and its own Universe of experiencing in and of itself. The phrase that says "We live each day only once" is not far from the truth. The formulas and calculations that are presented in this book are the legacy the originators of Chaldean Numerology have left us. To discover why and to what extent each day is new is yours for the asking, through understanding the language of the numbers and vibrational patterns of your Personal Days and Hours.

Number 1 Personal Day

The Number 1 Personal Day is a beneficial time for expressing your ambitions and taking the lead, asking for a promotion, asking for a raise, etc. Your ability to make progress is enhanced. It is a good period for starting things—new jobs, new projects, and meeting new associates are emphasized. This cycle could be signified by you becoming the main figure in an organization, if you take the first step.

Number 19/1 Personal Day

The Number 19/1 Personal Day brings with it the Number 1 of new beginnings, the 9 for completion or transformation and energy, and another Number 1 for confidence, individuality, and courage. This is a very powerful, inspiring vibration, and is a "blessing" to any environment, so the possibility of things going wrong is minimized, favoring an outcome that moves in a positive and successful forward direction.

Number 2 Personal Day

The Number 2 Personal Day is keynoted by cooperation, coordination, partnership, and receptivity. This is a good period to work in environments and situations that involve associations and teamwork activities. It is also a good period for resolving issues through mediation. This is a time for practicality, as well as follow-through effort. Your creative imagination is active; use it.

Number 11/2 Personal Day

The Number 11/2 Personal Day is a Master Number vibration which should find your intuition humming. This cycle is keynoted by metaphysics, philosophy and religion, where visions, revelations and psychic illumination are emphasized. You may be given the opportunity for limelight events. This period is also good for promoting and launching an invention. The symbolism of the 11 refers to balance or equilibrium between two extremes. The Root Number 2 is the number of idealism and emotional sensitivity, and combined with the aspirations of the 1, magnifies the imagination, romanticism, inventiveness, and emotional energy of the 2.

Number 3 Personal Day

The Number 3 Personal Day is a period when you have a happy, positive outlook. Social popularity is emphasized as well as many dealings with clubs and organizations. If your talents and energies are not scattered, it could be a very successful time for you. However, watch your desire to spend money—be wise.

Number 4 Personal Day

The Number 4 Personal Day puts you in a building cycle and you should sacrifice now for future benefits. This period may be restrictive in nature, in the sense of needing to pay attention to detail, and it will be of busyness. Discipline yourself and work with determination. Success will follow you more easily if you develop and express tolerance, mercy, and sympathy.

Number 13/4 Personal Day

The Number 13/4 Personal Day combines the forceful and aggressive energy of the Numbers 1 and 3, including the independence and individuality of the 1, and the highly dynamic and self-expressive energy of the 3. Their Root Number 4 provides structure, hard work, discipline, and foundation, which helps to focus and concentrate the power of the 13. However, the force and creativity of the 1 and the 3 are held within the structure of the solid 4, which may cause you to feel that your individuality is being held in check or that your creativity is being stifled.

Number 22/4 Personal Day

The Number 22/4 Personal Day is a Master vibration good for participation in humanitarian foundations or for laying a foundation upon which others can build. The 22 governs things of the earth (from the Root Number 4). The double 2 magnifies the cooperative spirit, emotional sensitivity, and ability to see both sides of the issues. Under the influence of the 22, you can make your dreams a reality. However, balance is needed between the sensitive and emotional 2, and the practical and disciplined 4.

Number 5 Personal Day

The Number 5 Personal Day is a period for change, travel, and movement. You should experience many and varied situations, people and events; this includes associations and acquaintances. Religious and spiritual work is signified (evangelistic in nature). This is an excellent time for speaking, writing, public relations and salesmanship, including promoting your own ideas. Beware of haste or speed in your decisions.

Number 14/5 Personal Day

The Number 14/5 Personal Day vibration may bring uncertainty, along with some dissatisfaction. That's because of the two active and versatile, masculine numbers (the 1 and 5) on the outside edges of the number, and the disciplined and structured feminine 4 in the center. The Number 1 expresses individuality, independence, and creative and original ideas. The Number 5 vibrational patterns express freedom, change, movement, and variety—while between these two numbers stands the 4, whose patterns dictate hard work, discipline, routine, and structure. In this case, the root Number 5 of the 14/5 suggests change, action, and uncertainty when dealing in money matters, particularly activities which involve speculation or investment. Be very watchful in regard to how you manage and use your resources and money.

Number 23/5 Personal Day

The Number 23/5 Personal Day sets up an environment of freedom, change, opportunities for growth and expansion, variety, and travel. The 23/5 vibration is the best of all of the 5 combinations. It has within it the patterns of cooperation, harmony, and receptivity of the Number 2, supported by the social vibrations, creative expression, charisma, and joy of the Number 3. The 2 and 3 combine to form the Root Number 5, which brings an energy of freedom and action, and sets the tone for pleasant, creative, and lively vibrational patterns of excitement. Since the "lead" number is the 2, any restlessness, impatience, and conflicting energies are held in balance. Changes under a 23/5 Personal Day are more easily accepted, while new ideas and associations are easier to incorporate into your experiences.

Number 6 Personal Day

The Number 6 Personal Day symbolizes the law of balance and responsibility. You should earn good money, but may be required to share it with many. This is a good period for study projects and gaining knowledge. Married life and romance are *highlighted.* You will find great enjoyment in things involving rhythm, beauty, culture, and fine arts.

Number 7 Personal Day

The Number 7 Personal Day is a good period for intellectual pursuits (quiet pleasures of the mind). Pursue studies of a mystical nature. This cycle is one in which you can put ideas into form. Be punctual; don't let delays cause disappointment. You can carry out plans in which personal contact is unnecessary. Be aware of a tendency to feel alone and lonely (it is a good period to contact your "center" but not to withdraw from the action).

Number 8 Personal Day

The Number 8 Personal Day puts force, energy, and power at your command. You should now be able to avail yourself of what is at hand. Actions regarding money, business, and career should result in favorable outcomes. Take the reins of your action and participation and set your own direction. (Note: Power has been entrusted to you—use discrimination.)

Number 9 Personal Day

The Number 9 Personal Day is signified by balance, growth, and gain, and is a very good period to eliminate negative influences. Cast off old modes, ways and attitudes, and cheerfully make way for the new. It is a number of completion and endings. This is a number of healing—all modalities of physical, mental, and emotional healing. A good use of this vibration comes in service to others—humanitarian associations in all fields of endeavor.

Number 18/9 Personal Day

The Number 18/9 Personal Day generates power, ambition, and emotional energies. It is the most powerful expression of the Number 9 vibrational patterns. The envelope of energy surrounding the 18/9 encourages social, political, military, financial, religious, and/or medical change and upheaval. The 18/9 blends the Number 1, leadership, originality, and creative ideas, the 8, power, sound judgment, and efficiency, and the Root 9, completion, healing, universality, and compassion. This combination could suggest some kind of completion or ending on corporate or management levels in business, medicine, and religious endeavors, as well as in military, political and social organizations.

###

Chapter 16:
Universal Numbers Defined

General Information

The Universal Year, Month, Day, and Hour represent the calendar year, month, day, and clock hour and generate overarching vibrational patterns that affect everyone in the world and everything that is going on around you. And these unfolding vibrational patterns are felt by everyone "equally." Since everyone starts out on a level playing field, so to speak, it is of prime importance that you grasp and understand how your personal reality and life experiences fit in. These "Universal" vibrational patterns form an envelope within which all people and things function and experience. This is especially true in regard to how the environment, in which your drama (story) takes place, is formed. Additionally, there are many potential events unfolding, and multiple conditions and situations occurring simultaneously. People of all walks of life, cultures, religions, political views, and more are interacting and reacting to those "Universal" events.

The nature of "Universal" vibrational patterns is such that you really have no control over them. You cannot manipulate or change them, in and of themselves. But the numbers of your "Personal" patterns can blend with the Universal numbers to create an environment which will be defined by "your" personal information contained within your design and blueprint.

Following are four tables which show you the "numbers" of the "Universal" vibrational patterns used in the formulas and calculations contained in the book.

See Tables on the Following Pages:

Example of Assigned Universal (Calendar) Year Numbers Reduced Down

2005 = 7	2014 = 7	2023 = 7
2006 = 8	2015 = 8	2024 = 8
2007 = 9	2016 = 9	2025 = 9
2008 = 1	2017 = 1	2026 = 1
2009 = 2	2018 = 2	2027 = 2
2010 = 3	2019 = 3	2028 = 3
2011 = 4	2020 = 4	2029 = 4
2012 = 5	2021 = 5	2030 = 5
2013 = 6	2022 = 6	2031 = 6

(For purposes of calculation, use the numbers shown in this table.)
Table 16–1

Example of Assigned Universal Month Numbers

Month	Assigned Numbers	Month	Assigned Numbers
January	1	July	7
February	2	August	8
March	3	September	9
April	4	October	10 reduced to 1
May	5	November	11 reduced to 2
June	6	December	12 reduced to 3

(For purposes of calculation, use the numbers shown in this table.)
Table 16–2

Example of Assigned Universal (Calendar) Day Numbers

1 = 1	10 = 10	19 = 19	28 = 28
2 = 2	11 = 11	20 = 20	29 = 29
3 = 3	12 = 12	21 = 21	30 = 30
4 = 4	13 = 13	22 = 22	31 = 31
5 = 5	14 = 14	23 = 23	
6 = 6	15 = 15	24 = 24	
7 = 7	16 = 16	25 = 25	
8 = 8	17 = 17	26 = 26	
9 = 9	18 = 18	27 = 27	

(For purposes of calculation, use the numbers shown in this table, do not reduce down.)
Table 16–3

The Special Case of Universal Hours

When listing the "numbers" of the Universal Hours, "time" is counted in the same manner as a measure from Greenwich Mean Time or Greenwich Meridian Time (GMT). However, GMT is not the origin of the "clock" hour determination, only a reflection in today's terms of the nature of the 24–hour day. The Universal Day is counted on a 24–hour clock. That is, the first twelve hours (AM) hours are 1:00 o'clock through 12:00 o'clock (noon), while the PM hours are 13:00 o'clock through 24:00 o'clock (midnight). Many countries have used the designation of 0100, 0200, etc., since time measurement was first deemed necessary by civilization.

These "24–hour" increments that we know as a "day" were originally determined by the Chaldean priest-scientist astronomers at least 6,000 years ago. The "24–hour" clock time was based on the movement of the planets around the Sun. (It is interesting to note that these ancient priest-scientists were aware Earth revolved around the Sun thousands of years before our "modern" day scientists "proved" that fact.) The "24" planetary hours are based on an ancient astrological system, known as the Chaldean order (or sequence) of the planets.

This order (or sequence) of the planets is defined here partially in technical terms as a means to convey the discovery that the Chaldeans made. The Chaldean order (sequence) refers to the velocity required by planets to achieve a circular orbit in relation to their primary or central point of orbit, that is, the speed required to stay in place around the Sun. From a heliocentric (having the sun as the center) perspective, this sequence also indicates the distance of the planets from the Sun. [These calculations are related to a standard equation for velocity (v), distance (d), and time (t), i.e., v = d divided by t or, is restated, t (time) = v (velocity) divided by d (distance).] These ancient priest-scientists discovered that once the velocity of the planets' orbits and the distance that they were from their primary star was known (in this case, the Sun), "time" could be calculated.

The result of this discovery was that the world's planetary hours use the mathematics of the Chaldean order of the planets to divide time into "hourly" increments. That is, each planetary day was divided into twelve increments of two (2) hours each or twenty-four (24) planetary hours. In the ancient past, the calendar-makers/astrologers settled on a seven-day week and a 24–hour day. The first hour was the 1st hour of the morning, now known as either 0100 hours, 1:00 o'clock, or 1 AM; the 12th hour or noon is known as 1200, 12:00 o'clock, or 12 PM; the 18th hour is considered the first hour of the evening (and is also known as 1800, 18:00 o'clock, or 6 PM), etc., with the last or 24th hour being "midnight" (2400 hours, 24:00 o'clock, or 12 AM). Most of today's nations used in the past and use today a 24–hour clock, 1 through 24 to designate the number of the hour. The United States of America (USA) is the rare nation that uses 12 hours in the AM and 12 hours in the PM (except for the Military, which uses a 24–hour clock). Interestingly enough, the United States Naval Observatory keeps the official time for the USA and converts the 24–hour clock time into 12 hours before noon and 12 hours after noon.

The Universal Clock Hours and their corresponding numbers listed in table 16–4 are a direct result and representation of the Chaldean discovery of how to determine planetary hours.

Assigned Universal Clock Hour Numbers

US Hour Number	US Hour Number	US Hour Number
1 AM = 1	10 AM = 10	7 PM = 19
2 AM = 2	11 AM = 11	8 PM = 20
3 AM = 3	12 AM = 12	9 PM = 21
4 AM = 4	1 PM = 13	10 PM = 22
5 AM = 5	2 PM = 14	11 PM = 23
6 AM = 6	3 PM = 15	12 PM = 24
7 AM = 7	4 PM = 16	
8 AM = 8	5 PM = 17	
9 AM = 9	6 PM = 18	

(For purposes of calculation, use the numbers shown in this table, do not reduce down.)
The Universal day is subdivided into 24–Universal Hour numbers.
Table 16–4

Conclusion

Remember, you can "personalize" all of your numbers. You can make the Universal Year "Personal" by bringing your Name and Birthdate numbers into the formula. You make the Universal Month "Personal" by bringing your Personal Year numbers into the formula. You make the Universal Day "Personal" by bringing your Personal Month numbers into the formula. And, you make the Universal Clock Hours "Personal" by bringing your Personal Day numbers into the formula. That is, you have the option of personalizing these "Universal" vibrational patterns within your design and blueprint. The primary factor in modifying these Universal environments is your knowledge and use of the vibrational patterns that are personal to you as defined by your name and birthdate numbers.

###

Chapter 17:
Sample Celebrity Numerology Charts

The purpose for including celebrity Numerology charts in *Numbers–The Powerful Bridge Beyond* was first, we thought it would be interesting to select some famous people and run their Numerology charts to show you just how the charts mirror who they appear to be or the role by which we identify them. Second, we wanted to show you how each celebrity is "designed," by briefly outlining their characteristics which are the same "characteristics" as yours. However, the combination of the "numbers" of their characteristics is very different from your combination. Third, we wanted to show you how a Numerology chart or complete character analysis can help you navigate your way to success by utilizing a scientific way of first and foremost understanding your make up so that you are more likely to feel confident about the choices you make as you go through transitional periods in life.

No matter how the number combinations play out in everyone's charts, the end result is always the same. Your Birthname and Birthdate form a blueprint of what you came into this lifetime to experience. This means that we all have a path that is thought to be predestined but certainly unique to each of us. However, you can alter that path at any time, if you consciously choose to change the numbers (and as a result the vibrational patterns) of your Birth Chart by merely changing your Name. This action, in and of itself, will eventually introduce "different" vibrational patterns into your environment than those that grew out of the numbers of your Birthname. This will most definitely bring about or attract other experiences. What separates successful people from non-successful people is simply exercising free will, making right "choices" and life-altering decisions in order to achieve set goals.

Mini-charts have been generated for the following eleven famous individuals listed in table 17–1 who are politicians, actors/actresses, or entrepreneurs. These celebrities were specially chosen so you can see how each of their unique blueprints (charts) will provide the character traits of each celebrity based on whether we run their "birth" or "stage" name which makes a big difference in the outcome.

Celebrity	Name on Mini-Charts
Walt Disney	Stage Name
Bill Gates	Birthname

Steve Jobs	Birthname
David Letterman	Birthname
Shirley MacLaine	Stage Name
Marilyn Monroe	Stage Name
Colin Powell	Birthname
Ronald Reagan	Birthname
Robert Redford	Birthname
Steven Spielberg	Birthname
Oprah Winfrey	Birthname

Table 17–1

What do all of these individuals have in common? Each has a unique blueprint but for purposes of this exercise, we will only generate a mini-blueprint that will outline five of their major characteristics from their Numerology charts: Destiny, Soul/Heart's Desire, Personality, Purpose, and Life Goal. The sum total of all these parts forms a holistic picture of these individuals in addition to those characteristics not discussed.

Knowing what each celebrity's image portrays, see if see if you think the mini-charts for the eleven celebrities generate an accurate read of how you envision each of these individuals to be.

It is probably safe to say that all of these famous people started with ambition, desire, drive, and passion. However, the truth of the matter is they accomplished what they did through a number of experiences or challenges they faced, trying times, and trial and error, which helped shape each individual's goals. That, along with making right choices and decisions eventually led them to success. Making sound decisions, based on insight and clarity can in fact expedite your steps to success by virtue of staying focused and determined. But is that the reality in your life today? Again, the answer is probably not. There are many influences that affect your decision-making process; namely, your emotions, income, family, education, etc.

Numbers–The Powerful Bridge Beyond

Chaldean Numerology for the New Millennium

Knowing the meaning behind the numbers of your characteristics simply gives you a better understanding of how you are "designed." Some are born lovers, leaders, diplomats, humanitarians, teachers, entertainers, or builders. By knowing what your blueprint reveals, you have a better understanding of your relationships, compatibilities, behaviors, strengths and weaknesses, so you can make better choices in life. Discover how your Numerology Chart, the Design and Blueprint of your Life, affects your destiny and gives you options for controlling changes in your life. Numerology charts and readings are valuable tools in helping to gain knowledge about various aspects and areas of your life, whether personal or business.

The Numerology charts for the eleven celebrities are shown on the following pages. The Birthdate and Name numbers generated represent five of the major characteristics of their original design and blueprint at birth. (Note: In some of the profiles, we have elected to use either the celebrity's birthname or stage name which they are known by in order to generate their chart. The information provided is the result of research from various resources to ensure accuracy of obtaining the birth information, so it is presumed the information is correct based on the research.)

WALT DISNEY

Born: **Walt Elias Disney**
Birthdate: **December 5, 1901**

Below is a "partial" Numerology mini-chart generated for Walt Elias Disney based on calculating his Birthdate and "Stage" Name as Walt Disney–not his full Birthname.

Missions in Life		Blueprint Description
Destiny (Birthdate)	1	Leader, pioneer, creative, independent, strong-willed, innovative, courageous, always looking to the future and moving in a forward direction, man of vision.
Soul/Heart's Desire (Vowels)	8	Lots of energy, ambitious, materialistic but generous, successful, organized.
Personality (Consonants)	7	Analytical, intelligent, reserved, perfectionist; an educator dedicated to sharing knowledge and truth.
Purpose (Total Name)	6	Devoted to serving family and community as a cosmic parent; strong influence in establishing harmony and beauty in every environment.
Life Goal (Midlife) (Birthdate + Name)	7	Educator of great wisdom and teachings, passing on intellectual and spiritual truths.

Summary

Walt Disney was a powerful man, leader and pioneer, creative, innovative, emotional, builder of structure and foundation, cosmic parent and always forged ahead in a positive direction to serve mankind.

BILL GATES

Born: William Henry Gates
Birthdate: October 28, 1955

Below is a "partial" Numerology mini-chart generated for William Henry Gates based on calculating his Birthdate and Birthname.

Missions in Life		Blueprint Description
Destiny (Birthdate)	4	The builder of structure and solid foundation with the task of bringing forth new ideas for the benefit of mankind.
Soul/Heart's Desire (Vowels)	6	The lover; represents harmony, beauty, truth, and justice. Idealist and an inspirational cosmic parent dedicated to family, friends, community, and mankind. Seen as being very solid and responsible.
Personality (Consonants)	11/2	Inspirational and motivational on a worldwide level. Leader, pioneer, visionary lead taker to bring about changes that benefit others. On the flip side, a diplomat/peacemaker and very detailed-oriented.
Purpose (Total Name)	8	Success and ambition to become the boss or authority, organized, and career-driven to acquire power and materialism; highly energetic.
Life Goal (Midlife) (Birthdate + Name)	3	Joyful time more than other times in life. This is meant to be social, successful, developing creativity, magnetic, imaginative, and inspirational.

Summary

Bill Gates is a powerful man, compassionate humanitarian, ambitious, organized, emotional, builder of structure and foundation, cosmic parent and always forging ahead in a positive direction to bring about change that serves mankind.

STEVE JOBS

Born: **Steven Paul Jobs**
Birthdate: **February 24, 1955**

Below is a "partial" Numerology chart generated for Steven Paul Jobs based on calculating his Birthdate and Birthname.

Missions in Life		Blueprint Description
Destiny (Birthdate)	1	A leader and pioneer who paves the road for others to follow. Aggressive, self-assured, and confident in his abilities to make a difference; always thinking in terms of progress and moving forward in a positive direction; putting forth new ideas to benefit mankind.
Soul/Heart's Desire (Vowels)	6	The lover, devoted to his family and friends, and serving as a cosmic parent. This is a domestic vibration and as such, the desire for his personal life becomes very important while he makes a difference in the world.
Personality (Consonants)	8	Ambitious, the authority, high energy, successful, driven, has vision, organized.
Purpose (Total Name)	14/5	The risk taker. Not afraid to pave new roads for others to follow or to take chances in going in a different direction, intent is to open up new opportunities for the benefit of mankind, may be stubborn and opinionated since he is the builder and very structured by nature.
Life Goal (Midlife) (Birthdate + Name)	6	Desire and focus shifts to his dedication to family, friends, and community in midlife.

Summary

Steve Jobs is a man of power, vision, compassionate humanitarian, leader, pioneer, creative, successful, emotional, builder of structure and foundation, cosmic parent and always forging ahead in a positive direction.

DAVID LETTERMAN

Born: **David Michael Letterman**
Birthdate: **April 12, 1947**

Below is a "partial" Numerology chart generated for David Michael Letterman based on calculating his Birthdate and Birthname.

Missions in Life		**Blueprint Description**
Destiny (Birthdate)	1	Leader, pioneer who takes the lead to bring about change and pave new roads, creative mind, aggressive.
Soul/Heart's Desire (Vowels)	2	Sensitive, non-aggressive, diplomat, peacemaker, negotiator, generally does not like confrontation, requires a partner in both personal and business affairs.
Personality (Consonants)	6	Cosmic parent for family, friends, and community; seen as being well-balanced, sympathetic to others, harmonious, neat, very much a caregiver and domestic by nature, quick-witted and clever.
Purpose (Total Name)	8	Ambitious, liking the finer things in life, aggressive, energetic, and driven.
Life Goal (Midlife) (Birthdate + Name)	9	Compassionate humanitarian devoted to serving mankind, emotional, and caring.

Summary

David Letterman is a leader and pioneer, and is creative, energetic, and ambitious by nature. The rest of his life will be devoted to serving mankind as the cosmic parent. Midlife will be more emotional, drawing out his compassion more than any other time.

SHIRLEY MACLAINE

Born: **Shirley MacLean Beaty**
Birthdate: **Date: April 24, 1934**

Below is a "partial" Numerology chart generated for Shirley MacLean Beaty based on calculating her Birthdate and "Stage" Name as Shirley MacLaine–not her Birthname.

Missions in Life		Blueprint Description
Destiny (Birthdate)	18/9	This name brings the power of a worldwide leader and pioneer, is ambitious and very devoted to serving mankind as the emotional, compassionate humanitarian and has vision.
Soul/Heart's Desire (Vowels)	6	The lover, caregiver, cosmic parent dedicated to family, friends, and people in general; seen as well-balanced and together.
Personality (Consonants)	1	Forging ahead always in a positive direction to serve as the leader/pioneer and pave the road for others to follow.
Purpose (Total Name)	7	The purpose is to educate teaching on all levels, very intellectual and knowledgeable with the desire to share knowledge learned through life's experiences and personal growth.
Life Goal (Midlife) (Birthdate + Name)	16/7	Continue leading, being devoted to family and friends with the intent of continuing to educate mankind on a worldwide basis.

Summary

Shirley MacLaine is an emotional, compassionate humanitarian, and leader/pioneer who came into this lifetime to serve mankind on a worldwide level. She's creative and known as a cosmic parent, and is always forging ahead in a positive direction to educate the world with her discoveries in life on a metaphysical plane.

MARILYN MONROE

Born: **Norma Jeane Mortenson** (AKA: Norma Jeane Baker)
Birthdate: **June 1, 1926**

Below is a "partial" Numerology chart generated for Normal Jeane Mortenson based on calculating her Birthdate and "Stage" Name as Marilyn Monroe–not her Birthname.

Missions in Life		Blueprint Description
Destiny (Birthdate)	16/7	Leader, pioneer, and cosmic parent serving family and community on a domestic level, while searching for knowledge and truth as an intellectual.
Soul/Heart's Desire (Vowels)	22/4	The Master builder is dedicated to serving mankind on a higher level so others may benefit.
Personality (Consonants)	7	Analytical, intelligent, reserved, perfectionist, an educator dedicated to sharing knowledge and truth.
Purpose (Total Name)	11/2	To inspire and motivate people.
Life Goal (Midlife) (Birthdate + Name)	18/9	The combination of all 3 number vibrations represents a worldwide leader and the ability to lead; is ambitious and serves all of mankind at the same time while being the compassionate humanitarian.

Summary

Marilyn Monroe was a leader, lover, and very intelligent. Her desire was to be inspiring and motivational which she accomplished by being an actress who was not only beautiful but mysterious.

COLIN POWELL

Born: **Colin Luther Powell**
Birthdate: **April 5, 1937**

Below is a "partial" Numerology chart generated for Colin Luther Powell based on calculating his Birthdate and Birthname.

Missions in Life		Blueprint Description
Destiny (Birthdate)	11/2	Powerful leader, pioneer, creative mind; a destiny to serve mankind in a highly inspirational and motivational manner. Not only as an aggressive leader but as a diplomat, peacemaker, and master negotiator; highly charged and emotional.
Soul/Heart's Desire (Vowels)	4	The builder of structure and foundation; must have affairs in order and is stubborn and opinionated; loyal, dedicated, reliable, and hard worker.
Personality (Consonants)	9	Compassionate humanitarian, emotional by nature as a result of this vibration; noble, sincere, well-balanced, truthful, dedicated to making or bringing about changes to benefit mankind.
Purpose (Total Name)	13/4	Always moving in a forward direction as the leader and pioneer in paving the roads for others to follow, socially-oriented and joyful, wanting to enjoy his life while forging ahead as the builder.
Life Goal (Midlife) (Birthdate + Name)	6	From midlife on, energies will be devoted to family and friends; seen as being well-balanced, sympathetic, having it together.

Summary

Colin Powell is a man of power, compassionate humanitarian, leader, pioneer, creative, emotional, builder of structure and foundation devoted to serving mankind, cosmic parent and always forging ahead in a positive direction.

RONALD REAGAN

Born: **Ronald Wilson Reagan**
Birthdate: **February 6, 1911**

Below is a "partial" Numerology chart generated for Ronald Wilson Reagan based on calculating his Birthdate and Birthname.

Missions in Life		Blueprint Description
Destiny (Birthdate)	11/2	Powerful leader, pioneer, creative mind; a destiny to serve mankind in a highly inspirational and motivational manner. Not only as an aggressive leader but as a diplomat, peacemaker, and master negotiator; highly charged and emotional.
Soul/Heart's Desire (Vowels)	23/5	Desired to be that of the diplomat/peacemaker and master negotiator; very sensitive in nature; thrives on freedom, changes, and traveling.
Personality (Consonants)	5	Quick-witted, progressive, needed constant changes to avoid boredom.
Purpose (Total Name)	1	To become a leader, pioneer who paved roads for others to follow; independent and self-reliant, having the confidence and ability to take the lead role.
Life Goal (Midlife) (Birthdate + Name)	3	Midlife should have been a time for enjoying life and socializing; included success and being the entertainer, as well as developing talents.

Summary

Ronald Reagan was a powerful man, a worldwide leader, pioneer, creative, and always forging ahead to bring about positive changes for the purpose of serving mankind.

ROBERT REDFORD

Born: **Charles Robert Redford**
Birthdate: **August 18, 1936**

Below is a "partial" Numerology chart generated for Charles Robert Redford based on calculating his Birthdate and Birthname.

Missions in Life		Blueprint Description
Destiny (Birthdate)	19/1	Powerful leader, pioneer, creative mind, emotional, compassionate humanitarian with a destiny to serve mankind and bring about change, letting go of the old for the new.
Soul/Heart's Desire (Vowels)	3	To be happy, joyful, social, successful and to simply enjoy life as he chooses.
Personality (Consonants)	1	Confident, aggressive, well-groomed, dignified, creative.
Purpose (Total Name)	13/4	Always moving in a forward direction as the leader and pioneer in paving the roads for others to follow; new beginnings, socially-oriented and joyful, wanting to enjoy life while forging ahead as the builder of structure and foundation, hard worker, may be set in his ways, opinionated, but loyal, dedicated, reliable and very structured.
Life Goal (Midlife) (Birthdate + Name)	5	From midlife on, this is a life full of changes based on choices. Includes changes, freedom, and travel. The desire for constant change keeps this man progressive and young.

Summary

Robert Redford is a powerful, compassionate humanitarian, leader, pioneer, creative, emotional, builder of structure and foundation in wanting to serve mankind but desiring changes to avoid boredom in life.

STEVEN SPIELBERG

Born: Steven Allan Spielberg
Birthdate: December 18, 1946

Below is a "partial" Numerology chart generated for Steven Allan Spielberg based on calculating his Birthdate and Birthname.

Missions in Life		**Blueprint Description**
Destiny (Birthdate)	14/5	The risk taker, not afraid to pave new roads for others to follow. A born leader, pioneer, thrives in an environment of constant changes, freedom, and travel. Typically stubborn and opinionated but very dedicated to work which is actually play time versus work, man of vision.
Soul/Heart's Desire (Vowels)	23/5	Diplomat, peacemaker, joyful, creative, enthusiastic, inspirational, the entertainer but desires freedom and a changing environment.
Personality (Consonants)	5	Rebellious, progressive, resourceful, magnetic, quick thinking, unconventional, and requires changes to add spice in his life versus boredom.
Purpose (Total Name)	1	Leader, pioneer, creative, determined, courageous, innovative, strong-willed, independent, strives to bring about change for serving mankind.
Life Goal (Midlife) (Birthdate + Name)	6	Cosmic parent, responsible, dedicated to family and friends, will continue the rest of his life to inspire mankind through his creativity.

Summary
Steven Spielberg is a risk taker, pioneer, and leader and is not afraid to pave new roads for the benefit of serving mankind. As a builder, he is structured and requires his affairs to be organized. His desire is for constant change, freedom, and travel to eliminate boredom which is not in his vocabulary.

OPRAH WINFREY

Born: Oprah Gail Winfrey
Birthdate: January 29, 1954

Below is a "partial" Numerology chart generated for Oprah Gail Winfrey based on calculating her Birthdate and Birthname.

Missions in Life		Blueprint Description
Destiny (Birthdate)	13/4	Has vision, new beginnings and always forging ahead in a positive direction with feeling joyful, successful, and social but primarily driven as the builder of structure and foundation, to bring about change for the betterment of mankind; may have a tendency to be stubborn and opinionated.
Soul/Heart's Desire (Vowels)	8	Lots of energy, ambitious, materialistic but generous, successful, organized.
Personality (Consonants)	6	That of the lover, the cosmic parent, well-balanced, and together. Devoted to family, friends, and community.
Purpose (Total Name)	14/5	The risk taker, not afraid to move forward to bring about change to streamline current reality, turning it into some humanitarian event; a hard worker who thrives on changes, freedom, and travel.
Life Goal (Midlife) (Birthdate + Name)	9	To serve mankind as the emotional, compassionate humanitarian.

Summary

Oprah Winfrey is a risk taker and builder of structure and foundation and is not afraid to go where no one has before. She is ambitious, while at the same time a compassionate humanitarian, but her heart is devoted to family, friends, and mankind, and is a very together human being. Her personality is that of the lover and is domestic, stemming from being the caregiver on a worldwide basis.

###

Appendix A:
More on Chaldean Alphabet Sound-Syllables

Chaldean Numerology recognized and applied certain characteristics and formulas which ensured that the accuracy of the calculated numerical values and the interpretations of the patterns of our names were maintained at all times. The primary reason for this accuracy is the assignment of specific numerical values to the "sound-syllables" (what appear to be "letters") of the Aramaean/Chaldean Alphabet.

Of the Twenty-Six (26) sound-syllables used in Chaldean "Numerology" (see table A–1), Twenty-Two (22) correlate directly to the 22 original letters (sound-syllables) of the Aramaean/Chaldean/Hebraic Sacred Alphabet. Although the four (4) additional letters/sound-syllables which evolved in the Chaldean Alphabet were not considered part of the original Sacred Alphabet (see table A–2), the additional Chaldean letters E, F, J, and W are either variations of or are in close "sound" proximity to the sound-syllables of the original Sacred Alphabet "Letters."

Twenty-Six (26) Letter Chaldean Alphabet

1	2	3	4	5	6	7	8
A	B	C	D	E	U	O	F
I	K	G	M	H	V	Z	P
J	R	L	T	N	W		
Q		S		X			
Y							

Table A–1

Twenty-Two (22) Letter Original Sacred Alphabet

1	2	3	4	5	6	7	8
(A) aleph	(B) beth	(C) chaf	(D) daleth	~~(E)~~ Not Original	(U) vau	(O) ayin	~~(F)~~ Not Original
(I) yod	(K) kaph	(G) gimel	(M) mem	(H) he	(V) vau	(Z) zain	(P) pe
~~(J)~~ Not Original	(R) resh	(L) lamed	(T) teth	(N) nun	~~(W)~~ Not Original		
(Q) qoph		(S) semakh		(X) tzaddi			
(Y) yod							

Table A–2

The "**E**" (with the Numerical value of 5) comes from the Proto-Greek (3rd millennium BCE) letter epsilon, which is a sound-syllable variation of (derived from) the Aramaic/Chaldean/Hebraic hê (pronounced "hey").

The letter "**F**" (with the Numerical value of 8) is a variation of the Aramaic/Chaldean/Hebraic letter pê (pronounced "pey"), which became "ph" (pronounced "eph") when incorporated into languages other than Aramaic/Chaldean/Hebraic.

The "**J**" (with the Numerical value of 1) has multiple origins, one as a later addition to the original 22 Aramaic/Chaldean/Hebraic Sacred Alphabet letters (variation of the letter "I"). The "J" is also included in the structure of the Sanskrit Alphabet. The letter "J" is pronounced as "Jey or Jay." However, the sound of "J" is pronounced "jh," as in major or "geh" as in sledgehammer.

> The "**W**" (with the Numerical value of 6) is a later addition to the Aramaic/Chaldean/Hebraic "Sacred" (22) and is a transliteration of the Aramaic/Chaldean/Hebraic Alphabet letter "wâw" pronounced "double u." However, the letter "W" is not a variation or derivation of the letter "u," but rather the combination of two Vs (VV), which, when enunciated, had the sound of a double "u."

While the pronunciation of the English letter "W" is double "u," the sound of "W" within a combination of sound-syllables can be, for instance, "wa" or "wh." The Latin (later became known as "Roman") Alphabet, as well as English, the Romance languages, Middle and Eastern European languages, languages of the Near East (Grecian peninsula/Asia Minor/Middle East—Greek, Egyptian, Aramaean, Chaldean, Hebrew, Persian, etc.), and Asia Major (Far East—India, Tibet, China, etc.), to some degree, incorporated the above variations into the structure of their languages. These variations (language structure changes) came about as a result of the development of language systems that followed the expansion and diversification of the human family from the lands of Ancient Aramaea, Chaldea, Sumeria, Mesopotamia, and Western Persia (now represents Eastern Syria, Southeastern Turkey, Southern Armenia, Iraq, and Western Iran).

These additional sound-syllables became necessary to describe "new" patterns that were a part of the interactions between people and these new experiences (unimagined before the expansion), and reflected the impact of humanity's ability to adapt to this "new" world encountered by each clan, culture, tribe, etc. In other words, certain vibrational patterns that were unfolding in the new experiences could not be fully described by the strict application of the Aramaic/Hebraic sound-syllables first identified in the original alphabet.

Now, as it worked out, the Chaldean priest-scientists developed a numerological science based on their research, experience with evolving language structures, knowledge of sound and energy, and the generation of vibrational patterns that defined the world around them. The potential spectrum of these vibrational patterns and their interpretation amazingly required only minimal sound-syllable ("letters") additions to the original Aramaic/Chaldean Alphabet sound-syllable structure. The Chaldean priest-scientists found that the addition of these "four" sound-syllables to the original Aramaean/Chaldean Sacred Alphabet completed the full range of generated vibrational patterns which operate within the living environment of the planet. As a result of this scientific research and discovery, the Chaldean Numerological alphabet was established to accommodate the whole family of languages which has spread throughout the modern world.

###

Appendix B:
"Y" is Always a Vowel and "W" is Always a Consonant

In Chaldean Numerology, the "Y" is always a Vowel, and only a Vowel, while the "W" is always a Consonant and only a Consonant in the determination of name vibrational patterns. This appendix is being presented to reinforce, clarify, and expand the explanations of the logic behind using "Y" only as a vowel and "W" only as a consonant.

A great deal of time, study, research, and testing was undertaken in order to validate and verify the appropriate usage of "Y" and "W," numerologically speaking, in calculating the correct numerical values for the numbers of your Name. In the original application of Chaldean Numerology, the "Y" was always a *Vowel* and the "W" always a *Consonant*. There were no exceptions, qualifications, modifications, or alternatives in regard to the specific use of the two sound-syllables "Y" and "W" for what they were intended to be used—"Y" as a vowel, and "W" as a consonant. Always remember that we are addressing sound-syllables which have vibrational resonance, not letters which are dormant. It was exceptionally important to be absolutely sure there was no uncertainty in the correct application of "Y" and "W" being used in our formulas and equations.

This resulted in an extensive investigation through the study of many cases to determine the accuracy of the alternate vowel/consonant (known as a semi-vowel/semi-consonant) usage of the "Y" and "W." (Note: A semi-vowel or semi-consonant is a letter that is for the most part a vowel or consonant, but occasionally is considered a consonant or vowel.) A comparative analysis was prepared using the "Y" as a semi-vowel and the "W" as a semi-consonant as compared to using the "Y" strictly as a vowel and the "W" strictly as a consonant. The issue to be resolved in conducting the comparative analysis was discovering and understanding the influence or affect on the interpretive process. That is, the ultimate goal of this analysis was to determine which "Y" and "W" application correctly and accurately interpreted the vibrational patterns that describe the design and blueprint of our Names.

After we completed the case studies, we compared the results of the vibrational patterns generated from calculating numerical values when applying a semi-vowel "Y" and semi-consonant "W" in the determination of the correct numerical values of a Name to the results of the accuracy when using "Y" only as a vowel and "W" only as a consonant. Those whose Numerology charts were used as case studies were presented two charts, one chart being calculated from the formulas of the original science of Chaldean Numerology, using the "Y" only as a vowel and the "W" only as a consonant, while the other chart was calculated using "Y" mostly as a vowel, but sometimes as a consonant, and the "W" mostly as a consonant, but sometimes as a vowel. There was total agreement that the charts calculated using the "Y" only as a vowel and the "W" only as a consonant (from the original science of Chaldean Numerology) were the only completely accurate charts.

At the end of the analysis, it was clearly demonstrated that the only "valid" and "true" conclusion of the investigation was that the application of "Y" only as a vowel and "W" only as a consonant provided the most appropriate and correct determination of the vibrational patterns within a Name. The semi-vowel "Y" and semi-consonant "W" application caused the numerical values of the Name to be erratic at best with inaccuracies in almost all interpretations. This further questions the validity of the Modern (Western) number system using such an application which is based on the modern linguistic understanding of the structure of a language's writing system, and has absolutely nothing to do with sound-syllables and the vibrational resonance of numbers which were the basis of the ancient science of Numerology and is still valid today. For this reason, the Modern (Western) number system *does not and cannot accurately* (if at all) interpret the meaning of the patterns of your Name.

As a mathematician with a science background, Mr. Mykian knew that in both physical and mathematical sciences, the proof of the pudding is in the taste. That is, the proof can be shown by reaching both a valid and true conclusion, based on the stated premises or assumptions. One of the ways to demonstrate a scientific outcome, in this case, the showing of the accuracy of strict usage of the "Y" as a vowel and the "W" as a consonant, is through the "results" of a scientific investigation, which, in no uncertain terms, fully supported the truth and validity that is assumed from the premises.

Additionally, to address the variations of application of "Y" or "W" as a vowel versus consonant in any language is complex to say the least. The phenomenon of "Y" and "W," being treated sometimes as a vowel and sometimes as a consonant, is caused by mixing up the meaning of (being confused by) linguistics (letters and structure of a written language) versus phonetics (sounds created when speaking the written letters of the language). In the instance of this controversy, the confusion is magnified by trying to liken phonetics, the definition of differing sounds created by the letters (linguistics) in speaking a language, with the sound of "Y" or "W" as sound-syllables in the interpretive aspects of Numerology.

For instance, by definition, a vowel, per phonetics, is a sound in spoken language which is characterized by a certain configuration of the vocal tract. The word *vowel* comes from the Latin word *vocalis*, meaning uttering voice or speaking. But phonetics is not meant to, nor can it, fully explain sound-syllables, which result in the generation of vibrational patterns, and require the use of the language behind numbers (Numerolinguistics) to interpret the numerical values that represent the patterns of a name. The "Y" and "W," as sound-syllables, in combination with other sound-syllables, form "word" (Name) sound-syllables which give off unique vibrational patterns and describe aspects of the design and blueprint of our life's experiences. Each sound-syllable resonates to unique numerical values which have specific descriptive meanings that flow from the sounds of our Names.

In the final analysis, the appropriateness of the use of "Y" only as a vowel and "W" only as a consonant has been known since the beginnings of Chaldean Numerology, is still valid today, and provides the greatest possible accuracy in describing the language of our life's design. The use of the "Y" as a vowel and "W" as a consonant, at all times, ensures a consistent and continual accuracy of the language of the numbers, which describes the design and blueprint of our unfolding life experiences.

Again, the patterns of a Name do not derive from the language of the number of a single letter, but of a specific combination of letters as "word" sounds (combination of sound-syllables). Each of these word sounds has a designated number (the sum of the letter/sound-syllables within a Name) that identifies the "vibrational patterns" of a Name, using language as the medium of translation. We sense that the confusion, which abounds in Numerology about the "Y" and "W" as a vowel versus consonant or sometimes both a vowel and a consonant, causes professed numerologists to "pick" one approach over another approach, giving the "Y" and "W" split personalities so to speak. This generally occurs because they have undertaken little or no independent research into (1) "proving" beyond a scientific doubt to themselves and their clients that their approach is valid and (2) understanding (or trying to understand) the origin of Chaldean Numerology and the basis of their system of numbers. (Note: As stated above, in terms of phonetics, the study of speech sounds (voice), a vowel is a sound in spoken language that is formed by an open configuration of the vocal tract. However, some languages allow sounds that usually would not be considered vowels to form the basis of a syllable, such as the sound of "m" in the English word prism. Does this make the "M" questionable as a consonant or when it is to be considered such? The word "vowel" is often used for the symbols which represent vowel sounds in a language's writing system, particularly if the language uses a letter-based alphabet. In the Roman Alphabet for instance, the vowel letters are usually A, E, I, O, U. However, in modern linguistic understanding, vowels are simply defined in terms of a language's structure.)

In contrast to vowels, consonants are characterized by a closure at one or more points along the vocal tract. This conception of consonants is also a modern linguistic understanding which defines and addresses consonants as a sound used in a language in terms of "vocal tract" constrictions, not sound-syllables that "resonate" (vibrate) and give off waves of energy that form vibrational patterns.

###

Numbers–The Powerful Bridge Beyond

Chaldean Numerology for the New Millennium

About the Author
Joanne Justis

Ms. Justis, born into a metaphysical family, has been a spiritual intuitive all of her life. She trained under her Mother, a Master Numerologist who originally founded Numbers R U. And together, they have provided charts and readings since 1984. Ms. Justis created and designed a comprehensive and responsive Chaldean Numerology Web site (NumbersRU.com). Her Chaldean Numerology computer software program, *Numerology for the New Era,* was inspired by and based on an original software program copyrighted in 1983-1984. The result of years of research, *Numerology for the New Era* is a unique, one-of-a-kind, newly redesigned and revised innovative PC and web-based application which utilizes leading-edge technology and has the ability to calculate dates between 1900 and 3004, a span of over a hundred years. This top-of-the-line software enables NumbersRU.com to provide clients with perfectly accurate Numerology charts specializing in complete character analysis, compatibility charts for children, singles, married couples, and business partners, in addition to baby naming with a twist, naming for business ventures, companies and product naming, pet and animal (pedigree) naming, and more.

Ms. Justis has degrees in Miracle Mastery Programs and has an extensive background in Marketing, Communications, and Operations and is a logistics expert by trade. She is a guest reader/lecturer at bookstores in Northern and Southern California, has been a guest on radio programs, and has published articles in a number of metaphysical magazines. Ms. Justis is one of five Consultants for the Association Internationale de Numerologues in the UK (Numerology.Org.UK), a member of Empire Who's Who, and various women's organizations, and has a numerological office located in Los Gatos, California.

###

Numbers–The Powerful Bridge Beyond

Chaldean Numerology for the New Millennium

About the Author
William Mykian

William Mykian graduated from the Pennsylvania State University where he majored in Mathematics and Philosophy. He has a diversified background and experience in business, financial and performance management, political consulting, professional writing, nutritional therapy, and counseling. Mykian has also spent almost half of his lifetime in active research, study, and practice of the science of Chaldean Numerology and the Language of Numbers in addition to being a Reiki Healing Master.

He is one of the few experts in the understanding and application of Chaldean Numerology in the tradition of Master Chaldean Numerologists Cheiro (Count Louis Hamon) and Gerun Moore, and the author of the book *Numerology Made Easy*. This is an introductory textbook, a first-of-its-kind Chaldean Numerology primer that explains the basic formulas and application of the Chaldean System of Numbers.

Mykian has written articles on Metaphysics, Meditation, and Numerology, conducted workshops and classes on Numerology based on his book, and is a motivational speaker. Not only is Mr. Mykian a mathematician and philosopher, he is a lifetime student of Spiritual and Metaphysical principles. This path has led him to the teachings and writings of Joel S. Goldsmith, Helena P. Blavatsky, Krishnamurti, Charles Fillmore, Corinne Helene, Alice Bailey, Christopher Isherwood, Annie Besant, Alan Watts, and Swami Prabhavananda, to name a few. Among the books that have influenced the shaping of William Mykian's life are *The Holographic Universe* (M. Talbot), *A New Science of Life* (R. Sheldrake), *Wholeness and the Implicate Order* (D. Bohm, Ph.D.), and *Cymatics: A Study of Wave Phenomena & Vibration* (H. Jenny).

###

Bibliography

Cheiro (Count Louis Hamon), *Cheiro's Book of Numbers.* New York: Star Books, 1932. Reprint, India: Hind Pocket Books, 1995.

Encyclopedia Britannica, Standard ed. 2004, s.v. "Pythagoras."

Encyclopedic Theosophical Glossary, online ed. Theosophical University Press, 1999. http://www.theosociety.org/passadena/etgloss/etg-hp.htm.

Forster, Charles. 1851. A facsimile reprint of an 1852 edition by Richard Bentley, London. *The One Primeval Language Traced Experimentally through Ancient Inscriptions in Alphabetic Characters of Lost Powers from the Four Continents: Including the Voice of Israel from the Rocks of Sinai.* Boston: Adamant Media Corp., 2006.

Huffman, Carl, "Pythagoras," *The Stanford Encyclopedia of Philosophy (Spring 2005 Edition),* Edward N. Zalta (ed.), http://plato.stanford.edu/archives/spr2005/entries/pythagoras.

Jordan, Juno. *Numerology: The Romance in Your Name.* Camarillo, CA: DeVorss Publications, 1965.

Justis, Joanne. Numbers R U. *Numerology for the New Era* (Computer Software Program), Copyright 1983–1984, 2003–2006.

Moore, Gerun, and Ruth Ericsen Setley. *Numbers Will Tell.* New York: Grosset & Dunlap, 1973.

Mykian, W. *Numerology Made Easy*. Chatsworth, CA: Wilshire Book Company, 1979.

O'Connor, J. J., and E. F. Robertson. "Pythagoras of Samos." *School of Mathematics and Statistics, University of St. Andrews, Scotland* (January, 1999). http://www-history.mcs.st-andrews.ac.uk/history/Biographies/Pythagoras.html.

Parfitt, Will. *The Elements of the Qabalah.* New York: Barnes and Noble Books, 1999.

Pursel, Jach and NPN Publishing, Inc. *Quote from a personal communication with Jach Pursel, Lazaris' only channel.* Copyright 2006, *Jach Pursel and NPN Publishing, Inc.* All rights reserved. For more information contact Concept: Synergy, P.O. Box 691867, Orlando, FL 32869, 800-678-2356, www.Lazaris.com.

Sitchin, Zecharia. *The 12th Planet: Book I of the Earth Chronicles.* New York: Avon, 1976.

———. *The Wars of Gods and Men: Book III of the Earth Chronicles.* New York: Avon, 1985.

———. *Genesis Revisited: Is Modern Science Catching Up with Ancient Knowledge?* New York: Avon, 1990.

Tanakh: The Holy Scriptures (The New JPS Translation according to the Traditional Hebrew Text) Philadelphia: Jewish Publication Society, 1985.

The Holy Scriptures According to the Masoretic Text: A New Translation with the Aid of Previous Versions and with Constant Consultation of Jewish Authorities. Philadelphia: Jewish Publication Society, 1917.

The King James Version of The Holy Bible. New York: American Bible Society, 2005.

The Theosophical Glossary by H. P. Blavatsky. Los Angeles: The Theosophy Company, 1930. A photographic reproduction of the original edition. First published 1892 by The Theosophical Publishing Society, London. http://www.phx-ult-lodge.org/Thegloss.htm.

Wikipedia: The Free Encyclopedia. Wikimedia Foundation, 2005. http://en.wikipedia.org.

###

Printed in the United States
73980LV00008B/57

9 781601 450791